A
COMMUNIST PARTY IN ACTION

An Account of the Organization and Operations in France

By

A. ROSSI

Translated and edited, with an Introduction,
by Willmoore Kendall

Archon Books
1970

ISBN: 0-208-00963-9
Library of Congress Catalog Card Number: 70-122396
Printed in the United States of America

Contents

Introduction

I

This book, a somewhat abridged English translation of A. Rossi's *Physiologie du Parti Communiste Français*,[1] goes to the printer's at a moment when the prevailing mood in the United States is one of ebullient optimism concerning the problems to which its conclusions are relevant.

Informed opinion, official and unofficial, holds that our domestic Communist movement, if indeed it ever constituted a significant threat to the existing social order (the clean bill of health obtained by all but a handful of United States Government employees from the recent loyalty investigation suggests that it never did), certainly constitutes no such threat today—as witness the "failure" of the Wallace movement in the 1948 election, the demonstrated incapacity of the Communist Party to recruit any significant number of Americans as Party members, and, most important of all perhaps, the continuous crystallization of public sentiment against the Communists through the years since the war. Press an exponent of this informed opinion for an explanation of this shift in public sentiment and he will tell you that it is the result of increased public awareness of the connection between the Communist Party and the Soviet Union (against which, as we have at last all admitted to ourselves, we are waging a cold war), or of heightened public understanding of the character and meaning of the Communist movement, both here and abroad. Press him for evidence of that shift of public sentiment and he will point to the mounting penalties, both institutional and social, that are now being visited upon men and women suspected of entertaining Communist views; press him further and he will point out that even the most convinced American disciples of John Stuart Mill now pause, before telling you why the loyalty program in its present form is a betrayal of the democratic faith of our fathers, or why the "hysteria" about Communists on the part of the trustees and regents of our universities should be deplored by all right-minded Americans, to say: "Let me be very clear about one thing: nobody hates Communism more than I do. But . . ." Press

him to say whether he can imagine circumstances in which the
Communist Party, or the Communist movement, or Communism,
might become a significant factor in American public life, and he
will have a ready answer for you: Let us so mismanage our affairs
as to have another great depression, let the day come when we
shall once again have ten or twelve or fourteen millions of unemployed men and women in the United States, and then yes, it
might well be that the masses of our people would respond favorably to Communist agitation and propaganda. But, he will add,
thanks to the late Lord Keynes and his American adepts, thanks
also to the "mandate" for the Fair Deal (increasingly generous
unemployment insurance, the ever-widening scope of Federal
Government activity in such areas as public health and housing,
and so on *and* so forth), that is a possibility we may safely dis-
count. In a word: Mr. Truman speaks with sober accuracy when,
encouraged no doubt by a celebrated statement on the subject
signed by twenty-odd professors of one of the nation's leading
law schools,[2] he refers to talk about the threat of domestic Communism as a "red herring," [3] calculated to distract attention from
our real problems.

The prevailing state of mind about Communism abroad is, I
should say, only less assertive than this, rather than less optimistic.
Of the Marshall Plan, and the policy of containment of the Soviet
Union of which that plan is an expression, we are already saying
—as Samuel Clemens said of the ocean when he saw it for the
first time— "Man! It's a success!" For all that the Plan is still only
in its second year, the evidence of economic recovery in Europe
is viewed as already overwhelming; [4] the election statistics from
Italy and France [5] are taken to show that economic recovery is
working just the sea-change, in the minds and hearts of certain
misguided Europeans, that we had confidently expected all
along; and the European Defense Pact to show that, *pari passu*
with the emancipation of those minds and hearts from the appeal
of Communism, Western Europe will re-emerge as a military
force. This force, given our own readiness to sustain and supplement it in the accomplishment of its mission, will it is assumed
render highly improbable for many years to come any aggressive
démarche on the part of the Soviet Union in the European theater.
In short: our simultaneous and intimately related advances toward
our three major objectives—containing the Soviet Union, cutting

the Communist movement down to manageable size in the countries outside the Iron Curtain, and preventing a third world war—are, it is supposed, already great and will be progressively greater as the years pass. We have, to be sure, been aided in all this by the presumed inability of the Russians, with their "ideological blinders," to come to grips with the realities of the world in which they live; but they, and the Communists outside the USSR as well, are regarded *inter alia* as our intellectual inferiors and as, therefore, ultimately powerless in our hands. We are, moreover, more than willing to settle for the relative showing of the several political parties in France and Italy as—if one be needed—a reliable index of the aforementioned advances: if the Communists have already lost x per cent of their voting strength in France and y per cent of their voting strength in Italy, the next elections—if only our Congress does not upset the applecart by witholding or reducing Marshall aid—will show that they have lost x-plus per cent in France and y-plus per cent in Italy. And no one in his senses believes otherwise!

It is true that an exhaustive account of the prevailing state of informed United States opinion on these questions would run to book length; that there are marked differences in terminology and emphasis from exponent to exponent of that opinion; and that—since this follows from the two foregoing concessions—the account here offered is an "oversimplification." (As, for instance, Mr. Myrdal's assertion that Americans in general believe in an American "creed" which places a high valuation upon freedom and equality [6] is an "oversimplification"—but not for that reason the less useful or the less instructive.) I should be the first to agree, moreover, for all the care with which I have tried to set the various propositions down in approximately the form in which I have heard them enunciated and defended at every cocktail and dinner party in New Haven or Washington I have attended in recent months, that, once brought together in this manner on the printed page, they look rather like a caricature of a position than like a reputable scholar's summary of a position. (Let him who wonders why attempt to summarize, for example, the views of the late Mr. Voliva regarding the shape of the world without ending up with something that looks like a caricature.) I am, nevertheless, prepared to stand upon it as accurate reportage, and to summon my readers either to confirm it (as I think they will), or to name the man

not readily identifiable as a voice crying in the wilderness whose
over-all position adds up to anything essentially different from
this. A Mr. Dewey, to be sure, returns from his junket through
Europe to inquire (he is speaking of the members of the Polit-
buro): "Why should these 13 men be stupid enough to change
from a cold war to a shooting war? They have won more in the
last four years of uneasy peace than any nation ever won by
war."[7] (He may, however, be thinking of China rather than
Europe; in any case the apparently inescapable inference is missing, that if the Russians are winning the cold war we must be losing it; and, in any case again, the voice's overtones are recognizably those of the wilderness of disappointed presidential ambition.) General Donovan, to be sure, is always there to remind us
that, on the Soviet side, the cold war has at no time been so cold
as we should like to think it,[8] that we must organize for the kind
of "subversive" warfare that the Russians are already waging, and
—out of his authoritative wartime experience with secret operations against the enemy—that the question to ask about the domestic Communists is not How numerous are they? but rather How
determined are they, how well trained, how evenly distributed
among the most vulnerable targets in the United States economy?
which is to say, How effective will they be behind our own lines
if and when we find ourselves at war with the Soviet Union?
There is the Educational Policies Commission of the National
Education Association, of which both General Eisenhower and
Mr. Conant are members, which is sufficiently concerned about
domestic Communists to resolve that "Members of the Communist
Party of the United States should not be employed as teachers"[9]
(but note that the ban, if *per impossibile* it were to be enforced,
would extend only to known cardholders). The World Federalists
are always there, saying one never knows quite what, and the
fellow travelers, saying what they are told to say, and, at opposite
ends of the wilderness, the Communists themselves and Mr.
Bullitt.[10] But, cry as they may, these voices are drowned out by
those of the optimists, who are always there fustest with the most-
est decibels.

I am much less concerned, for the purposes of the present Introduction, to argue the merits of this "prevailing informed opinion"
than to direct attention, as I shall in a moment, to the semi-articu-
late major premise upon which, as I believe, it rests. Since, how-

ever, I have already intimated that I regard it with a certain skepticism, I should be less than candid if I did not pause here to record in broad outline my reasons for dissociating myself from it. These are:

a. I have at no time, either as a functionary in the Department of State through the months before the Marshall Plan was taken out from under its wrappings or as an academic observer attempting to keep afloat in the flood of (domestic) propaganda that has subsequently been loosed in its behalf, believed that Marshall dollars would accomplish, *even on the level of economics,* a fraction of the miracles our Congressmen have been led to expect from them. Nor, as I turn for a last look, before this book is passed through the press, at the journals on which I rely for expert guidance on economic questions, do I find any eleventh-hour reason to join the optimists on this point. A recent (June 11) issue of the *Economist,*[11] which can hardly be suspected of animus against the Marshall Plan, has this to say about the economic situation of France: "The numerous developments in re-equipment and production during 1948 . . . had little impact on the country's *alarming balance of payments position. . . . It was thanks to very large doses of American aid that this deficit did not lead to disaster. Marshall dollars financed 45 per cent of French exports last year.*" (The *Economist's* analyst carefully avoids any suggestion that the balance-of-payments position has become less "alarming" during 1949 and any speculation as to what is to happen to France when the flow of Marshall dollars is, as we are told that it one day will be, discontinued.) Britain also, as I write these lines, seems to be on the threshold of a new balance-of-payments crisis, which appears to be unresolvable on any terms that do not run counter to ECA policies.[12] In a word: in so far as the prevailing American optimism is predicated upon a favorable prognosis regarding the economic health of Western Europe, it is not yet warranted.

b. The empirical evidence regarding the political gains that may putatively be attributed to the Marshall Plan to date (and thus the political gains that we are putatively entitled to expect from it over the next years) is by no means convincing. This is not to deny that the Communists have lost a certain percentage of their electoral support in the two countries which, equally with the Marshall Plan enthusiasts, I regard as crucial, namely, France and

Italy; and it is not to deny, and certainly not to refuse to welcome, the impressive increments of electoral strength that have accrued to the anti-Communist coalitions that have taken shape in those two countries since the war.[13] But there are three things that we must not forget: First, that any political party has, when the wind is in its sails, a certain number of "marginal" sympathizers who are barely willing to go along with it, and that the ease with which these marginal supporters can be drained off teaches us nothing whatever about the ease with which the intramarginal supporters can be drained off—which is to say that making inroads into the Communist Party's electoral strength is, like most excellent things, difficult, and difficult precisely because governed by the law of diminishing returns. Second, that the connection between the percentagewise electoral losses of the Communists (as, also, the percentagewise gains of the notoriously unstable anti-Communist coalitions in the two countries) and Marshall dollars may well be less simple than we are asked to believe. And, third, that the safest of safe generalizations about contemporary politics is that democratic institutions are, in any country, ultimately at the mercy of any totalitarian movement which can command the allegiance of as many as 25 per cent of the voters. In neither France nor Italy has Communist electoral support been rolled back, by any means, to a safe point beneath this danger mark. If, therefore, the preservation of democracy be one of the political gains we are interested in, the time for optimism is not yet.

c. Even assuming that the Marshall Plan *can* accomplish the economic rehabilitation of Western Europe, that European prosperity *will* affect the relative strength of Western Europe's political parties and coalitions in the manner envisaged by the prevailing informed opinion, and that we *are* about to see Western Europe begin to re-emerge, in consequence, as an effective military force, I am still unable to follow the strategic thinking by which one proceeds from these propositions to the conclusion that we shall have prevented, or even postponed, a third world war. Here, as it seems to me, the custodians of our wisdom about the Soviet Union (in our planning staffs, our intelligence agencies, our research institutes) have done the nation a great disservice by fixing their attention (and thus ours) upon the question, Does the Soviet Union want war?—and upon its variant, Can the Soviet planners, given the limited productive capacity of the Soviet economy, given also the proportions of the task of reconstruction imposed upon them by World War II, conceivably convince themselves that they can win any war they might fight with the United States within the foreseeable future? The answer to both these questions, assuming that they are worth answering at all, is clearly No; and this No has, as I see it, been the point of departure for our strategic thinking ever since it was first pronounced by a certain highly authoritative voice. If, in the Berlin crisis, we had the good sense not to act upon it, and chose the airlift in preference to sending through an armored convoy, still the fact that the Russians have been the first to say "uncle" in the ensuing battle of nerves has, unhappily, re-established it as the relevant axiom. And, meanwhile, we have not even begun to think through the question that we need to answer if we truly mean business about preventing a new war, namely, In what circumstances might the Soviet planners be obliged to choose war in preference to the realistic alternatives left open to them by United States foreign policy? (The good sense we displayed in Berlin was, be it noted, a tacit recognition of the urgency of this question as opposed to that which we were answering aloud. The same good sense appears, in general, to have presided over our budget allocations for the Air Forces.)

Once the strategic problem is posed in these terms one finds oneself face to face with the disturbing possibility that the more the Marshall Plan *succeeds* as a specific against economic paralysis, Communist influence, and military impotence in Western Europe, the more it *fails* as a means of preventing or postponing war between the United States and the Soviet Union. For the re-emergence of Western Europe as an effective military force may well be an alternative to war that the Soviet planners, given their purposes and commitments, will not accept without fighting, *whatever the odds against them may be*. To affirm flatly that it is not—and the informed opinion I have summarized above clearly presupposes some such flat affirmation—is either to insist that the Soviet Union is no longer in a position to advance to the Channel, which seems highly improbable, or to lay claim to a kind of insight into those purposes and commitments which one can only envy. I, for one, continue to suspect that the Soviet Union will strike before Western Europe is capable of offering more than token resistance to the Red Army; and even if I did not I should think twice before taking the contrary for granted for purposes of policy making.

d. I have spoken above of the empirical evidence on the basis of which we are asked to believe that economic recovery in Western Europe is and will continue to translate itself into political gains vis-à-vis the Communist movement; and I have thus reserved for separate treatment my major quarrel with the body of opinion I am here criticizing, which is this: That body of opinion takes it for granted, on recognizably *theoretical* grounds, that the "causes" of the Communist movement are ultimately economic, that therefore the measures appropriate to a struggle against that movement, whether at home or abroad, are as a matter of course economic measures, that, in fine, if we but solve the economic problems (ours, and those of other peoples) and keep them solved, the menace of Communism will disappear forever from those quarters in which it now exists.[14] In its most vulgar form, the position boils down to the axiom that there is in any country a simple one-one relation between the incidence of poverty and the strength of the Communist movement [15] (I shall not press the debater's point that the proposition comes straight out of the mouth of Karl Marx); in its more sophisticated forms it pays lip service to "political" (that is, other than economic) measures but insists that they are practicable only in an appropriate economic context [16]—or fixes attention not upon the incidence of poverty but upon the incidence of disappointed economic expectations. Always, however, whether the problem be explaining the presence of Communism where it is present, or accounting for its absence where it is absent, or planning means for combatting its growth or preventing its emergence, the strategic role is assigned to the data, and thus by implication to the skills, of the economist.[17]

Should any reader instinctively ask, at this point, If the causes of Communism are not economic what on earth could they be? or What kind of measures could we conceivably adopt, in the struggle against Communism, except economic measures? let him take comfort: the intellectual climate of his age and country is not congenial to any other response. Or, to put the same thing in another way, in order for him to cultivate any other response he would have first to seal himself off from virtually all the fountains of wisdom to which well-informed people in the United States normally turn when they require guidance on these matters. That is why I have clung, throughout the preceding paragraphs, to the phrase "prevailing *informed* opinion"; for I do not suppose that the broad masses of the American people (most of whom have had, at one time or another, firsthand experience of poverty) would, in the absence of false teaching by their presumptive intellectual betters, ever acquiesce in the notion that there is a simple one-one relation between poverty and Communism, or place their largest bets upon anti-Communist measures that take that notion for granted. That is also why I have devoted some five hundred hours of heavily mortgaged time,[18] over the last year, to translating M. Rossi's book, which beyond any other book on the Communist movement that has come to my attention seems to me capable of pointing us toward a sense-making answer to the question, Why do people become Communists? For without an answer to that question that represents the best thinking of which we are capable, that involves no uncriticized *petitio principii*, and that, above all, can bear confrontation with the empirical facts at our disposal, we shall continue to be the unintentional allies of world Communism in its brilliantly planned, brilliantly executed drive for world power.

II

Why do people become Communists? Will a significant number of people continue to become Communists from year to year through the years ahead? In what circumstances that we might move to create would the Communist movement cease to attract converts, or, better still, lose its hold upon the converts it has already attracted?

José Ortega y Gasset said it, nineteen incredibly long years ago, in his *Revolt of the Masses*. There is, he argued, absolutely nothing in the creed of Communism which, as such, is likely to commend itself to the people of Europe, because these people fail to see in Communist organization any future so tempting as to dispose them to turn their backs upon the individualism into which they have hitherto poured their energies. Does it then follow that the West [19] will not be "submerged by the Red torrent"? I once thought, he replied in effect, that that was the correct inference; and I thought so at a time when many, who have now "recovered their tranquillity, at precisely the moment when they might with reason lose it," thought otherwise. Today, however, it "seems to me quite possible that in the next few years Europe may grow enthusiastic for Bolshevism—*not for its own sake, but in spite of what it is.*" And why? Let us listen carefully, for these words deserve, to my mind, a place beside certain paragraphs in Keynes' *Economic Consequences of the Peace* on the honor roll of the great predictions of our age:

Whatever the content of Russian Communism may be, it represents a gigantic human enterprise. In it, men have resolutely embraced a purpose of reform, and live tensely under the discipline that such a faith instills into them. If natural forces . . . do not bring failure to this attempt . . . its wonderful character of a mighty enterprise will light up the continental horizon as with a new and flaming constellation. If Europe, in the meantime, persists in the ignoble vegetative existence of these last years, its muscles flabby for want of exercise, without any plan of a new life, how will it be able to resist [this] . . . contaminating influence? It is simply a misunderstanding of the European to expect that he can hear unmoved that call to new action when *he has no standard of a cause as great to unfurl in opposition.* For the sake of serving something that will give meaning to his existence, it is not impossible that the European may swallow his objections to Communism and feel himself *carried away not by the substance of the faith, but by the fervour of conduct which it inspires.*

And then this: "Communism is an extravagant moral code, but nothing less than a moral code . . . [Is it not our task] to oppose to that Slavonic code a new European code, the inspiration towards a new programme of life?" [20]

Richard Weaver has said it, too [21]—in familiar accents, and with an eye well-nigh exclusively to the course of events within the United States.[22] Make no mistake about it, he warns us in several passages which, craving his leave, I shall piece together and paraphrase in my own way: The "blue heaven" in which the Western Liberals are living is "precarious" to a degree that they do not even remotely suspect; and it is precarious above all because of the appeal of the "ideology fostered by their great rival to the East." [23] Soviet Communism, that is to say, has—for all its *ostensible* commitment to materialism—"generated a body of ideas with a terrifying power to spread; and it is precisely the Western Liberals' defeat in the "struggle to win adherents" that must finally drive them into "loss of judgment and panic"—or, if you like, has already driven them there, so that we "see before us the *paradox of materialist Russia expanding by the irresistible force of an idea,* while the United States, which supposedly has the heritage of values and ideals, *frantically throws up barricades of money around the globe.*" [24] The struggle, however fashionable it may be to suppose the contrary, is between "fanaticism" ("redoubling one's effort after one's aim has been forgotten") on the part of the United States [25] and clearheaded realism on the part of the Russians [26] ("nothing is more disturbing to modern men of the West than the logical clarity with which the Communists face all problems, . . . [for they recognize] that here are the first true realists in hundreds of years, and that no dodging about in the excluded middle will save Western liberalism" [27]). The remedy, if there is one? We must, for one thing, emancipate ourselves from the notion that it does not matter what a man believes "so long as he does not take his beliefs seriously," [28] and from the kindred notion that political society is possible without a "minimum consensus of value." [29] We must, for another, put behind us the idea that we are the helpless prisoners of our material circumstances ("When people set the highest value on relationships with one another, it does not take them long to find material accommodations for these" [30]). And we must, finally, relearn the truth that "some form of [shared] sentiment . . . lies at the basis of all congeniality," and that, in the absence of shared sentiment, cities and nations are merely "people living together in one place, without friendship or common understanding, and *without capacity, when the test comes, to pull together for survival.*" [31]

M. Rossi, in the book you are about to read, says it again—with immediate application, no doubt, to the society in which he lives but in terms which (as I know from many unforgettable conversations in his book-crammed house just outside Paris) he would unhesitatingly extend to any Western society that has certain characteristics in common with that of France. The Communist Party, he contends, "knows where it is going—even if the knowing is done in faraway Moscow"; it stands ready not only to tell a man what to do next but also to see to it that he does it; and because it does these things it is, for many Frenchmen, "*a welcome refuge from a way of life which, because it makes no demands,*

seems intolerably tame and enervating" (p. 215). Any complete
explanation of the Party's presence in France, of its remarkable
growth, must therefore "run, in large part, in terms of certain
characteristic features of French society which lend themselves
to exploitation by the possessors of the Soviet myth" (p. 223);
and if, as the election statistics of recent years clearly show, a
solid body of French voters remains loyal to the Party and its
slogans *"regardless of the policies it is supporting at any given
moment,"* we must recognize that this is because it "satisfies certain continuing needs that no student of French society and politics dares ignore" (p. 224). It knows, for instance, as the other
French political parties evidently do not, that "even the meanest
of men . . . have a deep-felt need for intellectual certainty . . .
[and] wish to be on the side of Truth"; it therefore offers them
"something to believe" (p. 206). It is, like it or not, "like *a great
river, fed from remote places by dependable tributaries,* and
swollen by innumerable objects which it tears loose from their
moorings and carries along with it" (p. 229). We merely play into
its power, however, when we accept Communist assurances that
the Party's success can be explained in terms of its defense of the
"interests" of the less prosperous classes of our society. Rossi
writes: "It *does* midwife . . . working-class demands. It *does,* in
backing up those demands, vigorously play the champion's role
that the other parties . . . fail to claim for themselves. . . . It
does, in this way, maintain close contact with the workers. But this
is not the aspect of Party strategy that wins it its hard core of militants, who are notoriously drawn from . . . elements . . . who
do not need to have their interests defended in the manner just described . . ." (p. 225). In the long run, furthermore, the Party's
strength is in direct proportion to the loyalty of this "solid core
of trained militants" (p. 229); and it is therefore the roots of this
loyalty that we must expose, and learn to understand, if we are
to arrest its growth.

   M. Rossi has, let us concede at once, no single, universally applicable answer to the questions implied in the concluding lines
of the foregoing paragraph. He is, however, deeply convinced
that "the Communist movement tends to thrive in societies whose
members are no longer held together by the bond of shared moral
principle and purpose" (p. 230). In such societies, he thinks, "men
tend to divide off into clanlike groupings whose very raison d'être

is their repudiation of the ideal of unity over a wider area," so
that the "citizen, unable to relate himself meaningfully to the
broader constituency, that is, the nation, seeks and finds his 'community' in one of these lesser groupings, of which the Communist
Party is merely the extreme instance" (*ibid.*). And if, sometimes,
he seems to be looking for the answer elsewhere (e.g., in the love
of power [p. 216] or in the sheer possession of the "Soviet myth"
[p. 223]), it is to this theme, or one very like it, that he always returns—as, for example, in what seems to me the most crucial of
the passages he addresses to those who seek in other directions for
guarantees against the ultimate triumph of the Communist movement: "[If the Communists win power in France, as one day they
well may] it will be because France is a country in which the
bonds of community have grown weak, a country in which pretty
much everybody is ready, at a moment's notice, to call into
question the moral foundations of national unity. For, make no
mistake about it, *where unity can be had on no other terms men
finally seek it in some political movement that is able and willing
to impose it*" (p. 243).

Let us agree at once that the three writers I have been quoting
are, to some extent, saying quite different things and would, at
the margin, move in quite different directions. Let us agree,
again, that even in so far as they are saying the same thing their
saying it does not make it so. And let us agree, finally, that I should
require more by far of the reader's time than I dare claim in this
Introduction in order to state the case for the points of view they
hold in common as over against those of the architects of the "prevailing informed opinion" in the United States—wherefore the
reader must not suppose me to think that I have done so. I shall
be content if these paragraphs have served merely to re-open
his mind to the fact that there are able students of contemporary
politics—three at least—who strongly believe that dominant
American theory regarding the "causes" of Communism is root-
and-branch wrong, that ruling American expectations regarding
the future of Communism are without foundation, and that
present American measures in the struggle against Communism
are the product—let us not mince words—of ignorance and
shoddy thinking. For, however much they may disagree about
other matters, the three writers I have been quoting—of whom
M. Rossi, because he shares our concern, my reader's and mine,

for the future of the democratic process, perhaps deserves the most sympathetic hearing—represent various degrees of approximation to a central position that can be summarized in the following propositions:

(1) people become Communists, for the most part, because of something they find *within* the Communist movement, i.e., in actual *participation* in that movement;

(2) people tend to seek that something within the Communist movement because, or rather in so far as, they do *not* find it in the political communities to which they belong;

(3) we may confidently expect ever larger numbers of people to seek that something within the Communist movement unless they begin to find it within their political communities;

(4) they will begin to find that something within their political communities only in so far as the latter are transformed, i.e., only in so far as we transform them, into communities of another kind;

(5) the characteristic of existing political communities that renders necessary their transformation (because it creates the strategic opportunities that the Communists exploit) is their *purposelessness*, i.e., their failure to make *demands* upon their members, i.e., their inability to infuse *meaning* into their members' lives;

(6) this purposelessness is precisely what we should expect to obtain in political communities that permit themselves the luxury of diverse and thus conflicting "belief-systems" (the phrase is de Grazia's), i.e., political communities that possess no *single* belief-system which their members are brought to accept and be loyal to, much as, shall we say, they are brought to obey the laws (Ortega would say "moral code," Weaver "some form of shared sentiment," Rossi "shared moral principle or purpose");

(7) in so far as we fail to discharge our responsibility for correcting this basic deficiency of our political communities we contribute, *nolens volens,* to the success of the Communist movement; and

(8) we are thinking wishfully when we tell ourselves that Communists are something less than our equals as regards insight into the realities of contemporary politics, as regards intellectual capacity, as regards emancipation from "ideological blinders," etc. (I, for one, feel about the alleged "stupidity" of Communist strategic planning and Communist propaganda, as compared to

ours, much as Mr. Lincoln felt about General Grant's whiskey.)

And it is, I think, possible to point to at least two other propositions which, though not actually asserted by any of the three writers, follow as a matter of course from the foregoing eight:

(9) we are very wide of the mark indeed when, in planning the means for combatting the growth of the Communist movement, we fix attention more than incidentally upon the data of the economist (the size of the national income, the distribution of that income, the ownership of property) or rely more than incidentally upon the skills of the economist; and

(10) the skills we need in the struggle against the Communist movement are clearly those of what Plato and Rousseau called the Legislator, i.e., those of the political theorist, whose business I should define, with them, as that of building the political community whose members willingly accept a single belief-system. It would follow, again, that there is a kind of poverty whose incidence, in any country, *does* stand in a one-one relation to the strength, actual and potential, of its Communist movement, namely, that which George Catlin calls "the poverty of political science." [32] And it would follow, finally, that if in any country, e.g., our own, the necessary skills do not exist (as I should be the last to suggest that they do), we can confidently point to that one of the learned disciplines in which the tempo of research and discovery must, at all costs, be quickened. Or, if you like, to that one of the learned disciplines whose carriers must be held accountable if, in Weaver's phrase, we are unable to pull together for survival when the test comes—as come now it must.

III

A recent writer in the *Economist* [33] speaks of Rossi's book as "useful," "well-documented," "illuminating," but "hostile" (i.e., to the Communists)—by contrast with, for example, Gérard Walter's *Histoire du Parti Communiste Français*,[34] which he deems "impartial." A previous reviewer, writing in the London *Times*,[35] makes much of the water that has flowed over the dams in France since the investigation that underlies the *Physiologie* was completed, leaving his readers with the impression that the book is out of date. I take vigorous exception to both these lines of criticism; neither, as I believe, shows any grasp of the character of the enterprise upon which M. Rossi is engaged, of the method he is using, or of the conclusions at which he arrives.

The *Physiologie* is indeed not a book that the French Communists were ever likely to accept for publication by one of their richly subsidized presses or to distribute through their bookstores or to welcome in the book-review columns of their mass-circulation dailies. In a sense, therefore, which is to say in so far as we are prepared to take our definitions of English words out of the Communists' own lexicon, "hostile" is the *mot juste*—and we must let it stand. The *Physiologie* is, again, not the book to which you would send the man trying to make up his mind whether a Communist victory might perhaps be a good thing for France, for a nice balancing, *sub specie aeternitatis*, of the relevant pro's and con's; and if that is what we mean by "impartial" then, well and good, it is a book that we must use with caution because of its *parti pris*. The *Physiologie*, still again, does not tell you what the Communists have been doing in France through the years 1942–49, so that if we insist upon reading it as "history" it is indeed incomplete, and old hat besides. But let us not overlook the following considerations:

a. There is as little point in applying the criteria of historical criticism to the *Physiologie* as there would be in applying them to, shall we say, the Yankee City Series [36] or to *Middletown*.[37] M. Rossi writes as a *political scientist,* seeking to analyze the political phenomenon known as the Communist Party—and along with it (this emphasis well-nigh all his reviewers have ignored) the relevant aspects of the political community which produces that phenomenon. His method, like the Lynds' and the Yankee City group's, is that of careful and patient observation of his subject's behavior *over a period sufficiently long* to enable the investigator to identify, and explain, the recurrent patterns of that behavior. He relies, like the Lynds and the Yankee City group, in large part upon what the subject says about itself, and upon what it reveals about itself in what it says about this or that (like Trotsky, Rossi rarely cites a non-Communist source for any fact that the Communists might wish to dispute). Now if we wish to discredit an investigation of this kind, it is never enough merely to point to the calendar: the intervening years may have modified the patterns upon which the investigator rests his conclusions; it is, if you like, even highly probable that the intervening years have modified them; but we are not, without bringing forward new data ourselves, entitled to an opinion as to the extent to which, or the direction in which, they have modified them (it may well be that the modifications, if we but knew them, would tend to re-enforce those conclusions). To suppose that we are entitled to is to engage—I paraphrase Collingwood—in persecution of the (social) sciences.[38] We can, of course, seek to show that the techniques by which the investigator has applied the method were not sufficiently refined for the task in hand; and I should say that M. Rossi has, to some extent, invited criticism with regard to the relative crudity of his techniques as compared with those of the Lynds and the Yankee City group, and his unfamiliarity with recent American developments in "content analysis." [39] But the critics have not been raising questions of this kind; and M. Rossi might well have replied to them, if they had, that the man about to be run down by an automobile requires neither a microscope nor a sextant but an observant naked eye.

b. M. Rossi does, to be sure, tell a story, i.e., the story of the campaign of propaganda and agitation by means of which the Communists fought their way up from outlawry (the weeks following the Nazi-Soviet Pact) to the position of odds-on favorite in the race for political power in France; and he is certainly accountable to the critics for the accuracy of that story. But the story is, for him, always incidental: his point always is, Don't you see that, other things being equal (especially as regards the impact of events outside France), the old-line parties, given the indefensible character of this (Western) society they must defend and the patent boyishness of their strategic thinking, cannot ultimately withstand this kind of attack? His point is not, This is what they did—that the reader can learn from some "impartial" historian like M. Walter—but rather, This is the kind of strategic thinking that clearly underlay their doing it, and This is what would have had to be done in order to keep them from getting by with it. Above all, his point is never, See how *wicked* they are, how *inconsistent*, how *shamelessly willing to follow the latest shift in the Party line*, though all this certainly emerges from his account; and this, I think, helps explain the failure of the book reviewers, whose ear is attuned to books that "prove" what M. Rossi knew about the Communists 'way back in the 'twenties, to come to grips with his argument. (From this point of view it is perhaps regrettable that the *Physiologie* is, inter alia, a relatively early statement of the "shocking" facts regarding the French Communists' willingness, or rather eagerness, to collaborate with the Nazi occupation; for this tickles the reviewers' taste for the sensational, whereas the beginning of wisdom in these matters is to recognize that, given the Communists' willingness to do and say whatever needs to be done and said in order to gain power, this is one area in which the sensational and the commonplace are quite indistinguishable.)

c. M. Rossi bids his non-Communist readers to recognize that they are responsible for the success, and even the existence of the Communist movement, and specifically warns them that, in the struggle against that movement, hatred is as a matter of course self-defeating. "We are ourselves responsible," he declares, "in large part, for every error on the part of our adversaries. We are . . . responsible both for the good we have failed to do and for the evil we have failed to prevent" (p. 256). And again: "If we advance . . . with hatred in our eyes, those of them whose faith in Communism is sorely taxed (as the Communists' faith often will be if the opposition takes the form envisaged here) will shake off their doubts and carry on as before" (p. 260). This, I should say, is the *reverse* of "hostile"; for the premise that underlies it is that a democratic society, in dealing with its Communists, should re-enact the parable of the lost sheep, whom the shepherd must bring back into the fold even at the risk of neglecting the sheep already there.[40]

These themes—our own responsibility for the existence of the Communist movement, the unwisdom, immorality even of "hating" the Communists, the need for reintegrating the Communists into our society—are, as it seems to me, among the great strengths of the *Physiologie;* and I hope that the reader will heed well all that M. Rossi has to say about them. At the same time, however, I should like to venture the following comments upon them—in part to dissociate M. Rossi from a certain interpretation that might be placed upon them, in part to dissociate myself from M. Rossi on some of the issues involved:

The shepherd in the parable, if I read it correctly, is quite clear in his head as to what he means by "lost," which is to say that he is not a man for whom all questions are open questions. Suppose him assailed by doubts as to the criteria by which he decides whether to regard a given sheep as lost, suppose him capable of conducting a debate with himself—or the sheep!—as to whether or not the lost sheep "may have a point," and the parable becomes, any way you look at it, nonsense. M. Rossi's use of it, therefore, must not be understood to align him with those of our fellow countrymen who believe, for instance, that the discussion process in our government departments profits from adequate representation of the lost sheep's (including the Communists') point of view [41]—especially in view of his argument (p. 259) in favor of the removal of Communist judges and army officers in France. For the brotherly love enjoined by the author of the parable does not—as M. Rossi, at least in this emphasis of his thought, has not forgotten—connive at, or even view with toleration, the defiling of the temple. The Communist Party, "whatever pose its future tactics may cause it to adopt, will remain . . . a cancer, whose natural function is to destroy healthy tissue and undermine vitality"; wherefore those "who think it can one day be assimilated are the victims of the most dangerous political illusion of our time" (p. 242).

Nevertheless—and for the reason just given—M. Rossi seems to me to have clouded his title to the parable of the lost sheep (and to have cut himself off from any possible appeal to the story of the money-changers) by adopting a position in political theory that points in a quite different direction. The Communist Party, he recognizes, "accepts the rules of the democratic process only while it is too weak to do otherwise, . . . demands freedom for itself only to carry on its struggle for power, and intends to take away the freedom of everyone else as soon as it can" (p. 255). But we are not entitled to conclude that "since it is to be a question of force in the long run anyway, the state must . . . stand with folded hands while freedom, the heritage of all, is being destroyed by the opportunism of the few" (p. 255). Why? Because "the search for truth cannot go forward in the absence of heresy and opposition," and because "when the unity of a democratic society is maintained through arbitrary imposition, even over a very small area, it ceases to be the kind of unity that is appropriate to a truth-seeking society," and finally because we cannot be sure, when we borrow the enemy's methods, "that we are not installing him permanently in our midst and delivering him our souls" (pp. 255–257). Now M. Rossi denies that this is "to place

error and truth and good and evil all on the same level" (p. 256);
but I find myself quite unable to apprehend the grounds upon
which he rests his denial, or to see how he can refuse to go the
rest of the way with the liberals and argue that you don't use
force against the man you believe to be in error because he
may after all be right (for we are not infallible), or to understand why, having said all that I have quoted him as saying, he
indulges the luxury of his analogy between the Communist
Party and a cancer (everybody knows what it is that you do
with a cancer) or of his views on the continuance in office of
Communist judges and army officers. (Suppose they refuse to
surrender their places? Or, if that be too easy to answer, what
about the inherently coercive character of the process which,
as we in America have now learned, you have to go through
in order to find out which judges and officers are Communists?) [42] M. Rossi must, I submit, give something up: Either
his nineteenth-century liberal political theory or his twentieth-
century police-state techniques; either the notion that it is
merely a "search" for truth we are engaged in, and not a defensive operation we mean business about on behalf of some truths
with respect to which we *are* prepared to assume our infallibility,
or his espousal of measures that make sense only as part of such an
operation.

M. Rossi's "better" view—and I call it that because it is the
view that has dominated the conception and execution of the
book you are about to read—is clearly that which assumes a distinction between healthy tissue and cancer and is, at the margin
anyhow, prepared to contemplate surgery. The parti pris which
the *Economist's* reviewer detects in the book, that is to say, is that
of the physician who, in the struggle between the diseased organ
and the malady that has attacked it, is indeed "on the side" of
the organ and "against" the malady. Or, as I should prefer to
put it, his parti pris is that of the political scientist who interprets
his oath as requiring him to investigate, and prescribe, the means
for curing sick societies of their sickness and thus making them
well again.

We must learn to welcome this kind of parti pris in the rare
book in which we find it.

Willmoore Kendall
Paris, July, 1949

I

On the Eve of the Defeat

1. At the time of the fall of France, in June, 1940, the French Communist Party was just beginning to surmount the difficulties it had brought down upon its head by endorsing the Nazi-Soviet Pact. A decree of September 26, 1939, had declared the Party, and all the other organizations associated with the Third International, dissolved. Its two mass-circulation dailies, *L'Humanité* and *Ce Soir*, had been put out of business. Thousands of its political spokesmen and trade-union leaders had been thrown in jail. Its parliamentary group, after a brief interlude as a "Workers and Peasants Group," had disappeared—and the repression, not content with unseating its members, had had most of them locked up. Within a few weeks, in a word, the Party had lost, almost without exception, the strategic positions it had won—in the press, in the municipalities, in the Chamber, in the Confédération Générale du Travail (CGT)—by participating in the so-called Popular Front.

Between September, 1939, and June, 1940, the Party has nevertheless published clandestinely some fifty numbers of *L'Humanité*. Over the same period it has completely transformed its structure, and is now made up of "groups of three." Each of the latter, in theory at least, is unaware of the others' identity; all communication among them takes place via the higher echelons. (In this, and in other respects as well, they reproduce the organizational formulae of the secret societies founded by Blanqui and Barbès.) * Though the Party's activities are indeed greatly reduced, it can now feel reasonably

* These societies, of which the Societé des Droits de l'Homme and the Societé des Saisons may be cited as examples, belong to the Louis-Philippe period of French history. They were antimonarchical, and were driven to adopt the organizational forms to which the author refers precisely by police "repression." Both Louis-Auguste Blanqui (1805–81) and Armand Barbès (1809–70) served terms in prison. W.K.

certain that it has ridden out the storm, and made the most of the domestic difficulties resulting from the war. Its instrument, for the latter purpose, has been a propaganda line that has become more openly defeatist with each passing day.

2. The signature of the Nazi-Soviet Pact, and the French Communists' obedient acceptance of the new Moscow line, earn the Party many new and indignant enemies. Up to this moment it has been demanding intransigent opposition to the foreign policy of the Reich and damning as traitors all who have sought to direct attention to the actual power relations between France and Germany. It has been insisting upon an immediate and unconditional alliance with the USSR. It has been singing the praises of Poland for its "resistant" attitude in the Danzig crisis—and those of England and France for the guarantees that have made that attitude possible. Within a few hours all that is turned upside down. For Stalin has reached an agreement with Hitler: the German-Soviet Pact becomes a "factor making for peace"; and uncompromising belligerency gives way to uncompromising pacifism as the order of the day.

The shift in line sets even the most seasoned Party members back on their heels; and the masses of the French workers are, to say the least, bewildered by it. The fellow travelers move promptly to neutral territory, where they can await further information; and for a time there are defections among the Party's own members. In general, however, the Party cadres hold firm, and those who, without openly "breaking," have drawn aside for a moment, come promptly back into the fold.

3. Let us turn back to the year 1934, when Russia suddenly adopts an activist role in international affairs (the Litvinov missions, "collective security" and regional pacts, the fight against the Pact of Four, the League of Nations, etc.). It can, as matters stand, include in its calculations only one foreign Communist Party that is neither illegal nor insignificant, namely, the PCF, the French section of the Communist International. In Germany—in the course of a few brief weeks after January, 1933—the Comintern has been obliged to write

off its strongest section. In England, where the 1926 strike brought the Soviet and British trade-unions together for a brief honeymoon, then put them asunder with reciprocal accusations of bad faith and treason, the Communist movement has never succeeded in putting down roots. In America, aside from a few professional agitators, the movement has at most a scattering of more or less influential "friends"; for instance, some of the "planners" in Roosevelt's entourage. In the Scandinavian countries and in Czechoslovakia the International has lost, in rapid succession, all the strong positions it conquered immediately after World War I. In Austria it has at no time been able to compete successfully with the Social Democrats, whose hold on the capital city can evidently be threatened only from the Right. In Spain the Communists have been caught between the Socialists and the Anarchosyndicalists, and are stopped dead in their tracks (their position is to improve after 1936, but we are speaking of 1934). In Belgium, Holland, Switzerland, the Communists have never ceased to be a minor party; and in the remaining European countries the Party is outside the law and without influence. In Hungary, in the Baltic countries, in Poland, in Italy, even in the Balkan countries (where the Communists' appeal to Left-wing agrarian sentiment had at one time won them strong positions)— in all these countries the tide has turned against them.

Nor have things gone any better in China, where the Party's membership has remained indeterminate and shifting and where its growth has been inhibited by continuous subordination to the USSR's policy in the Far East—most particularly, of course, its policy toward Chiang Kai-shek. The Party perhaps has some strength in certain peripheral provinces—for example, along the frontiers of Outer Mongolia; but in the interior the Kuomintang has kept a firm grip on its monopoly of power.

A slender balance sheet, undoubtedly, save as one looks at France, whose Communist Party is large, operating out in the open, and able to point to a real mass following. And this is all the more significant because, not long ago, the French

Communist Party was poorly thought of in Moscow, where its alleged "petty bourgeois" tendencies had earned it a reputation for "undependability"—the more since these tendencies were apparently shared by the French workers themselves. ("Undependable," in this context, means unreceptive to "Leninist" principles of organization and the class struggle—unreceptive, in other words, to "bolshevization.") The turning point here came in 1930, when, somewhat later than other countries, France entered a period of economic and social crisis; and over the next four years the French Communist Party quickly learns how to make its weight felt in French politics. By February, 1934, it has become an instrument through which Moscow can begin to sway the course of events in France. Moscow must, therefore, revise its opinion of the Party.

From the moment of Hitler's coming to power the Bolshevik planners have been trying to guess which of two tendencies Germany will follow in its foreign policy. Will it remain faithful to the tradition of Rapallo, or will it strike out along the lines indicated by the Nazis' anti-Communist declarations? Pending an answer to that question, Moscow must handle Berlin with kid gloves—and develop what strength it can in Western Europe. And since this cannot be done in England (as witness the latter's appeasement policy toward Hitlerite Germany through the years 1933 to 1935), it has a further reason for turning to France—where, for the rest, anxiety concerning the resurgence of Germany dates back to 1919.

After 1933, then, the course of Russian diplomacy runs increasingly parallel to the postwar French policy of pacts and alliances—this being the meaning, on one level, of Russia's active role in such matters as the definition of the aggressor, the strengthening of the Little Entente, the creation of a Balkan Entente (January, 1934), the rapprochement with Poland, and the Eastern Pact. And French policy itself, after April 16, 1934, comes into ever sharper conflict with Britain's policy of compromise and postponements. The Franco-Soviet

Pact of May, 1935, may thus be regarded as the coping stone of a new system. Henceforth the political and social line of the French Communist Party, which always acts as the Soviet Union's agent in France, will unabashedly echo Kremlin policy.

4. The Party's patent dependence on the Soviet Union soon produces at least one result of fundamental importance: thousands of Frenchmen—not only out-and-out Party members and sympathizers but also many who follow the Party at second remove, through the Popular Front—become vague about the border line between French politics and Soviet politics. They come, for instance, to consider Stalin their real leader in the struggle against fascism. They openly attribute the Party's success in 1936 to the wisdom of Stalin's directives. In a word, blind confidence in the leaders of the Russian state and of the Communist International (they are, of course, the same men) takes deep root within the Party and is gradually communicated to the readers of *L'Humanité*—so that before long one of the tenets of the Fascist decalogue, transformed to read "Stalin is always right," begins to be heard in strange quarters. The Popular Front, the Communist Party, the working-class gains of 1936, the Soviet Union—these four things are increasingly tied together in the Party's propaganda, so that to mention one of them to a Party sympathizer is to call to mind the other three. And this leads promptly to a further development: anyone who adopts a position against Stalin's Russia thereby confesses that he is an enemy of the social reforms of the Popular Front. This explains, in part, how easy it will be for the Communists, when the time comes to do so, to argue that a Soviet victory is a necessary first step toward the re-establishment of France's prewar "social gains."

The French Communist Party grows both in wisdom and in stature through continuous and effective participation in the struggle for power. At the beginning of the period of which we are speaking it is, paradoxically, both too rigid and too unstable to meet the demands upon it. It casts off both these vices at the same time; it becomes firm and purposeful;

it acquires tactical skill—most particularly, flexibility in maneuver. Moscow indicates its satisfaction, and soon after
Dimitrov is citing it as an example to Communist parties in
other countries. It even abandons its recalcitrant attitude toward "bolshevization," and this enables it to move up into the
front ranks of the Comintern, which admiringly describes its
activities as an "experiment of international value." The Party,
in short, has the wind in its sails and is ready for battle; and
what is not added to it by its own sagacity is duly bestowed
upon it by the stupidity of its adversaries, or, failing that, the
stupidity of its allies. That is why, when the August 25, 1939,
thunderbolt is unloosed, it possesses enough accumulated capital to carry it through the few days of crisis—during which,
moreover, it reveals a highly developed instinct for self-
preservation and an impressive forward momentum. From
the standpoint of strict logic, to be sure, the new line (the
"fight against all the capitalists" becomes once again the order
of the day) violently contradicts that adopted in 1934, when
the Party wrote off its "class struggle" slogans and became the
champion of "unity of the French nation." From the standpoint of resourceful tactics, however, the one about-face, by
making the Party a more manageable instrument, has prepared
the way for the other.

5. These internal factors would not, in themselves, suffice
to save the Party from extinction during these August days,
and we must notice that they were paralleled and reinforced
by certain aspects of the situation out over the country. For
one thing, France is at this time fundamentally pacifist in
its outlook: French opinion makes no sense of the "phony
war," and this means, inter alia, that the new Communist line
is more congenial to the country's mood than the old one, and
because more congenial it disposes people to overlook its in-
consistency with the old one. These points can hardly be overemphasized. The contradiction between the two lines would
perhaps prove fatal to the Party at this time if the discussion
were projected on the level of intense patriotism; but no one

forces it up to that level. For another thing, the administration of France's new laws has been placed in the hands of men whose antiworking-class bias seems to vindicate the Communist contention that the war is a "capitalist device" for recouping the losses the capitalists sustained in 1935. For the masses, happily from the Communist point of view, do not arrive at judgments in these matters along the paths either of logic or of history, or compare this year's Party slogans with last year's. They are, rather, swayed by their passions, by their short-term interests, and by the advantages (real or illusory) held out to them for the future. The man who chooses the right moment for "trafficking in hopes" can, therefore, easily enough buy back his past, which in this context is merely a series of phrases and gestures that nobody remembers.

6. The above statement needs to be modified, however, to take into account the psychology of the Communist militant —including under this heading even those Communist leaders who have been most deeply influenced by Bolshevik training. Let me put it this way. There are some things you can accomplish, in such a movement as that which we are considering, by means of discipline and indoctrination, and others that you cannot accomplish. For example, you can win the time you need in order to think up a suitable explanation for a new tactical plan. But you cannot dispense with the explanation altogether, particularly as far as your less seasoned (that is to say, less corrupt) elements are concerned. Now the Party's propaganda through the years since 1934 is still present to its militants' minds during these August days, and not all of them can be counted on to forget it—besides which the very fact of having made your appeal to them in terms of Stalin's infallibility makes them look for continuity between your present and your past actions. This continuity the Party now provides them by retelling the story of the years just passed around this theme: the objective of Soviet Russia, yesterday's as well as today's (yesterday it was demanding resistance to Hitler,

today it signs a pact with him), is to preserve peace. The USSR's methods may change, but the end in view is always the same.

Taken by itself, this explanation has the twofold disadvantage of being entirely defensive and of pointing no path into the future. The Party needs something more than a mere explanation—something forward-looking that will enable its militants to shake off the feelings of inferiority that have held many of them frozen in their tracks over a period of weeks. Peace, the Party therefore tells them, is only the short-term objective—a device for gaining time during which to strengthen the USSR and the Red Army; once this is accomplished the march toward the long-term objective of world revolution will be resumed. And, to drive the point home, the Party specifically instructs them to abandon the idiom of patriotic fancy: they must cease to be citizens and become, once again, proletarians, real proletarians. One might have expected here the words "who have no fatherland"; but the formula from the *Communist Manifesto* can serve the Party's present purposes only if it is given this new twist: World revolution and socialism are already victorious over "one sixth of the earth's surface." The workers therefore *do* have a fatherland, namely, the USSR; and it remains only to enlarge that fatherland's frontiers until they include the rest of the world. This, the Party points out, is the meaning of all the recent Soviet territorial annexations (eastern Poland, the Baltic countries, the Carelian Isthmus, Bessarabia, etc.): they are first steps along a road that leads far beyond the horizon. The war, which will be considerably prolonged, will give the two competing "capitalist" combines the time they need in order to wear themselves out. It will also give the USSR the time it needs to prepare for battle. To think of the end of the war is thus to think of a moment when the Communists will be able to say: The world is ours. The Red Army, what with internal revolutions in country after country the world over, will be irresistible, and socialism will rapidly spread to the earth's remotest corners.

All this has the desired effect, because it holds forth the apocalyptic vision the Communist cadres need—so as to have something to look forward to or, if you like, so as to have a sense-making reason for hanging on and keeping busy. As the capitalist countries, one after the other, plunge into war, as the ruins pile up, the USSR looks more and more like an oasis of peace and well-being: safe and secure on the edge of a world that is falling apart, it is easily recognizable as the promised land. Nor is this vision intended only for the Party cadres. The attempt will be made to communicate it to the entire French people, who once they have grasped it—so the Communists tell themselves—will speed its realization. For the events of June, 1940, have convinced France's Communist leaders that the moment has at last come when the masses of the miserable and demoralized French people can be brought to share the Communists' hopes and cooperate in the realization of the Communists' plan.

7. The Communists, in a word, see the fall of France primarily as a windfall that they must make the most of without delay. The Germans are on the outskirts of Paris. Italy has just declared war. The French Army has been routed, and the French people are undergoing the ordeal of the exodus from Paris. And the point to grasp is the promptness and confidence with which the Communists formulate their policy in this drastically changed situation. The pamphlet *How to Save Our Country* must have been written on June 11 or 12—on the 13th at the very latest. But it embodies all the themes that are to be picked up and developed through the weeks following the announcement of the Armistice. "France is encircled. It lies at the mercy of the invader. Its people have been betrayed by the two hundred families and the politicians to whom they give orders." The responsibility for this disorder is shared by "all but one" of France's political parties. "All but one" of the country's parties let themselves be "absorbed into the holy alliance" for war; and because the Communists were alone in opposing that holy alliance they were "accused of every crime in the book, and then thrown to the wolves."

The people of France must henceforth heed the voice of the Communist Party, which has never misled them.

Our country can achieve peace and security and independence; it can achieve liberty and social progress; but it can achieve these things only by depriving the agents of the two hundred families of their capacity to do harm. They are the true traitors; they are the men responsible for the country's present plight; they are the soldiers of the fifth column. And our country must, to these same ends, restore the political liberties of all its workers; it must restore to them the right to organize; it must liberate the Communist deputies and the workers now languishing in prison; it must make the rich pay.

People of France, unite! Fight for a government the French people will support! Fight for a government that will strike at fascism and reaction! Fight for a government that will strike at those who have betrayed the working class! Fight for a government capable of coming to an immediate understanding with the Soviet Union for the re-establishment of peace the world over![1]

The defeat is an accomplished fact: armistice negotiations are under way, and there are news leaks which indicate that Germany is driving a hard bargain. The nation responds in terms of humiliation, fatigue, and despair. France lies helpless at the feet of its ancient enemy.

After the Armistice: Communist Collaboration with the Occupation

8. Between June 17 and the beginning of July the Communists redefine their position. Their major premise for this purpose is that their hour has come.

On June 18, for instance, they distribute a pamphlet on the outskirts of Bordeaux in which they urge their readers to "demand the immediate arrest of the traitors and the establishment of a genuinely popular government, resting upon mass support." Such a government, they point out, "will of course free the workers now in jail, remove the ban on the Communist Party, and press the struggle against the fascism of Hitler and the two hundred families." It will come to an understanding with the USSR, based on plans for an equitable peace. It will "fight for France's independence, and take steps against all of the country's fascist organizations." This is, recognizably, from the source cited in Chapter I; that is, the authors are almost certainly men from the Party's central offices in Paris whom the exodus has deposited temporarily in Bordeaux. And the concluding note—of great interest for our inquiry— is an appeal for action by the "men in the shops, in the fields, in the stores, and in the offices," along with the merchants, the artisans, and the professionals, and, finally, the "soldiers, sailors, and aviators still under arms." [1] Some of the Party's local units, particularly in the unoccupied zone, go further still. A handbill distributed in Marseilles declares that "the moment has come for us to learn to use our weapons." [2] An issue of *Rouge-Midi* says the same thing, though in somewhat more guarded language: "Let the streets resound with your cries; let them seethe with your anger—your anger against the very men who are to fight with you for their possession." [3] The Party leaders soon see, however, that the struggle for power is a more complicated matter than these words would seem to suggest, and that, in any case, they can lead it only from Paris.

9. Upon their return to Paris shortly before the end of June the Communist leaders, having resumed liaison with the representatives of the Soviet Union, work out a concrete plan of action based on a new estimate both of the situation in France and the situation abroad. The broad outlines of this plan, certain elements of which have already turned up in the pamphlets and newspapers published during the exodus, may be recognized in the first number of *L'Humanité* to appear in occupied Paris; [4] and they are set forth again, also early in July, in a document from the Party's Central Committee—the *Manifesto to the People of France*. The central theme of both publications is this: The existing state of affairs, if only it can be handled "bravely and wisely," justifies the most extreme hopes the Communists have ever permitted themselves. This is to remain the Party line throughout the ensuing months. Even June 22, 1941, is to bring only such minor modifications as are unavoidable in view of the outbreak of war between Germany and the Soviet Union. The major emphases are as follows:

A. We are face to face with a genuine revolutionary situation. Because France has fallen, and because the two opposing "capitalist" blocs will wear themselves out as the war continues, the order of the day for French Communists is the conquest of power.

B. The conquest of power is out of the question unless peace is concluded with Germany within the immediate future. Only a Communist government can negotiate an early peace.

C. The Party's relations with the occupying power depend, and will continue to depend, on the German-Soviet Pact. These relations are of such character as to give the Party a relatively free hand in the present revolutionary situation, and will in no way jeopardize the Party's good name.

D. The Party will be effective only as it succeeds in tying itself to the broad masses of the population:

a. by couching its appeals in the language of outraged nationalist sentiment;

b. by aggravating and exploiting every manifestation of discontent;

c. by profiting from the political and psychological errors of other political groups, in so far as such errors enable the Communists to put themselves forward as the sole defenders of liberty, or the Republic, or the traditions of the French Revolution.

E. Our short-term objective is set by the struggle for social liberty and national independence. But this objective must at all times be subordinated to the necessities of the march to power and of the revolution, to which it is merely a means.

F. The revolutionary factors in the present situation can work themselves out only if there is an organization capable of manipulating them. The Communist Party is such an organization; and the removal of the legal ban on the Party is therefore a matter of the first importance.

G. "Committees of the people" must be created to mediate between the Party and the masses of the people. They will operate under continuous control by the Communist Party, and will serve as its instrument. Through them the Party can press its demands in every area of the nation's life.

H, a. The struggle over "immediate" and "small-scale" issues must at the earliest possible moment be translated into a fight for power in the broad sense of that term. This fight must be based upon a program comparable to that of the Bolsheviks on the eve of the October Revolution.

b. The "committees of the people" must be regarded as the nuclei of the future French Soviets.

I. The Party's action with respect to immediate issues is the essence of its political and economic strategy during the transitional period. This must be made to contribute to the installation of a new "popular" government, to be "created" and controlled by the Communists.

J. Such a government can come to power only if, through-out the preceding period, the Communists have (a) been so active in every phase of the nation's life as to keep the initiative in their hands, (b) completely overshadowed all other parties in this regard, and (c) won acceptance as the protagonists of "the unity of all Frenchmen."

K. Execution of the above plan calls for the maintenance of a certain climate of opinion, that is, a constantly rising fever of popular excitement. This in turn calls for a symbolic vision relating both to the present and to the remote future, that is, Soviet Russia, which both exemplifies and guarantees the victory of the revolution.

10, A.* The war, which up to the moment of the Nazi-Soviet Pact has in the Communists' view been a "crusade for popular liberty," now becomes a war for clearly recognizable imperialist ends. The Communists can therefore take as their guide the general Bolshevik doctrine regarding imperialism, the last stage of capitalism—and that regarding imperialist wars. Such wars, according to a course of study which the Party published clandestinely at the beginning of 1941, "some-times create situations in which the triumph of social revolution is an immediate possibility." [5] In Moscow, however, and thus in the Central Committee in Paris as well, ruling expectations run in terms of a long war—with a "further weakening of the forces of imperialism" and the assurance of handsome postwar opportunities for the Communist movement: "While the capitalist powers are all wearing each other out and under-mining each other's strength, the USSR is, with each passing day, expanding its economic, political, and military power, and thus its influence the world over." [6] Should the French Communist Party bide its time until the end of the war, or should it strike at some earlier date? Here also the answer is supplied by Bolshevik doctrine, that is, by the notion of the "unequal development" of capitalism and imperialism from country to country. Prolongation of the war will create "new

* Throughout the remainder of the book, M. Rossi thus relates each discussion to that paragraph of the outline in Section 9 on which it bears. W.K.

weak points along the imperialist front, and at each of these points a victorious proletarian revolution will become possi· ble." [7] Meanwhile the thing to do is to fix attention upon the weakest link in the chain. And, just as Russia was the weakest link in 1917, so France is the weakest link today.

The French Communists, then, tell themselves that they are to play, in the course of the "second imperialist war," the role the Bolsheviks played in the course of the first—and all the more easily because the Bolsheviks, now in command of a great state and an "invincible" army, will lend a helping hand. The reasoning here proceeds from the datum of France's post-Armistice helplessness to the conclusion that France is in an "immediately prerevolutionary" situation, which is to say: the defeat and disintegration of France are candidly recognized as the Communists' trump card. An internal instruction sheet circulated at the end of June or the beginning of July speaks unabashedly of a direct connection between the French defeat and the future triumph of the revolution and treats the one as, so to speak, the first stage of the other. "French imperialism," it asserts,

has just sustained the greatest defeat in its history. In every imperialist war the real enemy is within; and that enemy, in France, is today stretched full length on the ground. The working class, not only in France but the world over, should regard this development as a victory for its interests, because it means one enemy less. As for ourselves, we must leave no stone unturned in our attempt to make of this the definitive cataclysm of French imperialist activities. To put it briefly, the interests of the French people coincide with those of German imperialism in the latter's struggle against French imperialism; and it is not, from this point of view, too much to say that for the moment German imperialism is the French people's ally. The man who does not grasp this is no revolutionary.[8]

I have in my files a "Letter to Communist Militants," signed (in the name of the Central Committee) by Thorez and Duclos, which makes the same point. The present situation, it argues, is distinctly more favorable than that of 1914–18. Then the "imperialist front was penetrated only after three years of fighting"; this time one great imperialist stronghold, France, lies defeated only ten months after the outbreak of hostilities.[9] An issue of *Party Life* puts this even more strongly, and rounds out the reasoning. As the war spreads from country to country it is undermining "all the outposts of French imperialism" and shutting off the normal flow of "trade between France and other capitalist countries." France is being simultaneously weakened "from within" by the political ineptitude of the Vichy government, by the discrediting of the old-line parties, and by continued ministerial instability. The writer draws this conclusion:

Conditions are ripening for a formidable popular upsurge, to be led by the working class acting through its chosen instrument, the Communist Party. This party, despite the ordeal of the imperialist war and the difficulties imposed upon it by the current ban, today stands firm as a rock. The bourgeoisie, the constant prisoner of the innumerable economic and social problems it has itself created, is now playing its last cards. It has exhausted the potentialities of all the traditional political combines.[10]

11, B. The Bolsheviks, it will be remembered, had declared themselves in favor of "immediate peace" as early as March, 1917; and this fact had greatly strengthened their hand—both in the army and, in their subsequent campaign against "unity," out over the country. The French Communists now tell themselves that they also are in a position to exploit popular pacifist sentiment, since the people, demoralized as they are by defeat, ask nothing better than the restoration of the comforts they have known in the past.

Although the conclusion of the Armistice to some extent pulls the rug out from under the Communists in this regard, they speedily recover their equilibrium; and before long they are seizing every opportunity to call attention to the possibility of an immediate peace treaty, and to insist that the Vichy government is doing nothing whatever to bring it about. The following is typical of the comment in the Communist newspapers around this time: "How long must we wait for peace?

Three months have passed since the Armistice was signed. But what has the government done about it?" The French Government, the Party's newspapers insist, must "take all the necessary steps at once." [11] At the same time, however, they urge the apparently contradictory thesis that only the Communist Party, and a government following its lead, will in fact be able to take the necessary steps. Why? Because the Communist Party alone has the necessary string to its bow, namely, the friendship of the USSR, which is now in a position to intervene on France's behalf, prevail upon Germany to grant France peace on relatively favorable terms, and safeguard France's independence and territorial integrity. The French people ought, then, to demand not only peace but also "a Franco-Soviet pact of friendship patterned upon the German-Soviet Pact." [12] France *can* keep out of the present imperialist war; it *can* follow an independent policy. But it can do these things only as it is prepared to lean on the USSR, which is the "fortress of peace"; and this the Vichy government, blinded as it is by its anti-Soviet prepossessions, will of course never do, for all that its refusal is sure to sacrifice both peace and France's national independence. France can, for this purpose, turn only to the Communists, who are able to count on "aid from the Soviet Union" and are alone sufficiently strong and deserving to "rebuild, on the ruins piled up in our beautiful country, a nation that will be powerful, free, and happy." [13]

12, C. What the Communists are thinking, then, is that *if* they act quickly, *if* they make skillful use of the German-Soviet Pact, they can engineer a new Brest-Litovsk. But they have already lost precious time and shown insufficient presence of mind. And they know it. "We have," says the instruction sheet cited above,

made some political mistakes that we must now regret. The Soviet radio had broadcast the following order to Paris militants: Do not leave Paris, no matter what happens. *L'Humanité* was to resume open publication immediately following the arrival of German troops, who would thus find themselves faced with an accomplished fact. The copy for the projected issue was ready when the time came, but the necessary personnel was nowhere to be found.[14]

As a matter of fact, Moscow's instructions could not possibly have been carried out: the exodus had swept the Communists out of Paris along with everybody else. But the leaders were soon back and attempting to make up for lost time. "The Party"—we continue to quote from the instruction sheet just cited—

immediately opened negotiations with the Kommandatura about the publication of *L'Humanité*. The Germans took no exception to the copy we had prepared; but they did ask our comrades to publish the paper under a different name, suppress the words "Central Organ to the Communist Party," and leave off the hammer and sickle. This our comrades refused to do—on the grounds that *L'Humanité* is the symbol of the entire movement and must therefore be retained as the name of its newspaper. The German authorities replied that it was difficult for them to authorize open publication, since Mussolini and Franco, obliged as they were to keep up a fight against Communism, would disapprove.[15]

The document adds that there were parallel negotiations regarding the resumption of publication by *Ce Soir*, that for a time they seemed likely to prove more successful, but that "difficulties of every imaginable kind" caused these negotiations also to break down.[16]

Each of the two adversaries in this game intends, of course, to use the other for his own purposes. The German authorities wish to carry the French masses with them; and they think that the Communists, who alone have an organization that is a going concern, can help them do this—the more effectively since their strength lies in the Paris region. The Communists, in turn, wish for friendly neutrality on the part of the occupying power because once that is assured they will be free to direct their fire against the Vichy government—their hope here being either to unhorse that government or, failing that, to create a separate government for the occupied zone. The relevant negotiations nevertheless progress slowly; and for a

time the Germans attempt to work the Communist vein themselves by publishing a newspaper called *La France du travail*,
an undisguised imitation of the old *L'Humanité*. (This newspaper is a great success at first, and the Communists find it
necessary to warn their friends against it.)

The slow progress of the negotiations does not mean that
either the Communists or the German authorities are failing to
reap advantage from their modus vivendi. Communist propaganda, over a period of several months, refrains from even the
mildest attack on the occupying power, and speaks with deco-
rum even of Hitler and the Nazi Party. The German authorities, though unwilling to authorize its open publication, close
their eyes to the "clandestine" printing and distribution of
L'Humanité. On June 20, for instance, the French police pick
up three Communist militants and charge them with attempting to bring out an edition of *L'Humanité*. Several days later
they are set free—and it turns out that the occupation authorities have interceded on their behalf![17] The instruction sheet we
have been citing goes so far as to boast that the Party, thanks
to the tolerance of the Germans, "is not completely illegal."
And a later instruction sheet, which sets forth the objectives
the Party must accomplish through September and October,
pauses to explain the "policy of the occupying Power" and
offers the following counsel to the Communist cadres:

The occupying power winks at our propaganda. It does this in
part because its purpose is to extend and consolidate Hitler's
political system, in part because it wishes to create difficulties for
the French Government. In view of its attitude we must, while
pressing forward as energetically as possible with our underground activity against capitalism, act with skill and caution. We
must not give ourselves illusions about the toleration we enjoy:
it might, from one day to the next, be transformed into repression.[18]

The German military authorities are, in point of fact, more
interested in maintaining the kind of order appropriate to an
occupation than in forwarding the political designs of the
Nazi leaders. They are therefore displeased when the Com-

munists begin to organize demonstrations on behalf of the reinstatement of the "intervened" * municipalities on the out-skirts of Paris. When, however, the Kommandatura puts an energetic statement of its objections in writing and communi-cates it to the Communists, the demonstrations cease. And the Communists, despite numerous rebuffs, cling valiantly to their propaganda for a sort of "united front," which the occupying authorities are invited to join on grounds of both principle and interest.

The pamphlet *We Accuse*, which is distributed in October or November, 1940, belongs to a moment when the German authorities are beginning to share Vichy's views regarding the repression of the Communists. It nevertheless conveys a clear picture of the way in which the Party leaders conceive this united front:

Our party, by fighting against the Treaty of Versailles, fighting on behalf of fraternal relations between the French and German peoples, fighting against the imperialist war, has at all times held its head high. With head still held high, it today demands the restoration of the rights that have been taken from it. . . . The leaders of the Reich have repeatedly told the German people that the present war was thrust upon them by the governments of London and Paris. They have declared that the German Army's only enemy is Western plutocracy. They have made it clear that Germany congratulates itself upon the good-neighborly relations it has maintained with the USSR since August 23, 1939. To all this the French Communists reply as follows: If you are telling the truth, make your actions fit your words. Thousands of men are today in prisons and camps for having fought against the war. These men should be freed. Municipalities have been intervened on the grounds that their governments were made up of the most determined opponents of French plutocracy. These working-class municipalities should be reinstated. The newspapers that were suppressed because they expressed approval of the German-Soviet Pact (*L'Humanité, Ce Soir, L'Avant-garde, La Vie*

---

* "Intervention" is a legal process by which the central government ousts the popularly elected communal authorities in a locality, and itself assumes responsi-bility for their activities. It has points of similarity with the Anglo-Saxon device of "receivership." W.K.

ouvrière, the review *Russie d'aujourd'hui*) should be authorized to resume publication. This Communist reply has, furthermore, been stated in the only terms worthy of the French and German peoples. The occupying authorities have refused to listen. . . . However awkward this may be for these leaders, the German soldiers must now be told, simultaneously with the French people, that the real opponents of French plutocracy, the real enemies of the warmongers, are today languishing in prison on orders from German authorities. These persecutions admirably serve the interests of the capitalist oligarchs; and the German authorities are alone responsible for them.[19]

One recognizes here all the characteristic features of the united front tactics the Party has employed before: (1) the appeal for confidence, stated in terms of an attitude that the Party has adopted on some occasion in the past (in this case its attitude toward the war, which entitles it to the good will of the German authorities); (2) the identification of a "common ground" that justifies common action (the fight against the Western plutocracies, who are responsible for the war); (3) the demand that such and such leaders (formerly it was the Socialists, now it is the Germans) "make their actions fit their words"; and (4) the direct appeal to the masses (in this case the German soldiers and the French people) to bring pressure on the desired ally.

13, C. Through several weeks the Communists are able to indulge the illusion that they are operating, so to speak, in a closed container, where they have only to speed up the action of existing yeasts—popular fatigue, discontent, and exasperation—and power will automatically be delivered into their hands. Meantime, however, they must win acceptance—alike by the occupying power and by the French people—as the sole force for order that has survived the catastrophe. "The German Army and German officialdom," says the instruction sheet we have just cited, "found upon their arrival a single organization that possessed solid bases and enjoyed popular support—the Communist Party, despite its legal dissolution and despite the persecutions it had suffered." [20] The Germans are therefore obliged (so the instructions continue) not only to reckon with it but also to imitate, or take over, its methods of operation. From the Germans' point of view the important thing is the earliest possible restoration of normal economic and social activity, and the Communist Party is ready to bring about that restoration because that is the price it must pay in order to achieve power.

From the earliest moments of the occupation, then, the Communists' propaganda runs in terms of the "rebirth" or "restoration" of France, which they alone are in a position to midwife. France must, they declare, "have done with frivolousness and anarchy." [21] The first number of the (more-or-less) clandestine *L'Humanité* insists, for instance, that "every shop in France resume production at once." [22] The first *Manifesto to the People of France* stresses the necessity of "getting France back to work." [23]

The Soviet leaders themselves, furthermore, are urging the Party in this direction. Molotov, speaking before the Supreme Soviet on October 1, 1940, defines the mandate: "The French people now confront the difficult task of rebuilding their country. First they must heal the wounds they have sustained in the war; then they must devote themselves to reconstruction. But this regeneration cannot be accomplished by familiar methods." Other directives from within the USSR strike this same note. The Party knows, therefore, what Moscow expects of it.

This calls for an initial phase during which the Party must get itself identified as the only force capable of "healing the wounds" of France. Later, though it will continue to cling to this Red Cross nurse's role, it will inaugurate a second phase, in which its task will be to provoke a popular upsurge that will culminate in a political revolution, that is, in the installation of "its" government. This is the context in which we must consider the Party's persistent appeals for "peace" and national "independence," these being the objective conditions it regards as indispensable for success. "The People of France," says the first manifesto from the Central Committee, "faithful to their traditions and character, wish to make their own decisions regarding the social and political problems posed by the betrayal of the owning classes." [24] The Communists at Nièvre, declares a Party pamphlet, "backed up by their numerous friends and speaking through the great Party they have made their own, therefore demand that the French people be permitted to elect their own government." [25] The theme is reiterated by *Party Life:* the French workers "are determined to recover their independence, and to settle their accounts with their bourgeoisie in their own way." [26] "The French people," we read elsewhere, "are resolved to give themselves a government of their own—and to make it the ally of the USSR and the friend of all other peoples." [27]

The inarticulate premise here is clearly that the German occupation authorities are going to leave the Communists free to make their revolution. Here again the precedent in the leaders' minds is the Bolshevik experience of 1917–18. The French Communists' position is, in one sense, more favorable: Why, they ask themselves, if the Russians were able to make a revolution during a world war, should we not be able to do as much? And the question seems doubly sensible because the Bolsheviks were alone and isolated, while the revolution in France can count on assistance from the mighty USSR. There is other evidence of this well-nigh mystical identification with the Bolsheviks. The Party leaders denounce the Vichy government's "capitulation" and "treason" in the Montoire negotiations, but at the same time tell the cadres that Communists "do not refuse to negotiate with any government." Why? Again the Soviet pattern: the Bolsheviks proved, long ago, that a "proletarian government can negotiate successfully with non-Communist governments, and arrive at understandings consistent with the interests of all peoples." [28] And when all prospects of a profitable compromise with the German authorities seem to have vanished, the Party explains, in similar terms, how things would have fallen out if it had been able to carry out the plan it conceived at the end of June:

We unhesitatingly declare that if we had presided over the destinies of France in June, 1940, as the Bolsheviks presided over the destinies of Russia in 1918, we would have put an end to the war. . . . The peace that the Bolsheviks signed in 1918 was a very hard peace; but the government that signed it was a government of the people, committed to the reorganization of the country along socialist lines and to the expropriation of the capitalists and the landowners. This peace, which would have been suicidal for any other government, was for the Soviet Government a necessary first step toward the reconstruction of the country. The Laval-Pétain armistice, by contrast, makes France's destiny one of slavery and fear. It chains France to the conqueror; it leaves Frenchmen exposed to the danger of becoming, overnight, soldiers of Germany. The peace that a popular French government would have signed, a government that was the friend and ally of the Soviet Union, would have signalized the redemption of the country—that is, the resumption of its independence.[29]

The Communists' plan as of summer, 1940, looks to the rapid conquest of power, conceived, as we have seen, in terms of a "day of reckoning" between themselves and the men responsible for the war. Paradoxically, the group surrounding Pétain is thinking in similar terms. The Vichyites, like the Communists, are determined to effectuate their "national revolution"; and, again like the Communists, they define that revolution in the language of civil war. They seek, like the Communists yet again, to use the Germans for their own purposes, or, failing that, to neutralize them. The Vichyites, though only after several months during which the issue is undecided, win out, for all that the Communists hold in their hand the trump card of the Soviet Union. And the brochure *We Accuse* is only one of many Party publications which show how bitterly the Communists regret the "lack of understanding," on the part of the occupying power of course, that has made the Vichyites' victory possible.[30]

The Conquest of the Unorganized Masses

14, D, a. The Communists know that they are ineffective save as they succeed in carrying the masses along with them. According to Stalin, who learned his mythology in a seminary at Tiflis, the Party draws its strength from the masses as Anteas drew his from the earth, which is to say: it must keep in the closest possible touch with them, place itself always on their level, understand their needs and their reactions. To fail to do so is to cut itself off from all possibility of leading them and getting results from them.

To the agonies of the war there have now been added those associated with the defeat, so that the Communists can, without inaccuracy, speak of the "ever more insistent curses of an entire people that has been betrayed." Curses against whom? Against those who willed the present plight of France. They must be driven out of the country "forever and a day"; [1] let the man who thinks otherwise look about him and see the disasters "that have overtaken France because of the mistakes of a series of governments made up of criminals." The Communists, in other words, recognize in the "disasters" a unique opportunity to establish the desired contact with the masses. Their effect, according to the Party's analysts, has been (a) "to develop in the masses a distrust for their leaders," (b) "to create a climate of opinion unfavorable to the men responsible for the war," (c) "to line the masses up against the profiteers and capitalists," and (d) "to demonstrate to the masses the emptiness of the accusations leveled against the Party." [2] And it follows that the Party has only to nurse every grievance, aggravate every form of discontent, in the knowledge that the masses, in due time, will haul down the building. Furthermore national feeling, however weakened and obscured by the events of the past weeks, is sure to revive as soon as the nightmare of the exodus is over; and the Communists think of this also as a formidable weapon they can turn against the Vichy government, which will then pay the price for having accepted power on the terms laid down in the Armistice.

The earliest Party documents of the period under consideration, those published in Bordeaux on June 18 and those published in Paris at the beginning of July, accordingly summon the "masses" to join the "struggle for national independence." As the months pass the overtones of this summons will vary somewhat, as the Party's language is adjusted to the game it is playing vis-à-vis Vichy, the occupation authorities, and the USSR; but it will at no time cease to be the leitmotiv of the Party's propaganda.

The defeat, in this context, admits of only one explanation: France was betrayed. It is, then, to the category of treason that the Communists will refer the policies and, for that matter, the very existence of the Pétain government.

The reshuffling of ministers in September, 1940, for instance, has been carried out on "orders from Hitler," which is not surprising, the Party points out, since the Vichy government is not "a French government at all, but rather a government of marionettes manipulated by foreigners." [3] When Flandin replaces Laval, the country has merely moved "from one traitor to another." [4] Admiral Darlan's conversations in Paris can have no other result than the "enslavement of France"; [5] and the admiral's meeting with Hitler in Berchtesgaden is the signal for a special edition of *L'Humanité* excoriating the "odious bargain" to which he has committed a "government of defeatists and traitors." [6] The Party, in a word, gets on with its task of undermining the Vichy government by wrapping itself in the mantle of nationalism and by teaching its tongue the language of abuse. Through the twelve months' period between the Armistice and the outbreak of the German-Soviet war Vichy is the chief obstacle in the Party's path, and nothing must be left undone that might contribute to its downfall.

15, D, b. In one of the first instruction sheets forwarded to

its militants, the Communist Party sets forth the agitational
themes it is counting on to give it sway over the masses:

The Communists' task is to assume leadership of the unemployed
workers, who demand unemployment benefits and a job; of the
recently demobilized soldiers and sailors, who are seeking employment and want their rights respected; of France's women,
who are raising their voices against the high cost of living and
the shortage of food; of the peasants, who are demanding assistance in restocking their farms and insisting upon deliveries of
tools and seeds; of the youths, who with their bellies full of the
servitude that awaits them in the government camps cry out for
vocational training, admission to a trade, a job. We must, with
an eye to the organizational forms appropriate to each of these
categories, as also to local conditions, organize mutual aid and
solidarity committees that will keep us in touch with the masses
and allow us to take action on behalf of the demands each situation appears to call for. For this purpose we can use any or all
of a large number of techniques, including representations to
public authorities, demonstrations in the streets, occupation of
factories by laid-off workers who are demanding employment,
etc. In short, the task of the Communist is by no means limited to
the distribution of handbills. He must maintain contact with the
workers and farm laborers everywhere; he must mingle with the
crowd; he must take his place in the queues and make his appearance in the cafés; he must take part in intimate discussion groups;
he must visit the amusement centers. He must become the mouthpiece of popular dissatisfaction, the tribune of the people.[7]

The above is an accurate forecast of the Communists' actual
activities during the period following the Armistice. The
plight of the several social classes, their privations and sufferings, are kindling that the Communists busily accumulate
against the day on which they will start the big fire. Any dis-
turbance that they can initiate and perpetuate will, they feel,
increase the hazards of an already hopeless situation and create
new difficulties for the government; or, to vary the metaphor,
the dissatisfaction of the workers, the farmers, the housewives,
and the families of the prisoners of war is a crown of thorns
to press upon the government's brow. Nor does the govern-

ment have an easy way out: if it acts, if, for example, it con-
cedes pensions to aged wage earners, the Communists will
show that it has done this "under pressure from the masses,"
that is, as a result of the Communist Party's own representations, which will accordingly continue as before. Sometimes
you use violent language; sometimes you raise the bid; sometimes you do both. The essential thing is to keep the situation
at white heat and prevent crystallization around any center
other than the Communist Party. You do not judge propaganda in terms of its intellectual content but in terms of its
effectiveness for demolition purposes. The governing principle is set forth on the masthead of a publication used in connection with the training of Communist cadres: "When you
press demands, you weaken the enemy." [8]

16, D, b. Hunger may never have made a revolution but
it has prompted many a popular revolt. Knowing this, the
Communists go all out in their attempt to exploit the difficulties caused by the food shortage, which is no respecter of persons. They do not, of course, wish any uprisings that might
get out of hand: the people's sufferings are, we repeat, merely
a "workable" vein from which they must mine out every last
long-term political advantage—as their discontent is only one
of several ingredients that go, in specified quantities, into the
Communists' beakers. The latter do not, therefore, wish to
be immediately successful in the struggle for more food, which
makes sense for them only as a means of conquering strategic
positions in the hearts of the workers. And since they do not
so wish, they content themselves with creating "committees
of the people" (preferably, of course, committees that they
can control), which will enable them to manipulate the supply
of food at some time in the indefinite future. "The time has
come," writes *L'Enchaîné*, "for the men and women of every
street, of every quarter, of every locality, to get together and
form an end-the-food-shortages committee. This committee
will then name deputies, whose task it will be to keep watch
over the sources of supply and the prices at which goods are
bought and sold. The poor man has the same right to live as

the rich man. The question of ability to pay should not arise." [9]

The food problem, quite independently of anything the Communists say about it, is urgent in the extreme, and the truth about it is, in all conscience, sufficiently heartbreaking without touching up by a skillful propagandist. But the conscious purpose of the Communists is to exasperate—if possible to the point of frenzy—the pity people feel for the children, the women, and the aged, and the hatred people feel toward "the starvers of the poor, the organizers of the famine." The Party appeals now to the one and now to the other, according to the result it wishes to obtain.

One device upon which the Party seizes is that of urging the women of the country to demonstrate, to make representations to the public authorities, and to demand increased rations. Numberless Party tracts and handbills are addressed to woman in her triple role of mother, housewife, and worker —claiming for her, as worker, "rights equal to those of men in all branches of activity." The ideas underlying this tactic are explained in one of the Party's instruction sheets:

Wherever you look, the difficulties of finding food, the scarcity of jobs, the inadequacy of unemployment benefits, etc., have put women in a state of unprecedented dissatisfaction. They are complaining at the top of their voices, and for good reason. They are merciless in their condemnation of the political parties responsible for their plight, although they often fail to draw the conclusions appropriate to the resentment and anger they feel. In the queues, indeed wherever women are brought together, their grumbling is the first thing you notice; but they speak of the Party only when conversation is deliberately steered in that direction. If, therefore, we wish to bring large numbers of workers' wives into the movement, our militants must seek places in the queues, keep their ears open, slip in a sympathetic word now and then, and sometimes go so far as to guide the discussion and most especially the protests into particular channels. We must point up the contrast between the misery of the many and the war profits accruing to the bankers and capitalists. Above all, we must get across the idea that the rich must be made to pay. If our militants do this, it will soon be possible to organize women's committees, and put them into action against the high cost of living, the shortages of basic commodities, etc. Our female comrades in particular must make it their urgent task to organize the masses of women—in the hope of influencing them and keeping them informed not only of the Party's activities but also of the great social and humanitarian accomplishments of the land of the Soviets.[10]

The Party's slogans and posters emphasize the difference between the living conditions of the poor and those of the rich, the contrast between the popular soup kitchens and the restaurants supplied by the black market. Over and above the physical suffering, rendering it more intolerable, there is the sense of injustice; winter, which brings a coal shortage, a transport crisis, and new requisitions by the occupying authorities,[11] exaggerates both. The details of the situation are, in short, such as to speak movingly for themselves, without need for propagandistic emphasis; and the Party, as it tells about them, merely projects them against the background of the USSR, the country of abundance, and appends the invitation "to do as they have done in Russia," that is, set up a true "government of the people."

The defeat and its aftermath, we repeat, produce a whole series of hardships, which the Communists seize upon at once as "good material"—those of the refugees, those of the unemployed, those of the recently demobilized soldiers and sailors, those of the men not yet demobilized, and those of the young people. The speedy repatriation of the refugees soon takes away the first of these resources. But large numbers of people, especially during the first months after the Armistice, have no job; and the instruction sheets direct the militants' attention to them: "We must organize committees of the unemployed everywhere; we must express and support their claims; we must organize delegations to wait upon the authorities in order to urge these claims; we must demand authorization for public meetings of the unemployed so that they may talk their problems over together." [12] As the weeks pass a certain number of factories get back their managerial and other personnel and are able to resume production. But a Communist pamphlet published as late as January, 1941, confidently insists that "the employment problem is as serious as ever" and summons the unemployed to take up the fight against "humiliation and impoverishment." [13]

Among the unemployed there are a great many recently demobilized soldiers and sailors and large numbers of young people. The Party, speaking to the former, tells them to demand "work, not charity, veterans' preference at the employment exchanges, and pensions for all the victims of this war that the capitalists have brought upon us." [14] It tells them to demand for the 1939–40 veterans all the rights enjoyed by the 1914–18 veterans. The chief objectives of Communist agitation among the veterans, however, are political. "Those who fought in the recent war, having witnessed so many acts of treason, will surely have a piece to speak at the present moment." [15] Much more than anyone else, that is to say, they are in position to press the campaign against "those who are responsible for the war" and to insist upon a "day of reckoning." "The Communists in each locality must bring the recently demobilized veterans together and assemble the evidence needed to establish the guilt of their commanding officers"; they must "cause the veterans" to point an accusing finger at the civil and military traitors "who willed the war and concocted the defeat." [16] The traitors in question, be it noted, are not to be tried at Riom but before popular tribunals made up of workers, peasants, and soldiers.

Demobilization deprives the Communists of much of the raw material for another of the major operations listed above: that among soldiers on active duty. The Party can, and does, demand that the 1938 and 1939 classes be "returned at once to their homes"; [17] aside from these classes, however, there is nothing left save the so-called Armistice Army, which is made up entirely of volunteers and is for this reason not particularly susceptible to Communist propaganda. The Party nevertheless decides to have a go at them, and as late as the eve of the Nazi-Soviet war it is still bidding for their support. The major theme of the tracts composed for this purpose is the bugaboo of

French participation in the war—that is, of French soldiers under orders from England or Germany; but there is also the usual list of "demands," some of which (for example, that of doing away with the salute outside hours of duty) are reminiscent of the famous *Prikase Number 1* of the Kerensky period, which helped to hasten the disintegration of the Russian Army.[18]

The Party, needing support from the nation's young people, gives generous support to *L'Avant-garde*, organ of the Federation of Communist Youth, and to a magazine called *Notre jeunesse*, and reminds its militants that "everything that is of concern to young people is close to our hearts." [19] The propaganda directed at the young people differs little in tendency from that intended for other groups; that is, we find the same political slogans here as elsewhere. But young people like to think in terms of personalities; the Party accordingly gives them articles that make heroes of the Party leaders, particularly the Number One Leader, Maurice Thorez; and his picture, and the slogan "Power for Thorez" as well, appear with notable frequency in the youth publications. The young people must have "demands" of their own; and the Party program, published in January, 1941, under the title *All Out for the Well-being of the French People*, provides an appropriate list—a so-called "Proclamation of the Rights of Young People": "the right to a job, the right to vacations, the right to recreation, and the right to a home." [20]

We must remember that at this time a million prisoners of war, most of them young men, are absent. This is the most painful station of the nation's cross and an opportunity that the Communists are not likely to overlook. They move to create "prisoners' aid committees," made up of the "prisoners' wives and relations, along with all French women of good will"; [21] they launch—and keep control of—a program of packages-for-prisoners and "adoptions"-of-prisoners; [22] they publish two newspapers which describe themselves as "organs" of the French prisoners of war.[23] They denounce the government for its "do-nothing" policy and accuse it of not even wishing to do anything for the prisoners. They demand "the liberation of all France's prisoners of war." [24] They offer the families the blackest possible picture of the lot of their loved ones in the camps; they offer the loved ones the most dismal possible accounts of the plight of the families from whom they are so cruelly separated—the objective here being, of course, to create a mood of exasperation calculated to make of each prisoner, when he returns, a proponent of the great "day of reckoning." Through the first months after the Armistice, when many families still do not know what has happened to their soldier sons, the Party has its local sections send them a circular telling them, "just in case they have not yet been informed," that So-and-So is a prisoner of war. The circular adds: "We take this opportunity to express to you, along with our deep-felt sympathy, the hope that we shall soon be able, one and all, to visit punishment upon those who are responsible for the misfortunes of France, and force those who have profited from this war, in which the people have suffered so much and from which they are suffering still, to disgorge their ill-gotten gains." [25] The notification, of course, is merely the pretext, the anguish of the prisoners' families merely another string to a guitar picked by an unmoved but capable instrumentalist.

The Call to the Workers, the Peasants, and the Middle Class

17, D, b. The Party directs a steady flow of propaganda at those sections of the population that have been torn loose from their moorings (the refugees, the prisoners of war and their families, the veterans, and the unemployed, whom the defeat has deposited upon the nation's highways and in the nation's camps), at the women, at the young people—at all whose susceptibility is likely to have been sharpened by recent hardship. But this is not enough; it must also penetrate the enemy's own territory and strike at the sources of his power; and the strategy for this purpose is ready, fully worked out, in the literature of Marxism and Bolshevism. First you make an inventory of the "social forces" that can conceivably be channeled into revolutionary action. Then you seek the means of establishing contact with each of them. Then you bring them together behind a common program. The Communists see three "classes" that they can hope to mobilize against the "capitalist" system and the government and draw into an alliance looking to the overthrow of both. These are, in descending order of importance, the industrial proletariat, the peasants, and the middle classes. The Party must, then, do everything in its power to win the confidence of each—in order, subsequently, to gain sway over the mind of each.

It addresses itself, first and foremost, to the industrial workers, especially to the "avant-garde," or, if you like, the shock troops of the working-class army: the metal workers, the railway workers, and the miners. Alongside of *Workers' Life,* which has kept the name of the traditional organ of the CGT, there now appear newspapers intended for particular trades: *Le Métallo* and *La Tribune des cheminots* are conspicuous examples. (There are also newspapers intended for workers in particular shops.) The principal Communist "demands," which are such as to do service for each of the trades, appear again and again in each issue of each newspaper and in each Party tract: higher wages, more food. But the Party also espouses demands calculated to appeal to the particular trades, and it assigns to its "Bureau of Social Studies" the task of preparing so-called "notebooks" in which these demands are treasured up.[1] The original intention is to have these notebooks presented to management either by employee delegations or by the familiar "committees of the people." When the repression makes this too dangerous, the Party contents itself with circulating them—clandestinely, of course—among the workers, the purpose being to force the officials of the renegade trade-unions to adopt an unambiguous position, and to make sure that the Party shall become the spokesman for the discontent its notebooks will create.

The Party is, as we know, under a legal ban. It therefore seeks trade-union cover for its activities, and to this end launches a propaganda campaign in which it calls not only upon its own militants but upon the masses of the workers as well to rally once again behind the unions. Beginning in August, 1940, the instruction sheets, denouncing the new "corporative" type of organization envisaged by the government, speak to the cadres in the following terms:

These measures must be answered by a powerful working-class movement. That is why work within the trade-unions has become one of the principal tasks of every Communist. . . . What has been done in some places can be done in others—if our comrades show initiative. . . . Communists everywhere must prevail upon their fellow workers to join the unions; they themselves must resume their places in the unions and take the lead in elaborating slogans expressing the workers' demands, as also in organizing for the defense of the workers' interests. We are witnessing at the present moment a general trend toward lower wages; the unions' protest must be made in terms of reasoned arguments, facts, and figures.

Each day's delay in the accomplishment of this task "may make it all the harder to accomplish in the future." [2] *Workers' Life*, speaking to the working class as a whole, makes the same point:

The time has come to act. The time has come, as it did in 1936, for everybody to act. This time, moreover, we must set our sights higher than we did last time, for this time we go into action without the turncoat Social Democratic leaders and without the CGT fat cats. This time, instead, we go into action against the turncoats and the fat cats, who have once and for all joined the ranks of the makers of war and poverty. In order that we may fight as we did in 1936, let us resume our places in our unions and in our shop committees. Let us, hand in hand, travel once again the road to the employment bureaus. The trade-unions are today the only legal base for working-class organization and working-class action; and so long as that is true our place is inside the trade-unions. [3]

"Just as in 1936": this theme is insistently repeated in the Communist propaganda of the period. The workers need rallying points; and they also need a golden age, whether to look back on with nostalgia or to look forward to with enthusiasm. The Communists give them such an age in both directions: 1936 and the Soviet Union, the promised land of the past and that of the future. Both are served up to prospective converts in unscrupulously glorified form. Both, because they are in sharp contrast with present reality, offer a welcome refuge. The annual May Day celebration, for instance, is associated with 1936: this holiday, at least, the workers will not "permit the government to steal from them"; this year it must be respected, as it used to be in the past, as *their* day of days. [4] The "popular government" of which the Communists dream is also associated with 1936, and it begins to sound as if what they intend is not something new but a restoration. This government, when it comes to power, will "re-establish the liberties of the people, the rights of the trades-unions, and the forty-hour week—along with paid vacations and the social gains of June, 1936." [5]

18, D, b. Even if the Communist Party in any given country were to win all the workers to its cause, it would not be able to make the revolution and achieve power with their support alone. It urgently needs the support of the peasants—especially in France; Paris cannot do without the provinces, and these remain basically agrarian. The "alliance of workers and peasants" is, therefore, a fundamental principle of Communist strategy the world over, and its indispensability has been clearly demonstrated in a number of Marxist texts. The sharpest statement of the position, however, is to be found in the literature of the Bolsheviks, who insist that it was the Party's agitation on behalf of "land for the peasants" that made possible its October victory.

In its early days the French Communist Party showed scant understanding of this aspect of the problem of making a revolution—probably because the "revolutionary syndicalists," with their eyes fixed almost exclusively upon the working class in the large cities, were still influential in its councils. It learned very slowly the lesson that Bolshevik experience had to teach, and even when it got around to applying it—for instance, in its earliest prewar campaign for a "workers' and peasants' government"—this was done clumsily and unimaginatively. The kind of political maturity the Party began to show in its Popular Front days was, therefore, a reflection of great progress in this regard; only then did it begin to develop strength in the countryside. The 1936 elections were the first sure indication of that strength—a major contributing factor here being, let us notice, the Communists' sudden adoption of the "tradition" of the French Revolution. For the peasants are still remarkably faithful to that tradition.

That is the background in which we can understand the extent to which the Party, following the Armistice, aims its propaganda at the peasants and embodies their demands in its program. On the first of these points, this is the record: Entire issues of *L'Humanité* are given over completely to the problems of the countryside. The Party launches a newspaper called *La Terre*, "defender of the peasants," and keeps it alive through several issues. And it finds paper and ink for a flood of pamphlets—some of them for the peasantry as a whole,[6] some for peasant youth,[7] some for growers of particular crops (the winegrowers, for instance),[8] some for agricultural laborers,[9] and some for peasants in this or that region.[10]

On the second point, we have only to look at the Party's program for the peasants as summed up in the manifesto from the Central Committee entitled *All Out for the Well-being of the French People*. The major slogans are:

1. Confiscation of landed estates owned by capitalists; immediate allocation of the land thus confiscated to the agricultural laborers and the owners of small and middle-sized holdings; the creation, for this purpose, of special commissions made up of representatives of these three groups.

2. Cancellation of all debts owed by peasants and agricultural laborers to large landowners, bankers, and moneylenders.

3. Stabilization of agricultural prices at the production stage, to assure the peasant a just reward for his work; suppression of capitalist middlemen, the architects of the present structure of high prices.

4. Payment for harvests destroyed or lost due to the war.

5. Payment of damages for rebuilding houses and replacing farm equipment destroyed or injured during the war.

6. Help for peasants who have been forced off the land and for those victimized by excessive requisitions; this help to take the form of immediate replacement of missing livestock.

7. Fertilizer for all peasants at cost price; peasant representation on the board of directors of the factories producing chemical fertilizers.

8. Reconversion of war plants to the manufacture of farm tools and machinery, with peasant participation in the boards of directors of these factories.

A program of this kind, though worked out with an eye both to 1789 and 1917, will not be taken seriously by the peasants unless it is accompanied by an intensive propaganda campaign—itself skillfully worked out in terms of the interests and cherished beliefs of agrarian France. The Party's propagandists proceed therefore to describe the rural districts as "delivered into the hands of the pillagers," that is, the "latter-day gabelles from Vichy" and the occupation authorities, to stir up resentment against the arbitrary practices of the tax collectors, and to expose flagrant examples of "victimization and red tape." They fix attention on the gap between agricultural and industrial prices, which is all the more outrageous, they insist, because the peasants are receiving payment in "monkey money." And they make constant appeal to the underdog sentiments which prevail in the rural areas: they range the "little fellows" against the "big fellows," and show how France has been "handed over to the trusts" and to the "two hundred families"; they point an accusing finger at the banks, the finance corporations, the insurance companies, the millers, the sugar monopolists, and the chemical fertilizer trusts; and they let the "little fellows" in on the things the "big fellows" are doing so as to recoup their past losses. They report, for example, the latest measures adopted in the National Wheat Administration, which are forcing the small producers —and the consumers as well—out of the agricultural market. As for the so-called "agrarian corporation," provided for by a law promulgated on November 2, 1940, the government, they insist, is reserving almost all the key positions for "noblemen, large landowners, big business executives, and representatives of the agricultural trusts." Its purpose, clearly, is to return the peasants to "serfdom." [11]

Now: the crisis, together with Vichy's new economic legislation, is indeed crushing the small owners. Vichy, moreover, is full of talk about "getting back to the land." The two things together provide still further grist for the Communists' mill; that is, they permit the Communists to capitalize on the peasants' deep-seated distrust of the townsman, the man who "doesn't belong." If Vichy wishes to get someone back somewhere, the Communists declare, "let it begin by getting the prisoners of war back to France." [12]

The major appeal, however, is to the tradition of the Great Revolution, a vein which the Communists worked profitably between 1935 and 1939, and one which now promises even greater returns. The new regime is compared to the government of France in "feudal times": "now as in the days of the great lords, the gabelles and the gendarmes are overseeing every detail" of the peasant's life; the political and social gains for which Frenchmen fought in 1789 are one at a time disappearing before the onslaught of the Vichyites; the latters' first official act was to "assassinate the Republic, which became part of your personal heritage when your ancestors stormed the chateaux of the great lords." [13] At the same time, lest all of this redound to the benefit of certain Frenchmen in London, the Party points out that the Gaullists are no better: "the British lackeys, General de Gaulle and General de Larminat, both of them men of noble birth, are the spokesmen for a reactionary, antidemocratic movement which looks eagerly forward to the day when our country will be governed by a dictatorship." [14]

Vichy, then, is spiriting away the gains achieved by the French Revolution; and this means that France must rise in arms once more—to repossess the ground that has been lost and make new advances.

In 1789, peasants of France, your forefathers annihilated the old world of feudalism and along with it the power of the great lords. Your forefathers also were miserable; they also were oppressed by the tax collectors; they also were humiliated. They therefore set their hearts on a change; and soon, having allied themselves with the workers in the towns, they put an end to the power of the feudal lords. Today we have a new set of feudal lords to strike down: the steel barons and bankers and tycoons of commerce and industry, together with the scions of ancient families and a whole retinue of robbers, speculators, and usurers, whose task it is to pillage our unhappy land and hold it for ransom. [15]

Today, just as in 1789, it is a man's patriotic duty to fight back against the enemy within: "in 1789 the word 'patriot' was synonymous with the notion of revolutionary struggle against the agents of feudalism; in 1941 the word 'patriot' is synonymous with the notion of revolutionary struggle against the agents of capitalism"; and, just as the old feudal world went down before peasant buckshot, so the government of Vichy will be laid low by peasant grievances. [16] Grievances, then, are the present-day equivalent of buckshot, and what is needed besides, in order to make victory certain, is peasant unity, fortified by an alliance with the workers and the common people in the towns: The workers and the common people are "at one with you, peasants of the Republic, in their determination to prevent the great lords and landowners of the old regime from recapturing the strategic positions in France's economic and political system." [17]

The Communists insist, for the rest, that the kind of alliance envisaged in all this is already an accomplished fact in the USSR, "a Socialist State of Workers and Peasants." The case the Communists are making ultimately rests, here as elsewhere, upon the example of the USSR; and since the audience are typical French peasants, whose ties are to their land and whose experience, unlike that of the Russian peasants, has done nothing to prepare them for collectivist forms of ownership, this could easily prove embarrassing. Other things being equal, that is to say, the French peasant is likely to turn a deaf ear to the notion that Soviet Russia is the promised land for the peasantry. If they did not have an inexhaustible fund of falsehoods the Communists would, indeed, know better than to approach him with it at all; and, once they have decided to approach him with it, they must stand ready to make large drafts on that fund of falsehoods. They accordingly assure the French peasant that the Government of the USSR "has not so much as touched the land of the poorer peasants," [18] that the Stalin Constitution guarantees "respect for personal property and for the right of the citizens to inherit personal property," and that "nobody is forced to join a kolkhoz, since Article Nine of the Constitution underwrites the small private economy of individual peasants and handicraftsmen, based on their own labor rather than upon exploitation of the labor of other people." [19] All this, I repeat, takes some doing, as anyone will recognize who knows the story of what the "superindustrialization" of the five-year plans has done to the Russian peasantry, of how millions have been expropriated and deported, and of how four or five millions have been condemned to death by starvation. But the Communists do not shrink from the task of presenting the USSR as an Arcadia where all is abundance, peace, and freedom.

19, D, b. So much for the Party's wooing of the peasants. The remaining middle-class categories, the merchants, artisans, and functionaries, are by no means neglected, since the Party recognizes the extent to which they have kept their hold upon the French economy, upon French society, and upon French politics. Several of the Party's tracts are, for example, aimed directly at the merchants. They, like everyone else, are urged to organize committees of the people for the defense of their interests and, above all, for action on the food problem. And the Party calls upon all three groups, as upon the peasants, to form an alliance with the working class, from which there is "nothing to divide them." For only the workers (under the leadership of the Communist Party)—with whom, for the rest, these groups have no real conflict of interest—are capable of guaranteeing the victory that all Frenchmen desire.[20]

The Communists, the Intellectuals, and the Principles of 1789

20, D, b. The social group the French call the "intellectuals" are of special interest to the Party for two reasons: (a) its members are as a matter of course members of the "middle classes," whom, as we have seen, the Party is determined to win; and (b) they enjoy (purely aside from the influence they exercise in the quarters in which they themselves actually move) great prestige among the masses of the French people.

There are, for instance, the nation's teachers, whom Vichy has placed at the mercy of representatives of the most vicious forces at work in the nation. The teachers, "Left-wingers" and "Right-wingers" alike, are in a rebellious mood, and this makes it easy for the Communists to turn to their own political advantage each and every new outrage perpetrated against their profession. In some localities, indeed, teachers with Communist sympathies have succeeded in enlisting their colleagues in the Party's cause even before the Central Committee discovers their potentialities.[1] And the annals of the anti-Communist repression are full of the names of teachers who, we may be sure, but for Vichy's campaign of discrimination and persecution, could never have been persuaded to participate in the Party's activities.

Nor does the Party overlook the students, to whom it devotes, over and above the usual stream of pamphlets and handbills, the newspaper *La Relève*, which puts itself forward as the "organ of the Union of Communist Students." And when the occupation authorities first arrest Paul Langevin (November 13, 1940), the Communists, recognizing that public opinion has reacted sharply in his favor, redouble their efforts in the country's educational institutions.[2]

First of all, the Party urges the students to join the Communist Youth Movement, its twofold purpose here being (a) to capture their patriotic fervor for its own ends, and (b) to see to it that their enthusiasm shall at no time become embarrassing. That the second of these objectives is at least equally important with the first may be seen clearly from the *Manifesto to the Students of France*, which bears the date January, 1941: it praises the students for their November 11, 1940, demonstration at the Arc de Triomphe but also reminds them that "the country's independence is to be sought along the avenues of peace," that France will become free again not through war but "as a result of a Socialist Revolution," that, in any case, the ideal of independence is oceans apart from that of military revenge, and that what that ideal calls for is above all "the freeing of our country from its subordination to Britain." [3] The manifesto's major concern, in a word, is the nationalist drives of the young people, which it wishes them to project not on the level of international warfare but on that of social action. In turning their backs on war, says a pamphlet addressed to the students of France in May, 1941, they will be following the Party's long-standing example: "During the storm, only the Communist Party and the Communist Youth had the courage to raise their voices against the war, and to cry out, even before the decisive battles had occurred, for peace." [4]

The Party is, then, addressing itself to each category of the intellectuals; and it invites them also "to form a solid bond with the working class for the fight against obscurantism." [5] To this end, of course, they must organize; and their committees, which are to work hand in hand with the committees of the people created by the workers, are to be called "committees to resist reaction."

21, D, c. Communist propaganda and agitation never rely exclusively on appeals to immediate interests; they know how to arouse and exploit other psychological responses, both individual and collective—as anyone will quickly learn who studies the Party's 1934–39 campaign, conducted under the new slogan of "unity of all Frenchmen," for the "launching" of a Popular Front. During the period following the Armistice the Party has recourse to these same procedures, and this time it is able to take their effectiveness for granted. For, far from being artificial and arbitrary, these procedures rest upon a correct reading of sentiments that have deep roots in the popular consciousness and date back at least to the French Revolution.

Let me put it this way. The ideas and symbols of patriotism and good citizenship, of France's independence on the one hand and of its influence and prestige abroad on the other, have come to be associated in the popular mind with the Great Revolution, and can therefore be evoked by even the most casual reference to 1789. The relation is, moreover, reversible, so that these ideas and symbols, when aroused by the skillful propagandist, promptly call into play the drives and purposes that went into the making of 1789. The "Nation-People-Fatherland" complex has, in short, been a constant in French popular psychology for many decades, so that anyone who thinks, as Vichy is doing, in terms of merely wiping it off the slate, or treating it as a "lapse" in French history, is working against the main stream of French national sentiment—and doing the Communists' work for them. The Communists accordingly welcome—and milk for every possible advantage—the monopoly of the Great Revolution that Vichy is delivering into their hands. Increasingly, as time passes, their agitational objectives are related to the slogan of 1789; and the "notebooks of demands" mentioned in an earlier chapter are romanticized as today's *cahiers* of grievances and thus as the first step toward a new revolution.

The Party's task, in fine, is cut out for it: it must win acceptance as the heir and carrier of the traditions of 1789 and as the sole defender of the Republic, which "they" are attempting to wipe out of existence. Such mistakes by the enemy as the so-called "punitive expeditions" against the statues of Marianne in France's town halls prove genuinely useful to it in this regard. Rural folk and urban dwellers alike are deeply disturbed by these attacks upon the symbol of the Republic; for even those who have viewed more or less indifferently the attack on parliamentary institutions themselves have continued to be staunch republicans—most of them not out of attachment to any particular political theory but because traditionalist sentiment makes no distinction between France and the Republic.

22, D, c. The Communists also discover at this time that they are the true representatives of the main stream of French philosophy, "which begins with Descartes, flows through Diderot, and leads to eighteenth-century rationalism." This philosophy, "once the rallying cry of the bourgeois revolution" and later the "scourge of capitalism, ally of the Church," has now degenerated, "in the context of the occupation and the anti-French reaction in Vichy," into an act of treason.[6] Its purpose is to deliver into the hands of the enemy, along with the soil of the fatherland, the strategic positions from which the nation's opinions are influenced. The result is that "obscurantism today has at its command not only the resources of the occupying power but also the very apparatus of the state";[7] and the fight against it must therefore go forward simultaneously on the level of theory and that of practice. The intellectuals must take an active part in this struggle: it is their task to prepare the way for the new revolution, just as the philosophers of the eighteenth century prepared the way for 1789. Above all, they must grasp the fact that a situation congenial to a rebirth of French philosophy is now taking shape: "This rebirth will, beyond all doubt, occur in the course of this great struggle, which is to restore to the word 'philosopher' the meaning it had in the eighteenth century. . . . Side by side with a nation fighting for its liberty and independence, the philosophers of France will wage their war on behalf of truth."[8]

The defeat, it is emphasized, is not without its antecedents in the intellectual sphere: "the attack on humanism by the propagandists of mysticism, the attack on science by the refurbishers of metaphysics—for example, the followers of

Heidegger and Kierkegaard, the philosophers and novelists and poets of anguish and fear and trembling." [9] Rosenberg's Paris speech entitled "A Settling of Accounts with the Ideas of 1789" is, the Communists allege, "the completion and the crowning of this work of decomposition." [10]

The Communist intellectuals valiantly take their stand, in this context, against "the racist obscurantism" that "they" are attempting to impose upon France, and mercilessly expose it as a "meticulous systematization of false doctrines." Its purpose, the Communists point out, is to "replace science with pseudoscience, literature with fabricated delirium, history with fable, philosophy with myth, and art with crude fakery." [11] And, before they have done, they have gone so far as to present themselves as the sole defenders—in part, to be sure, because of abdication and compliance on the part of everybody else—of the spiritual values associated with the name of France. The Vichy government is again a useful if unintentional ally: if Rosenberg, like Vichy, thinks that the year 1789 will be stricken from the history books, Vichy, like Rosenberg, is seeking to put into practice the racist theories of the Nazis. When the Communists reply to Rosenberg's November, 1940, speech at the Palais-Bourbon in a clandestine brochure, they are therefore able to stress the fact that they are the sole claimants to the honor of making such a reply: "A vigorous struggle," they say at the beginning of this brochure, against every attempt at intellectual colonization—and it is precisely this of which Herr Rosenberg's trip [to Paris] is symbolic —is inseparable from the struggle for the liberty and independence of France. The Communist Party is proud of being in the vanguard of this struggle. It is the French Communists, and they alone, who lift their voices in reply to Herr Rosenberg; and this shows how true it is that the defeat has brought with it the ideological bankruptcy of the other parties.[12]

The point cannot be overemphasized. A courageous reaffirmation of the principles of 1789 from some group able and willing to restate them in terms of contemporary reality, a courageous reassertion of the human values which these principles embody and which are, accordingly, an integral part of the spiritual wealth of France, would have been a sufficient answer to this piece of Communist impudence. Vichy's attempt at an out-of-hand "liquidation" of 1789 has, however, created an air pocket for the Communist current to rush into—all the more since that attempt, compounded of historical ignorance and philosophical impotence, permits the Communists to exploit and attack the principles of 1789 at one and the same time. For Marx and his followers, of course, the ideas of each historical period are the ideas of its ruling classes, so that eighteenth-century thought, for all that it once played a revolutionary role, was then and is now a class philosophy. But the scholarly publicists to whom the fall of France has given their long-sought opportunity to impose ideas belonging to an even remoter past are as ready as the Marxists to deny to the principles of 1789 any claim to general and permanent validity. And this, I say, facilitates the ideological task of the Communists by encouraging them to have it both ways with the "class" interpretation of ideas and the espousal of the principles cherished by most Frenchmen—and cherished precisely because they fulfill man's need for truths he can regard as "universal." This need, which lies at the root of all systems of philosophy, also underlies the act of awareness that makes each nation a nation. And this is especially true in France, where even the Socialist movement, to the extent it has escaped complete capture by the Marxists, conceives its mission as that of "completing" the Great Revolution and realizing the fullest development of that revolution's potentialities for human betterment. The Communists, on the other hand, have always opposed the Socialists on this point; so that, while as we have seen they make the most of the humanitarian and patriotic symbols of 1789, they are still busy warning the faithful against the ideas of the Revolution, which are merely "blinders fixed upon the eyes of the revolutionary proletariat of the twentieth century." [13] Similarly, while they pretend to fight the battle of eighteenth-century humanism against Herr Rosenberg, their real quarrel with him is, demonstrably, that he speaks of race where they wish to speak of class, that he appeals to racial unity where they wish to appeal to "class consciousness." [14] But this, on any showing, is a family quarrel between two opponents of humanism, which the one attacks in the name of racism and the other in the name of the class struggle. And this is all the more true because the Communists recognize in Hitler Germany their only real competitor in the struggle for hegemony in Europe: "During the postwar period," they say, "we have seen three rivals step forward to claim the succession to the old spirit of Europe: (1) the American and European carriers of old-fashioned liberal humanism; (2) Communist internationalism; (3) Hitler's 'Pan-Germanism' "; [15] and, since liberalism is now "outmoded," only Bolshevism and Nazism remain in the lists. The USSR becomes the promised land of a new *Aufklärung*, which will tear off the "blinders" of humanism. The "evil conscience," or, if you like, absence of conscience, that has tormented the "old" world even in its dying moments, will at last be exorcised. And upon the ruins of humanism there will be built the kingdom of the "dialectic."

Social Revolution
and National Liberation

23, E. We have seen that the Party, ready as it is to make arrows out of any wood that happens to be lying about, appeals now to social restlessness, now to outraged national sentiment. But it is from the two things *in combination* that it expects the revolutionary uprising finally to emerge; and we must notice now how social and nationalist demands are tied together in its propaganda,[1] as when, for example, it accuses Vichy of directing its policy "at one and the same time against the working masses and against the national independence of the country,"[2] or when it declares itself to be "at one and the same time the Party of the French people's liberation from bondage to capital and the Party of the liberty and independence of France"[3]—and adds that if it were not both these things it would not be persecuted as it is.[4]

The French Communists are repeating here the political strategy of the German Communist Party after 1930, that is, during the period when its slogan was "social and national liberation." The strategy failed in Germany because the Nazis stole the Communists' thunder—on the social level by adopting an "anticapitalist" program, on the national level by putting forward a policy that was both more coherent and more extremist than the Communists' own. There is no reason, however, to expect it to fail in France. The French Communist Party, though hampered like the German Communist Party by direct and total subordination to Moscow, is more experienced. And it is operating in a much more favorable situation: For its opponents are not the Nazis but the Vichy government, together with certain early nuclei of the resistance whom the Party will make it its business to discredit.

The emphasis upon social and national objectives is associated, in the minds of the Communists, with the broader notion of the so-called "motive forces" of the revolution. According to this phase of Communist theory, the proletarian revolution can triumph "in the age of capitalism" only if it succeeds in bringing colonial and oppressed peoples into the movement. This thesis dates back, of course, to Lenin, who in 1916 formulated it as follows: "To think that social revolution is conceivable without uprisings by small nations, both in the colonial areas and in Europe; without revolutionary upsurges by a section of the petty bourgeoisie, with all its prejudices; without revolts by proletarian and semi-proletarian groups not yet aware that they are being oppressed by the land-owners, the church, the monarchy, the mother country, etc.—to think this is to deny the social revolution." [5] This thesis set the tone of the propaganda which Lenin and the Bolsheviks, once in power, directed at the peoples of the Orient, at the colonies, and at the countries controlled and exploited by the various imperialisms. The Communist International and its French section are, then, following Lenin when they state their strategic problem to themselves in terms of the following three revolutionary "factors": (1) the class struggle in the belligerent countries, which the economic and social consequences of the war have intensified; (2) the struggle for liberation on the part of occupied and oppressed countries; and (3) the struggle of the colonial peoples for freedom. [6] The victory, if this large-scale maneuver can be brought off, is assured, since one hears on all sides "the rumbling discontent of the oppressed peoples and of the enslaved masses in the colonies, as well as the mounting anger of the starved proletarians, who have been deprived of all their rights." [7] To the three Leninist factors already mentioned it is now possible, however, to add a fourth: the USSR, the workers' ally, which is strong because it is the only country in which "there is no such thing as capitalist exploitation and national subjection." [8]

No one can understand French Communist policy and tactics if he overlooks this: National sentiment and patriotism are, for the Communists, merely "factors" that one utilizes, along with other themes that can be translated into discontent, in order to bring about the social revolution. They claim for the "people of Alsace"—as for all other colonial and oppressed peoples—the right of free self-determination; [9] they urge French soldiers in Indo-China to "fraternize" with the Annamite insurgents; [10] they publish a manifesto to the "Algerian people" in which they call upon them to rebel against France.[11] Simultaneously, however, they summon the French people to rally to the nation that would presumably strike down the Algerian rebellion if it occurred! The nation, unless of course that nation be the USSR, is merely a means to other ends.

This emerges with great clarity from the Communists' handling of the theme of French "national liberation" from Vichy and the Germans. In order to bring that liberation about, they say, one must first bring about a social revolution, "as they have done in Russia"; and the extent to which this is merely bait to draw French patriots into a temporary alliance with the Communists can be inferred from the Party's vagueness about the form that liberation is to take. (This vagueness does not mean, of course, that the Communists are other than clear about this in their own minds.)

The new Soviet France will cast its lot with the USSR, "the workers' state," and will thus be liberated—like the Baltic States, like Poland, like Bessarabia. Once liberated it will "freely" join the Union of Soviet States of Europe.[12] When, therefore, the Communists say "the fatherland is in danger," what they really mean is that the USSR is in danger—not France itself but the "union" in which France is to take its place, with of course "the equality of rights among free peoples which is guaranteed by the Constitution of the USSR." [13] This is, moreover, not always concealed. A leaflet distributed in Epinal in September, 1940, summons its readers to struggle "for the defense of our Soviet fatherland, for the proletarian revolution in France, and for the world revolution" [14]—nor

could one ask for a clearer statement of the Communist hierarchy of values. The socialist revolution is always high on the
list: "The example of the Soviet Union shows that by over-
throwing capitalism in our country we will be able to recover
France's liberty and independence, and that the first step toward national liberation is that of social emancipation." [15]

The present war, in short, is to afford the opportunity for
putting into action Lenin's Zimmerwald slogan: "Let us transform the imperialist war into civil war." The Communists are
fighting for "a revolutionary outcome for the grave crisis that
has swept over the entire capitalist world" [16]—an outcome
which, for the rest, is assured because "the proletariat of the
oppressed countries has as its powerful allies the colonial peoples, along with exploited peoples everywhere, along with all
those who are struggling for national liberation." With these
allies the proletariat becomes "a huge army whose strength
constantly increases while that of imperialism wanes. This
army is already powerful enough to win the day. It will surely
prevent the plutocrats from ending their war without imperialism being overthrown—as it was in Russia in 1917—at
other points of the globe." [17] In the words of the "Internationale," it is the final conflict that has begun.[18] The Communists intend to write an entirely different ending to the war
than that desired by its bourgeois authors: "the capitalists have
begun the war; the proletariat will finish it." [19]

The German-Soviet war, when it comes, will force no
basic change on these points: at most it will render necessary
certain new overtones. Until June, 1941, the French Communists are intending to take power, then wait until the USSR,
having achieved in peacetime its aim of military preparedness,
can lay down its law to the war-weary belligerents and thus
"expand the frontiers of socialism" [20] until one day they will
include France.[21] Hitler's sudden attack on the USSR upsets
this plan, but without changing the basic character of the
Party's long-run intentions. The USSR, no longer able to
"settle its accounts" with all the imperialist nations at once,

must defend itself by making an alliance with one of them—Anglo-Saxon "imperialism," which, for the moment, is "democratic" once again. The data thus become somewhat more complicated, but the major inference to be drawn from them remains: "Hitler began the war, Stalin will finish it." [22]

The March to Power: The Committees of the People to Become Soviets

24, F. During the period immediately following the Armistice the Communist Party has, as we have seen, high ambitions. It believes its hour has come and that it can turn the defeat, despite Germany and perhaps even with a little help from Germany, into a complete reversal of the situation—for which read a "government of the people" that will consolidate a Communist victory and dictatorship. In order to bring this off, however, the Communists must, at an early moment, get themselves accepted by the country (and also by the Germans) as the only political force capable of organizing the masses and keeping them satisfied—a task of such magnitude that only a large organization, one furthermore that can operate more in the open with each passing day, can possibly accomplish it. The latter point is of crucial importance; and the Communist leaders, caught off balance for once, lose the few precious days or hours they need in order to confront the Germans with the fait accompli of a "legal" *L'Humanité* —and thus get out into the open. With this opportunity gone, the problem becomes, as a late June, 1940, instruction sheet puts it, that of "matching wits and speed" with the occupying power—a problem which is all the more urgent because the latter is offering in its propaganda "all the things the people desire—the entire program of the Communist Party." This propaganda is, moreover, "skillful in the extreme," and shows "a profound knowledge of the character and aspirations of the French people." From the Party's point of view, then, the "immediate objective is the struggle for legality." It must make it its business "to set up machinery for popular representation that will win recognition from the authorities." And this must be done rapidly, adroitly, so that "at the end of this period of confusion and disorganization the Party will be in a position to take over the control of public affairs." [1]

The Party's objectives, and its tactics as well, remain unchanged through September:

In the present circumstances, it is of first importance that our party not be left behind by the course of events, that it show a maximum of initiative, and that it not remain shut up inside itself. The situation is moving rapidly. Popular dissatisfaction continues to grow; objective conditions thus favor an outburst of unparalleled new activity on our part. Everything depends on our capacity to provide leadership for the popular movement; but in order to do that we must first take courageous action to shake off the ban upon the Party, the Party's militants, and the Party's propaganda organs. [2]

This means, inter alia, mobilizing popular feeling behind the deputies and the other Communists who are in prison, the reinstatement of Communist union officials, the reconstitution of the "intervened" Communist municipalities, and the open publication of *L'Humanité* and the Party's other banned newspapers. The propaganda campaign backing this venture must be "intense and spectacular"; there must be "large-scale and open" circulation of the Party's tracts and newspapers in the working-class districts and along the approaches to the factories and the railway stations; and the Party must organize to give the distributors the protection they will need.

The Party will, to these ends, proceed now to modify its organizational structure. First of all it must increase the size of its basic units, which through the period of illegality have been held to three members each; and it must explain to its militants the extent to which, in view of the new situation, the Party's other instrumentalities must be transformed:

Let us not hesitate to carry our membership drive to the thousands of sympathizers who, by adhering to the Party, will forward its activities. We must not impair the Party's security; we must maintain in force all necessary measures of caution; but within those limits we must see to it that each Party member gets across, in his immediate environment, the Party's slogans and policies. We must seize upon every opportunity, take advantage of every shift in sentiment on the part of the masses, in order to get out of our present rut and force the Party's activities out into the open. The Party's future depends, in part at least, on our success in rounding the present corner. In so far as this can be done without neglecting obvious security considerations, we must give top priority to bold and decisive action for the purpose of breaking through the cordon of illegality with which our enemies mean to keep us surrounded.[3]

25, G. Partly to hasten this transition to legal status, partly to bind itself more securely to the masses, the Party soon after the Armistice moves to create the committees of the people. The two objectives coincide: if the Party's activities can be extended to "hundreds of thousands and even millions of people," [4] it will find it all the easier to get those activities out into the open and give them needed protection; and this, in turn, will help it to recruit more people.

From the beginning, when the Party releases its first Paris *Manifesto to the People of France*, it therefore demands that "all men and women of good will, young and old, in each city, each village, in fact everywhere, unite in solidarity and mutual aid committees of the people, which will assume responsibility for getting the factories reopened, for putting France back to work"—in a word, for organizing the country's economic life.[5] These committees multiply rapidly, at least on paper; soon, too, they begin to be specialized—always with an eye to circumstances and to the types of people being organized as well. In August one of the Party's publications gives the following picture:

Committees of the people have already organized themselves in several dozens of firms, and have been able, through their activities, to collect back pay and get action on other demands. If its factory is in production, such a committee permits all the workers to unite behind a program of demands, and facilitates the rebirth of the factory local; if the factory is shut down, the Committee enables the workers to keep in touch with one another. Our comrades in each neighborhood and locality must, in addition to what they are doing in the factories, turn their energies to the creation of solidarity and mutual aid committees of the people [for general purposes]. In certain localities these committees are already busy attacking the food shortage and are rendering other great services to the inhabitants. Elsewhere the committees concern themselves with the problem of the evacuees, especially that of finding them places to live. In all the localities in which they exist they intercede with the municipal authorities on behalf of aged persons who are demanding old-age assistance, of mothers of families, of tenants threatened with eviction, etc., and defend other local interests. When they take their business seriously these committees become a rallying point for the population, and when militants throw themselves into their work they thereby increase our party's influence.[6]

By the beginning of September *L'Humanité* is able to report that "more than 110 committees of the people have been organized in and around Paris and are busy defending the interests of the working masses; with the approach of bad weather their activity should be intensified, with a view to winning increases in unemployment benefits, moratoria on rents for the unemployed, cancellation of gas, water, and electricity bills, etc."[7]

Activity of this kind is highly appropriate to the Party's general policy and purposes. It will go full speed ahead if the Party has estimated the situation correctly; it will be abandoned if the bold plan conceived in June proves unrealizable.

26, H, a. The fight for "immediate" or ad hoc demands is, as we have pointed out, intended to bind the masses of the people to the Party. It does not mean at all that the Party has written off either its wider demands or its struggle for power. On the contrary, the militants are told repeatedly that the matters just mentioned are merely means to the achievement of the final goal. And here, as elsewhere, the example of the Great Revolution is called into play:

When, early in 1789, the bourgeoisie and the peasants even in the smallest hamlets were drawing up their cahiers of grievances large and small, they were preparing the Great French Revolution which only a short time later was to sweep away the old feudal world. Now as then every fight over issues, every notebook of demands (for these are today's cahiers of grievances), every instance of mass action, however limited the objective, helps to rally the social forces which will tomorrow sweep away the old capitalist world.[8]

Only the people, it is emphasized, can cause the Party's revolutionary program to triumph: for the moment "the masses of the people must, if they fall back at all, fall back fighting; and they must press the day-to-day struggle over day-to-day issues, for this struggle is the prelude to the people's great drive for power." [9] Certain of the militants, euphoric over the Party's prospects for an early large-scale victory— the Party, we must remember, is constantly reminding them that victory is just around the corner—tend to regard the day-to-day struggle as so much wasted time or, worse still, as tainted with "reformism." But *Party Life* reads them a lesson:

Some worthy comrades refuse to attribute to the struggle on behalf of the unions and to the pressing of workers' demands all the importance that these things deserve. Their reasoning on this question is as follows: Is this the right moment for us to worry over day-to-day issues? Do not these issues eat up energies that we should husband for use in some period when large political problems will have been posed, and when it will be our task to get across to the masses the necessity of a socialist revolution? The obvious answer is: The problem of immediate demands must at no time be ignored or neglected by a revolutionary movement. When we organize action on the masses' immediate demands we rally those masses around our standards and mobilize them against the bourgeoisie. This kind of struggle, far from being a brake upon the struggle for power, is part and parcel of it.[10]

The distance between agitation on demands and the struggle for power is not, however, to be covered in a single leap. You must indeed begin by fighting out such matters as better pay for the workers; but before you can lead those workers into a fight for power you must sell them on slogans relating to wider problems than those of the factory. These slogans must, more-over, be of such character as to speed the "radicalization" of the working-class movement and force it upward to the po-litical level. All of this clearly calls for a "program" capable of rallying the masses; and this program must be of such character as to require the overthrow of the present govern-ment and the establishment of a Communist-led "popular" government.

We must remember, in this connection, the tactics used by Lenin between March and October, 1917—most particularly after the end of July, when the Sixth Congress of the Bol-shevik Party decided that the "democratic bourgeois" revolu-tion could and must create the opportunity for the socialist revolution.[11] The program formulated by the Bolsheviks at that time was intended not only to see the country through the transition between the two phases of the revolution but also to provide a plan of action for the first Soviet Govern-ment. And the program published by the Central Committee of the French Communist Party in January, 1941, under the title of *All Out for the Well-being of the French People*, is similar, both in tone and tendency, to that put forward by the Bolsheviks when they found themselves traveling "down the road of insurrection." [12]

With respect to foreign policy, for example, this program continues the plan conceived by the Party immediately after the Armistice, that is to say, the quest for a separate peace to be achieved thanks primarily to support by the Soviet Union. This parallels the Bolsheviks' 1917 foreign policy theme, "peace above everything," with only this difference: The Bolsheviks aimed at stopping the war and concluding an im-mediate armistice. In France, the armistice is unfortunately already an accomplished fact, so that what the Communists want is the cessation of hostilities in a war in which the country is not participating. And the reason they want it is that it will enable them to carry to a successful conclusion an internal operation which, in their eyes, has become possible as a result of the country's defeat. The program, again, proclaims the right "of national minorities and colonial peoples, of mandated territories and protectorates, to independence and to self-determination," which is the Leninist formula on the question —as the reader may see by consulting the records of the Bolshevik Party conference in April, 1917.[13] And the program follows the Russian precedent on yet another point of external policy: the government of the people will repudiate "all engagements, whether public or secret, entered into before its coming to power, where these conflict with the principles of its policy of peace and national independence."

With respect to domestic policy, the January, 1941, program parrots the resolutions of the Sixth Congress of the Bolshevik Party almost word for word. It demands, for example, "nationalization—without compensation—of the banks, the insurance companies, the mines, the railroads, and of each and every capitalist corporation, whether Aryan or Jewish owned, in such industries as electricity, chemical products, textiles, metals, etc."; confiscation of war profits and large-scale levies upon the fortunes and property of the big capitalists; confiscation of large estates; creation of a state monopoly to control foreign and wholesale trade; nationalization—again without compensation—of large stores; confiscation of private dwellings and big buildings owned by capitalists, etc.

The Party is, in a word, speaking with real candor when it declares, as it does repeatedly, that it is a question of doing "as they have done in Russia," and that France must choose between "two roads"—one that leads to decadence and vassaldom, another that will make of France "a socialist country destined to undergo rich development." [14]

27, H, b. As the demands pressed by the Party are moved up from the economic to the political level, its combat units must—for reasons that we have already noticed in part—be transformed: hitherto mere instruments of propaganda, they must now become organs of power. The task of the projected "government of the people" is, quite simply, that of creating a Soviet regime; and the committees of the people are merely the rough outline for, and preparatory stage of, the future Soviets.

"The Government of the People"—so the Party tells its potential sympathizers—

in order to assure itself of support from the masses of the people and control by those masses, of whose aspirations it will itself be a faithful expression, will proceed to set up machinery for popular consultation. This will call for:

1. Committees of the people on the·local level, to guarantee that municipal and village administration shall be popularly controlled;

2. Committees of the people on the factory level, to mobilize and express working-class energies within the production unit.

The activities of the Government of the People will be controlled by representatives of the aforesaid committees of the people, that is to say, by the representatives of the popular sovereign.

In order to assure continuing control by the people, the members chosen from the aforesaid committees shall be removable at the pleasure of those from whom they have received their mandates.[15]

"Committees of the people" and "Soviets" are evidently identical in structure and in meaning. The former term is, for the moment, preferable: it attracts less attention, and the situation is such that it would be unwise to rush matters. This does not mean, however, that outright conversion of the one into the other is to be postponed until the actual taking of power: at a certain point in the struggle that will precede (and, indeed, make possible) this event, the committees of the people will tend to become actual organs of power, and thus replace the existing governmental machinery in the various localities—in anticipation of the day on which they will replace the central government itself. They are, in short, destined to play on an ever larger scale the role of "second power," just as their Russian counterparts came to play that role. They will, little by little, take over the prerogatives of the existing government. They will, bit by bit, wear the government down and paralyze it. And, once they have fully drained it of its life's blood, they will proceed to liquidate it.

Where this is possible, therefore, the workers themselves must make arrangements for the reopening of the factories: "Organize a committee of the people in each factory. Open the factories and make them produce. Each factory must have its management committee appointed from among its own personnel." [16] In this area of the nation's life, in other words, the step from control to management is to be made well in advance of the revolutionary victory—which is to say that the state of affairs which, in Russia, *followed* the taking of power, the imposition of so-called workers' control, the crushing of resistance on the part of the factory managers, and the latter's subsequent flight or liquidation, *is to emerge in France out of the disorder and difficulties caused by the defeat.* In a manifesto published in July, 1940, the Party—for similar reasons—demands that a committee of the people in each Commune designate a deputy to be "charged with responsibility for resolving all problems relating to the supply of food to the Commune's inhabitants." And it demands comparable machinery on the level of the prefecture: a group made up of spokesmen of local committees of the people—one for each canton, to be exact—and empowered to "make decisions on administrative issues arising within the department." [17] The end result, of course, will be a "second power" nucleus in every factory, every town hall, every canton, and every department—so that a single step will remain to be taken in order for the "second power" to become the new government. The Party's program is, on the face of it, the Bolshevik program for "the dictatorship of the proletariat."

This formula, to be sure, is kept out of the tracts and newspapers devoted to agitation and propaganda. The Communists, needing peasant and middle-class support and obliged to take into account the suspicions and resistances the formula would arouse among the workers themselves, do not dare use it in their public utterances. For the rest, what's in a name—when you are clear in your own mind about the thing for which it stands? The word "proletariat" disappears and the word "people" takes its place; but what is in question is still dictatorship via "direct democracy"—dictatorship by a regime analagous to that which emerged from the October Revolution, that is, "dictatorship of the proletariat" in principle and dictatorship of the Communist Party in practice. In fine: the Communists need to regain legal status because illegality restrains their freedom of political action, and they need to recover the cadres that are still missing as a result of the post-September, 1939, repression; they are, therefore, willing to speak in terms of "reinstating" the liberties of "the people." But their use of this vocabulary by no means divests their program of its basic character as a program for dictatorship by a class and by a party.

The "democratic" measures proposed by the manifesto *All Out for the Well-being of the French People* leave no room for doubt on this point. The Communists are demanding:

withdrawal of civil and political rights from the executives and big stockholders of all capitalist corporations; denial to the capitalists of the right of association; removal of the restrictions upon free publication [of working-class newspapers]; a ban on the educational activities of religious congregations and on the continued operation of private schools; elimination of reactionary and obscurantist ideas from classrooms throughout the nation; removal of restrictions upon the people's right of free assembly, their right to a free press, and their freedom to organize; the suppression of newspapers financed or subsidized by the capitalists, who are enemies of the people, etc.

The dictatorship must, when it comes, have at its disposal the arms it will need in order to impose its will, so there is a further demand to round out the list: the "creation of worker and peasant militias to block all attempts to restore the privileges of the capitalists." What the French Communists have in mind, in short, is less a dictatorship comparable to that in Stalin's Russia, which after a quarter of a century of suffering and bloodshed has acquired a certain stability, than a dictatorship like that of the early years after the October Revolution— the period of "war communism" and civil war.

28, I. Agitation on behalf of short-term demands, formulae for the "period of transition," mass mobilization against the existing regime—all of these are of interest only as they contribute to the final struggle for power. The Communists must find a political slogan that will catch up within it their other slogans and at the same time—through every twist of the Party line—serve to remind the militants of their ultimate objective. The Party has such a slogan on ice—one which it devised back in the days of the Popular Front and which, now that it wishes to relate its current activity to the Popular Front, is all the more useful for that reason: "a government resting on the masses of the people" [18]—or, as it appears in a manifesto published in Bordeaux around June 18, a "popular government resting on the masses." [19] This slogan is ceaselessly repeated in every pamphlet, newspaper, and handbill the Party publishes from that moment forward, for Communist propaganda relies even more heavily than that of other totalitarian movements upon the hypnotic effect of the endlessly reiterated phrase. It elaborates for the purpose, to be sure, a whole series of minor variations, but all of them say recognizably the same thing: "popular government," "government of the people and in the people's interest," "government of the sovereign people," "government of the people for the people," "a popular French government," "a government of the workers, the peasants, and the common folk, who together make up the people," etc. As we shall see, the Party does not abandon the slogan even after June 22, 1941; it merely introduces one or two new nuances, devised with an eye to the new situation: for example, "a truly French government elected by the people."

The form of government to which the Party thus commits itself is not regarded as minimizing the dominant role that it is itself to play: rather the idea is that the vagueness of the formula is the best possible mask for the dictatorship through its early days. For the moment, the Party must do everything in its power to associate the idea of "government of the people" with that of Communist participation in, and even control of, that government. And to this end it puts back into circulation certain other phrases that did good service during Popular Front days and that, for one reason or another, are associated with the Party in the people's minds: "A popular government that will guarantee peace, bread, and freedom"; "give power to the people and make France free, happy, and strong"; etc. And it also revives the battle cry it used in its meetings and parades through the Popular Front period: "Power for Thorez."

29, J, a. The government of the people will turn the factories over to the men who work them and give the land to the peasants. It will make the rich pay. It will be the architect of a firm Franco-Soviet friendship. It will be the agent of France's "national and social liberation." [20] This is clearly a program which no one is likely to read or hear without thinking of the October Revolution and of the French Communists' own pronouncements during the period of the Popular Front. And, for all the tame language it is using in other contexts (as we have just seen), this is a recognizably frank expression of the Party's aspiration for power. So also is this other emphasis: the government called upon to carry out the program will naturally include the Communists,[21] and this means *led by* the Communists.[22] Government of the people and Communist leadership are thus deliberately identified in the popular mind:

The rebirth of France and its advance toward socialism can be the work only of a government that has sprung from the people and acts for the people. It is incumbent upon the Communist Party, the Party of the people, the hope of young people the world over, to perform that mission. Long live the glorious Communist Party, which alone has the strength and capacity to restore to us a France that is independent, strong, and happy.

Thus reads the Party's *Manifesto to the Students of France;* [23] and the following excerpt from a text which the Party leaders send out for nation-wide reproduction as a pamphlet sets the tone of its propaganda on this point:

ONLY ONE PARTY
is worthy of governing France.
Only one party
opposed the war.
Only one party
works in the people's interest.
Only one party
symbolizes the friendship between France
and the Soviet Union.
Only one party
can rebuild France in the midst of its ruins.
That party is
THE COMMUNIST PARTY [24]

All the Party's documents have recourse to these themes. Only the Communist Party "is qualified to point the way to salvation for the French people"; [25] the Communist Party is France's only hope; [26] only the Party can eradicate forever the causes of imperialist wars, because it is at one and the same time patriotic and internationalist; [27] only the Party can save France and restore its liberty and independence in a context of peace; [28] a free and independent France is the kind of France "that Communists wish for and intend to build." [29]

Eliminating the Competition

30, J, a. The fall of France has, at one blow, refuted the
"accusations leveled against the Communist Party." [1] So at
least the Party leaders hope; and, since today's sufferings always weigh more heavily with the masses than yesterday's
polemics, the objective situation certainly does not exclude
this interpretation. The war has ended in catastrophe; ergo,
those who opposed it, whether from the extreme Right or
from the extreme Left and whatever reason they may have
had for doing so, can now hold their heads high. The Communists' volte-face at the end of August, 1939, and, for that
matter, the widespread popular disapproval and relentless
oppression it brought down upon them, should now be regarded as titles to glory. What did the Communists do—save
"make the mistake of being right?" [2]

The Party, that is to say, now makes capital out of its anti-
war stand, which, in its view, subsequent events have completely vindicated. Never reluctant to insist upon its own
merits, it now claims as its *chief* merit that of having wished
for peace and opposed war; [3] and it makes this claim all the
more vigorously because it intends to capitalize upon it as a
means of obtaining certain political privileges that only the
occupation authorities can bestow. Its fight against potential
and at present more favored competitors therefore becomes,
in large part, a matter of keeping people reminded of those
competitors' "prowar" past. (Among its commonest targets
here are the Paris newspapers, which it hopes to discredit in
German and French eyes alike.) [4]

Its monopoly position as a champion of peace does not,
to be sure, yield the quick dividends which the Party has
promised itself. It nevertheless continues to draw attention to
it and to bring forward further evidence of its title to it. It
could do otherwise only if it were prepared to let the Ger-

mans think well of recently converted pacifists, that is, of the elements whose "eleventh-hour opposition to the war" contrasts so sharply with its own long-term and unwavering "revolutionary defeatism."

In their letter of October, 1940, Thorez and Duclos put this point as follows: "When we raised our voices against the imperialist war into which France had been forced by a government which enjoyed the guilty support of all members of Parliament except the Communists, we were fulfilling our obligations as proletarian revolutionaries. At no time did we lose sight of the fact that—in Karl Liebknecht's admirable phrase—the enemy is within." [5]

The Party must, to be sure, walk a tight rope here. It wishes to press its bid for a considerable measure of toleration from the German authorities. But it wishes also to exploit the sufferings inflicted by the occupation. This means that it must be stridently anti-German in one context, at least conciliatory toward the Germans in the other. But let there be no mistake as to whether or not the second context exists: the Party's attacks on Marcel Déat * and his friends for having "switched sides" in September, 1939, are, to cite but one example, comprehensible only when regarded as an attempt to eliminate a rival form of collaboration.

The Party does not give up easily on its dream of acceptance by the Germans—not even when there are indisputable signs that French public opinion is becoming irretrievably hostile to the occupying power, and this despite the fact that these signs appear more or less simultaneously with the early indications of an end to the Nazi-Soviet honeymoon. The Party—necessarily—adapts its propaganda to this new situation, and in a neopatriotic sense. But it by no means abandons the central theme: "The workers, the peasants, the small businessmen, the masses of common people—all these remember what the Communists have done for them. They know that the Communist Party was the sole opponent of the imperialist war,

* Leader and theorist of the prewar Neo-Socialist Party in France, who adopted a "pacifist-defeatist" attitude through the months just before the war and through those of the "phony war" period. As the context suggests, he "collaborated" with Laval. His name is frequently linked with those of Doriot and Faure. W.K.

as it is today the only party that is fighting against the nation-wide oppression which is crushing our country." [6]

31, J, b. If it is to extend its monopoly to other areas, the Party must break the bonds that continue to tie the masses to the country's traditional political groupings. This means doing whatever has to be done in order to get the largest possible number of its opponents, especially those who are genuine competitors for power, into hot water; [7] and through the months following the armistice the question of responsibility for the war and the disaster to which it has led are, naturally enough, the Party's most serviceable propaganda weapon for this purpose. Beginning therefore with a manifesto published shortly before June 14, it continually poses the question: "Who is guilty?" And over several months it repeats, again and again, approximately the same answer to this question: "In our country the guilty ones are the two hundred families plus their confidential agents who head up the political parties that form a holy alliance at the beginning of every war." [8] All of them are traitors: the political leaders, the two hundred families, and the generals.[9] All of them ought to be beaten "with the same stick"—those who did the job yesterday equally with those who are doing it today.[10]

The first Party manifesto from Paris (August, 1940) in-cludes a more detailed list of those whom the Communist Party accuses:

The time has come to fix the guilt of all the men who led France to its downfall. The political bankrupts who put the war policy into effect enjoyed the support of an inclusive coalition of parties, brought together not only by common treasonable objectives but also by common hatred for the working class and for Com-munism: the Radical Party . . . the Socialist Party . . . the Rightist parties . . . the Union of Socialist Republicans . . . the Doriot * gang, and the officials whom Vichy has put in charge of the CGT, the Jouhaux, Belins † [etc.], . . . These are the men responsible for France's ordeal.[11]

* Jacques Doriot, a major Communist spokesman in Parliament in the early '30's, was expelled from the Party in the days preceding the Popular Front. He later organized the Parti Populaire Français. W.K.

† Léon Jouhaux became Secretary of the CGT in 1909, and was still holding that office when this book was written. René Belin, for a long while editor of the trade-union weekly *Syndicats,* was the major spokesman of the "moderate" ele-ments in the CGT. W.K.

The Party, be it noted, makes no attempt to conceal its purpose in this démarche: it is out to discredit *all* other political parties, and it intends to do this by discrediting their leaders. It will, in this way, clear the ground that it intends to occupy.

The Riom trials, though a windfall, are not, of course, so great a windfall as they would have been had they been conducted under Communist auspices. The Party therefore indulges in endless fantasies about the trials *it* would conduct if it were in power; and soon its propaganda is demanding that Riom make way for a tribunal composed of "delegates of the soldiers, the workers, and the peasants, all united in an Assembly of the people" [12]—above all, of delegates of the recently demobilized soldiers, who have "witnessed high treason." [13]

To facilitate this tribunal's task when the time comes for it to be constituted, the Communists proceed to draw up lists of the persons who are to be tried. The first list of this type, presented in *Party Life*, includes "the former President of the Republic; the members of the government that declared war; everyone who has served as Prime Minister or Minister of War since 1919; the high staff officers of the Army, the Navy, and the Air Force as of the moment when war was declared; the commanding generals; the members of Parliament, journalists, and other public figures who supported the war policy of Daladier and Reynaud." [14] This list is republished, with minor variations, until it takes definitive· shape in the program the Party adopts early in 1941.[15] Meantime—in October, 1940—the Party, which by this time has extensive funds at its disposal, has showered Paris with small silk parachutes bearing the legend: "The warmongers shall be punished by the people." Earlier still—in September, 1940—it has taken its stand with Maurras * and Déat (who, for reasons of their own, wish to draw a distinction between the guilt of France and the guilt of France's prewar leaders) to proclaim that the people of France "did not want war" and that forcing them

---

* Charles Maurras, one of the editors of the distinguished prewar French newspaper, *L'Action française*, and one of the leaders of the antidemocratic, monarchist political movement of that name, was the major non-Communist spokesman for the view that France's prewar leaders were directly "responsible" for the fall of France. W.K.

to pay the expense of the occupation is therefore a "terrible injustice." [16]

32, J, b. The Communists would like, besides eliminating the competing parties as parties, to win over their rank-and-file members. To this end they make a direct appeal to the Socialists, the Radicals, and the Catholics—sometimes taking them by turns, sometimes blanketing them together. For example: "the workers who yesterday were still following the Socialist Party, the Radical Party, etc." are urged to join forces now with "their Communist brethren." [17] Usually, however, the Party takes these groups one at a time and fits its language to the milieu to be conquered.

The Party pays its respects most often to the Socialists, who, as it likes to put it, remain brothers even when they are enemies. During the period when Communist activity looks to the rapid conquest of power, that is, up until the first months of 1941, the Party's tactics are calculated to drive a wedge between the rank-and-file Socialists and their "traitorous" leaders. Both the Socialist Party and its leaders have "wallowed in shame and dishonor" [18]—the leaders especially, who betrayed the workers by making them accept the war, and thus placed them at the mercy of the munitions manufacturers.[19] All these leaders, the "prowar" Blum and Dormoy and the "pacifist" Paul Faure alike, are equally guilty; all have committed the same "crimes." [20] They have, clearly, left their followers no alternative but to line up with the Communists and join the Party. Here again, of course, Party policy coincides to some extent with that of Vichy, which is taking punitive measures against certain Socialist leaders; and the Party must, if it can, see to it that the victims of these measures gain no sympathy from its own potential recruits. This leads to some curious results. When Marx Dormoy * is arrested, the Party recognizes a "cunning trick on the part of

* Marx Dormoy, a member of the prewar Socialist government of Léon Blum. Late in the period covered by this book he was assassinated by the "Cagoulards." W.K.

the bourgeoisie, calculated to restore prestige to a personage who has served it well." [21] When Léon Blum, whom the Party has always listed among the men responsible for the war and the defeat, is allowed "to see his lawyer every day," the Party fumes over the "favored treatment" accorded him: "Why does the Marshal concede the status of political prisoners to traitors like Blum, Daladier, and Reynaud?" [22] When, on the other hand, Vichy unexpectedly frees some of the Socialist leaders, *L'Humanité* vociferously "deplores" their liberation, and suddenly adopts a new tack about Léon Blum: "What has become of the Marshal's promise to punish the men responsible for the disaster?" [23] (Here as elsewhere it reserves its most abusive language for its former partners in the Popular Front, for whom its hatred, though sometimes concealed for tactical reasons, never flags.) With respect to the Socialist heroes of other days, however, the Party must carry water on the other shoulder. When the reaction effaces yet another revered name from the street markers, the Communists' propaganda seeks to exploit the resentment of the Socialist rank and file, though not without adding its usual *veni mecum*: "The Vichy gang, under the protection of foreign bayonets, has just removed the monument to Jean Jaurès at Albi. . . . Join the Party of triumphant socialism." [24]

As time passes the Communists see that their bid for the Socialist militants is encountering more tenacious "party patriotism" than they have expected, and that—especially in view of the heightened repression—there are to be few takers. Their *Letter to the Socialist Worker*, distributed in March, 1941, accordingly begins and ends with these reassuring words: "In sending this letter, we do not mean to ask you to renounce your Socialist faith, or the fraternal ties that bind you to your party comrades. . . . Let us again join together, shoulder to shoulder, just as we did in the campaign that preceded our victory in June, 1936." [25] Even now, however, there is no let-up in the attacks on the Socialist Party organization and its leaders. The Party is simply getting back to the familiar tactical slogan of "unity with the rank-and-file Socialist workers," whose details are explained at length in one of the standard "courses" on Communist doctrine.[26]

There is a similar evolution with respect to the workers affiliated with the Radical Party: At first the Party concentrates its fire upon the leaders: Daladier, Sarraut, Herriot, Bonnet, Chautemps, etc., who "led the country into war and defeat" and are "discredited forever," so that there is nothing left for their followers to do but to join the Communist Party.[27] Later, when it has become clear that this approach is unsuccessful, the Party sweetens its utterances with such phrases as "worthy fellow citizen" and "worthy comrade," and tells itself that it can win over the peasants, the small businessmen, the functionaries, and the workers in the Radical Party by a direct appeal in terms of the "great ideal of liberty and progress." It says to them the things they wish to hear about Vichy's attacks on freedom, on France's corpus of anticlerical legislation, and on the rights of man. And it does not insist that the Radicals actually join the Party:

Come to us. If, in the face of the miseries piled high around you, you feel that it is your duty to take your place in our ranks, the Party's doors are open to you; but if you do not wish to go that far, it is clearly your duty, still more clearly your interest, to help us . . . as well as to bring your friends along. In this way we can all move forward together in the struggle against the traitors of Vichy and work for the liberty, independence, and rebirth of France.[28]

The Communists' propaganda among the Catholic workers falls far short, during this period, of their usual standards of adroitness and vigor. This is, in general, part of the price the Party must pay in order to ride the wave of anticlerical sentiment that Vichy has set in motion with its educational reforms. The Catholic workers, that is to say, favor many things (teaching by members of religious congregations, continuation of private schools, etc.) to which the Party's program is unambiguously opposed; [29] so that, for the moment at least, the only possible approach to them is through (a) themes calculated to undermine their confidence in the church hierarchy and the leaders of the Catholic unions, and (b) the "outstretched hand" *tout court*.[30] Neither is sufficiently promising to merit intensive cultivation. Not until June 22, 1941, will the Communists make a direct and determined effort to abate the distrust of the Catholics and entice them under the Party's tent.

33, J, b. From June, 1940, to June, 1941, the great Communist onslaught is that against the Gaullists, who are in several senses the Party's major rival. They also are militant; they also have shown a flair for operations underground; they also appeal to outraged national sentiment against Vichy and the occupying power. It would be difficult to find a single Party newspaper or tract of this period that does not contain some unfavorable reference to the "felonious" and "opportunistic" general and his alleged "sell-out" to British capitalism. *L'Humanité* sets the tone for this campaign with its first appearance in Paris following the defeat:

General de Gaulle, along with the other agents of British finance capitalism, has his heart set on getting the French to fight for the City of London. He—like the others—is bent upon getting the colonial peoples into the war. The French reply to these gentlemen is "Go chase yourselves." As for the colonial peoples, the thing for them to do is to seize upon the opportunity afforded by the present difficulties of their oppressors, and free themselves.[31]

After a time the Party reformulates its charges against the Gaullists so as to associate them with the "collaborationists"— and since both groups do in fact wish to get France back into the war this is less difficult than it sounds. Right down to June 22, 1941, it will be devising new slogans—all variants of the same idea—calculated to drive this point home: "Neither Churchill nor Hitler!" "Neither London nor Berlin!" "Neither a British Dominion nor a German protectorate!" The two immediate objectives are (a) to show that there is no ideological justification for the battle the Gaullists and their British allies are fighting, and (b) to insist upon the identity of character of the two warring "imperialisms." "De Gaulle," we read in the very issue of *L'Humanité* that applauds the Russo-German economic agreements of January, 1941,

says over the London radio that he intends to rally behind his standard all Frenchmen who are fighting for liberty. This same General de Gaulle was, a short time ago, a member of the general staff which . . . knew well how the armies stacked up as regards matériel, and yet led the troops forth to be slaughtered. . . . He is now seeking his fortune in England, where he has allied himself with the reactionary British Government, the nobility, and the bankers.[32]

Gaullism, the Party insists, is purely and simply a conspiracy to get France back into uniform, so that the beginning of wisdom lies in recognizing that the bitter-enders in London offer no solution to the problems of France. Even in May, 1941, when, a few weeks before the outbreak of the Nazi-Soviet War, the Party launches its campaign for a National Front, it continues to treat de Gaulle as an enemy. Some of our fellow countrymen, says the manifesto distributed on this occasion, "are mistakenly pinning their hopes on the Gaullist movement. We say to these fellow countrymen that the unity of the French people behind the cause of national liberation will never be achieved under the leadership of a movement made in the image of British imperialism and led by the defenders of colonial exploitation." [33]

The struggle for "national liberation" must not be permitted to overshadow the Party's other interests. Pending a decision to the contrary by the USSR, for example, there can be no question of withdrawing support from the Nazi-Soviet Pact—not even when the Party becomes aware that the pact is endangered (the drive for a National Front is a reflection of Kremlin anxiety on this point), and not even when new repressive measures and the rising tide of anti-German sentiment among the French people point up the advisability of taking a different stand. The USSR, though indeed looking to its defenses, still hopes to avoid a rupture with Germany, so that the Party must go right on saying what it has been saying all along (on the level of action, of course, it can begin to

draw in its horns). The manifesto distributed following Darlan's negotiations at Berchtesgaden—the calendar, be it noted,
already reads May 11—is a conspicuous example of the Party's
fidelity to its instructions. These negotiations, opening up as
they do the possibility of military cooperation between Vichy
France and Germany, force the Party to raise its voice in
opposition. But this opposition is articulated in the very terms
the Party was using before the new situation arose, that is to
say, in terms of a "national liberation" to be achieved thanks
to the Nazi-Soviet Pact, and on the basis of strict neutrality
vis-à-vis the war!

The Party thus denounces Darlan and his aides on these
grounds: "instead of keeping our country out of the war of
conquest between the rival Axis and Anglo-Saxon imperialisms" they are traveling "the road to war, and without giving
a moment's thought to the ruin and sorrow this criminal policy
will bring upon the French people." "Our cities and factories
will become targets for aerial bombardment, and the people
will once more pay in blood and tears for the criminal policy
of governments made up of scoundrels and traitors." [34]

Is this the language of peace at any price? No; the authors
of this manifesto wisely refrain from giving any such hostages
to fortune: "The peace the French people demand is a peace
that will bring with it freedom and independence. Our chief
objective in our fight for peace must be this: to prevent our
people, our national resources, and our territory from being
used in the conflict between Germany and England."

In what terms does the Party conceive the "fight" for "peace
that will bring with it freedom and independence"—the fight
that its new National Front is to win? The first task, as we
know, is to create a "government of the people." Let us suppose, however, that this government of the people has already
been formed. What will its policy be? Will it declare war on
Germany? Certainly not, since its aim is to prevent France
from being drawn into the war so long as Russia has not gone
into it, and since its program, in the last analysis, implies collaboration with Germany. The National Front manifesto can,

therefore, only reiterate the familiar list of "demands": (a) "the wiping-out of the line of demarcation between occupied and Vichy France"; (b) "the repatriation of all French prisoners of war"; and (c) "the cancellation of the war indemnity of 400 million francs per day." [35] Nothing has changed, on this showing, since the manifesto of January, 1941, *All Out for the Well-being of the French People*. Nor are the demands perceptibly different from those put forward by Laval as he pursues, and seeks to justify, his policy of collaboration!

34, J, b. The Party's propaganda campaign against the Gaullist movement goes forward along two lines: it is denounced as "reactionary," and it is denounced as "prowar."

In pressing the first of these charges, the Party—and here we see one of its propaganda techniques in its most naked form—finds itself with nothing whatever to offer in the way of proof. The technique the Party employs in such predicaments calls for, first, oversimplifying the objective situation of which you are speaking, and then, second, tying the elements to which you have reduced it together in a series of assertions which, to the militant at least, will sound like clear reasoning. England equals capitalism, London equals the City. Churchill is Prime Minister of England. Ergo, Churchill is the representative of capitalism and the City. England is waging war; the war it is waging is therefore capitalistic. De Gaulle's name shows him to be a member of an aristocratic family; therefore he is a "reactionary." De Gaulle, moreover, is in London; you have only to juxtapose the reality "de Gaulle" and the reality "England" (as just defined), and you have before you all you need in order to arrive at definitive conclusions regarding the character of the war and the role England and Gaullism are playing in it.

As for the second of the two charges, this is easy enough to support out of de Gaulle's own mouth. There is, for example, his June 18, 1940, message in which he urged France to keep on fighting, and insisted that the war, though indeed lost for the moment in France itself, was to be won over the world as a whole. The Communists' initial response to this message ran in we-know-better-than-that terms; but by October, 1940, when Maurice Thorez and Jacques Duclos compose their "Letter to Communist Militants," the answer has become much more specific: they denounce not only de Gaulle himself but "the agents of de Gaulle" (that is, the resistance movement within France), who are determined "to get Frenchmen killed in order to help England in its war with Germany." From this moment forward, "peace" and "absolute neutrality" [36] are the major emphases of the Communist line. They serve many purposes. In the first place, as we have seen, they provide ample justification for the Party's every posture through 1939–40: the war has ended in defeat and invasion,[37] and the Communists were, therefore, quite right in opposing it. In the second place they vindicate the Nazi-Soviet Pact: Russia signed merely to save the peace; [38] and if England and France chose to declare war instead of associating themselves with the pact,[39] this is merely another way of saying that they are primarily responsible for the war.[40] And what is true of the pact is true also of Soviet foreign policy in general: Stalin's mission in life is that of bringing peace to all men of good will. He has conferred the blessings of peace on the people of the USSR.[41] He has, thanks to the accord with Hitler,[42] brought peace to the "liberated peoples." He has "served the cause of peace" by signing the friendship pact with Japan.[43] If, now that Germany has occupied Bulgaria, Stalin contents himself with a verbal protest, this, too, is because his policy is that of "determined defense" of the peace.[44] If, again, after concluding a friendship pact with Yugoslavia on the eve of German aggression (to prevent the spread of war), he fails to intervene on behalf of his new ally, this also is because the USSR is—first, last, and always—the bastion of peace.[45]

The pacifist emphasis also fits in admirably with the Party's domestic strategy, most of all by enabling it to speak a language to which the French people, exhausted and bewildered as they are, will for some time listen far more readily than to the language de Gaulle is speaking. It holds out the hope of "peace now" (or at least by next week) and of all the good things peace would bring in its train: rapid demobilization, liberation of the French prisoners of war, the end of shortages (thanks to the commercial treaty with the USSR).[46] With the aid of the USSR, France will be able to keep out of the war,[47] maintain its "absolute neutrality," and take part in the great postwar straightening out of the world's affairs, which will of course go forward under Stalin's supervision. This calls for the Communists' taking power in France at the earliest practicable moment; and since a Communist government in France is conceivable only as agreed to or tolerated by the Germans, the Communists must eschew all forms of direct attack upon the occupation authorities.

35, J, c. The Party, now as in the days of the Popular Front (which it would like to revive at this time, though under its direct control and without participation by other political parties), stands forth as the party of "unity." [48] Its propaganda summons up memories of 1936 at every opportunity and by means of every rhetorical and logical device at its command, and draws the appropriate moral with respect to the present situation: In 1936 the danger was fascism, which was defeated by "unity"; what will save France today is unity, which will keep it out of the war and at the same time create conditions favorable to the installation of a "government of the people." The evolution of the "unity" theme over the months is itself, however, a matter of no small interest. The first *Manifesto to the People of France*, published in Paris in mid-August, insists that unity can and must be achieved at once, though only if it has the working class, that is to say, the Communist Party, as its nucleus. A special issue of *L'Humanité* toward the end of August, 1940, repeats the point in extenso; but in the October issue of the same publication Thorez and Duclos take a much more daring position, leaving out the words "working class" and speaking only of the Party, which is "alone worthy" to unify the nation. Marshal Pétain also, of course, is appealing to "French unity"; and the Communists, who during the early weeks have tended to handle him with kid gloves, are finally obliged to carry the battle into his camp.[49] A September,

1940, instruction sheet accordingly speaks of unifying "the French nation against the Vichy government," and of the need, for this purpose, of arousing confidence in the Party and in its leaders; [50] indeed the slogan "Power for Thorez," which is used on a large scale through September and October, 1940, is calculated precisely to direct the sympathies of the masses away from Pétain to another leader.

The campaign for unity, then, both narrows and broadens as the months pass. The Communists address themselves, at first, to all who earn an honest living, and thus propose an "alliance" between the peasants, the middle classes, and the intellectuals on the one hand and the workers on the other. Soon, however, they are appealing also to members of the old Popular Front and to the Catholic parties; and before they have done they go to the length of courting elements on the Right [51] —or, as they like to put it, "all honest men," [52] "all free men." [53] By May, 1941, when relations between Germany and the USSR are becoming tense and the Party initiates its drive for a "National Front," it is indeed 1936 all over again: the Party is prepared "to support any French government, any organization, any individuals whose efforts will be channeled into a sincere struggle against the national oppression under which France is suffering." [54] It is, however, careful to explain in the same document that such a struggle is possible only "under two conditions":

1. We must unify the entire nation, which means that we must exclude only the traitors and the defeatists who are the errand boys and supporters of the invader; we must form a broad national fighting front for French independence.

2. This National Front for independence, if it is to fulfill its liberating mission, must be based on the working class of France with the Communist Party at its head.

The front must never, in any case, become so broad as to resist subordination to the Party. It is to be the Party's direct instrument, and the Party will control both its policy and its organization.

The Communists, the Nazi-Soviet Pact, and the Foreign Policy of the USSR

36, K. The Party, as it presses forward with its national unity program, finds itself paying dearly for the Nazi-Soviet Pact. The masses, which is to say the individuals who make up the masses, no doubt have short memories. But the crisis of late August, 1939, has left behind it recollections too vivid to be easily erased; and the defeat has at most blurred these recollections, without by any means depriving them of their power to sway men's actions. The Communists, always quick to sense this sort of thing, recognize the difficulty, and drive themselves hard in their attempt to cope with it.

The pact, as we know, figures prominently in the plans the Communists elaborate in June and July of 1940—as we should expect it to do since the leaders regard it as a short cut on the road to power. Clearly, however, this view of the pact's significance will not serve for purposes of propaganda, which call for emphasis upon the benefits it will confer on France as a whole; and the Party elaborates for these purposes the following formula: Thanks to the good relations between Germany and the USSR, Franco-Soviet friendship will now be rounded out by friendship between France and Germany, and France will enjoy a kind of security it has never known before. Equally clearly, however, this formula alone is not enough; it is therefore supplemented by a long series of carefully prepared documents in which the most persistent objections urged against the Party's policies through 1938 and 1939 are taken up one at a time, minutely examined, and refuted [1]—as often as not by directing attention to the alleged claudications, weaknesses, and "betrayals" of the democratic governments between 1935 and 1939. Ethiopia, Austria, Albania, Spain, Munich—each of these receives due attention, subject, however, to this proviso: too much emphasis, too much detail, might expose the extent to which the general European situation had changed by the time the pact was negotiated. The major objective, clearly visible between the lines whatever the topic in hand may be, is to prove the necessity and justice of the Nazi-Soviet Pact. Here is a real challenge to the Party's inventiveness; and we must not be surprised if, in responding to the challenge, it resorts to several different—at the margin contradictory—explanations.

First explanation. The USSR entered into its pact with Germany because it had been unable to negotiate such a pact with England and France. The latter countries had refused to give the USSR the military guarantees—in the Baltic countries, in Finland, and in Poland—that it was clearly entitled to demand; up to the last moment, indeed, they had hoped to hurl Germany against Russia. Moreover, they did not abandon this dream even in the face of the Nazi-Soviet Pact: rather they egged Poland into adopting a policy of intransigence that would force Germany to declare war and advance—they of course regarded a German victory as a sure thing—to the Russo-Polish border. "The signature of the Nazi-Soviet Non-aggression Pact on August 23, 1939," Thorez and Duclos write in *L'Humanité,*

created the conditions for peace in Eastern Europe. Daladier and Chamberlain, however, wanted war. They encouraged the Polish Government to resist a peaceful settlement of the Danzig question. Then, when Poland was attacked, these fine fellows in Paris and London did not so much as lift a finger in its behalf. They lived in the hope that the course of military events in Poland would smash the Nazi-Soviet Nonaggression Pact and pit the Nazi Army against the Red Army. This hope has been disappointed.[2]

Second explanation. The USSR signed the pact with Germany in order to save the peace. "The entire foreign policy of the USSR can be summed up in the words 'keeping the peace.' "[3] Why? Because the USSR is "the land of peace."[4] The record for 1939 shows clearly, furthermore, that the

USSR at no time abated its efforts to bring about a peaceful settlement of the problems that were dividing Europe; and it would have succeeded in doing just that if the world had only been willing to listen, for example, by joining the "Peace Front" [5] that could so easily have taken shape in the spring. Moreover, the organization of such a front would have been simplicity itself following—and as a result of—the Nazi-Soviet Pact.

The Communists thus repudiate the contention that the choice, in 1939, was a "choice between another Munich on the one hand and war on the other." The authors of this contention, they assert, are putting it forward with an eye to the trials at Riom, that is, in order to establish the innocence of the Riom culprits:

Not on your life. The choice the ministers had to make in 1939 was between alternatives of an entirely different character. The Munich pact failed to bring peace to Europe because it did not include the USSR. In August, 1939, the German leaders, aware of what the Soviet Union's power really amounted to, signed their salutary nonaggression pact with that country. From that moment forward the saving of the peace called for a general European settlement in which the USSR, thanks to the new friendly relations between itself and Germany, would take an active part. It had ceased to be a matter of a discriminatory treaty—limited in scope, thus ineffective and even explosive—among four powers.[6]

Even after the Polish debacle, in short, the peace could have been saved, if only people had heeded the proposals from Germany—of which, be it remembered, the Communist deputies in Parliament had made themselves the spokesmen in their October 1 letter to President Herriot.[7]

Third explanation. The USSR was inspired purely by the wish to gain time, and thus to get itself into a more favorable position for initiating—and carrying through—the world revolution. We may take the *Course in Communist Doctrine*, published between January and June, 1941, as the *locus classicus* for this point: By signing the August 23 pact "Stalin won a victory of incalculable importance for Soviet foreign policy." The pact not only enabled the USSR to keep out of the imperialist war but also "assured it a few additional months in which to get on with building the socialist state" and completing the apparatus of power it will one day place at the service of the proletarian revolution.[8] The grand theorem here is that of the "objective coincidence" of the interests of the USSR and the interests of the revolution—this being the compass by which Communist leaders the world over are able to guide themselves through the trackless wilderness of political maneuvering: "The maintenance of peace," affirm the *Notebooks of Bolshevism*, "is to the interest of the USSR. This is self-evident." And it is equally self-evident that the "maintenance of peace between the USSR and Germany" is to the interest of the workers of the entire world—is, moreover, what they consciously desire:

The workers wish to free themselves from nationalist oppression and from capitalist exploitation. They would like the war to produce a world in which there would be no imperialism. The USSR is, in their eyes, the one great force in the world over which capitalist exploitation and nationalist oppression have no influence —the one great force that is anti-imperialist. It is, therefore, the one force that the workers regard as their ally. And the more tightly the Soviet fortress is sealed off from the hazards of the war, the more certain it becomes that the proletariat will call the tricks when the war is over.[9]

The Nazi-Soviet Pact is thus presented as, variously, (a) a *pis aller* the Soviet Union was forced to accept because of lack of understanding and hostility on the part of England and France, (b) a sacrificial offering laid by the Soviet Union upon the altar of peace in Europe, and (c) an indispensable cogwheel in the machinery of the coming revolution. Each of these explanations clearly excludes the other two. They nevertheless appear together sometimes in one and the same document—naturally enough, as it happens, because in Communist algebra one plus falsehood and one minus falsehood add up to one truth. As for the motives that led Germany to sign the pact of August, 1939, the Communists take this problem also in their stride: pure fear and nothing but fear threw Hitler into Stalin's arms.[10]

37, K. The interests of the USSR coincide at every point with those of the world proletariat, as also with those of all the world's peoples. Government and people in the USSR are one and the same thing.[11] Stalin does everything that the identical interests in question call for, and has no time for anything else.

Soviet policy, since it can always be deduced from these axioms, should in strict logic never require explanation. Day-to-day action and propaganda, however, impose their own requirements: the line of conduct appropriate to this or that situation does not leap to the eye, even for the man who has mastered the appropriate axioms; even if it did, moreover, one must remember that the faith of the "masses" is less firm than that of the cadres, so that the latter must stand ready to drive the appropriate line of conduct home to the former. Worse still, Moscow policy sometimes expresses itself in actions that, to the untrained eye, appear contradictory, and that the Party nevertheless dares not explain in terms of messianic inspiration. On any showing, furthermore, Moscow policy is something to be accepted—and implemented. All these considerations clearly point up the need for "popularizations" explaining Soviet policy, and for permanent mobilization for the purpose of getting such popularizations across. This, therefore, is an activity to which the Party must devote itself with unflagging zeal.

During the days following the Armistice, while they are cut off from Paris and thus from Moscow, the Communist leaders suddenly take out from under its wraps a slogan that has gone unused since October, 1939, namely, that demanding an "accord" with the USSR. It first reappears in a pamphlet published about June 12, in which the Party, in putting forward its demand for a government of the people, defines the latter as, inter alia, a government "capable of reaching an immediate agreement with the Soviet Union for the re-establishment of world peace." [12] Another pamphlet, distributed in Bordeaux around June 18, describes the objective as an agreement "with the USSR looking toward an equitable peace." [13] Whatever the particular form of words, this leitmotiv will dominate Communist propaganda throughout the ensuing months. At first, to be sure, such statements still have recognizable anti-Hitlerian overtones,[14] but this means only that one further step has yet to be taken. It is taken in the next days. For once the Communist leaders have returned to Paris, once they are back in touch with their Muscovite advisers in the Rue de Grenelle, and have had time to work out, with their assistance, the details of their plan of action, every emphasis that might conceivably give offense to the occupation authorities is scrupulously eliminated from their propaganda, and the very words "Hitlerism" and "Hitlerian" drop out of their vocabulary. One could, for the rest, ask for no better proof of the cadres' training in strict Party discipline than the suddenness with which this change becomes effective all the way down the line. One would expect an occasional slip; but the Party's newspapers and pamphlets yield none up to the researcher.

The Party's earliest documents for circulation *extra muros* charge the Allies, among other things, with having abetted the expansion of Hitler's military might through their policy of "weakness," of unilateral appeasement. This also is now slated to disappear—or, to be more accurate, the accusation must be given a twist appropriate to the new situation. The Allies—so runs the new, recognizably collaborationist formula —"sabotaged" the peace; so that, as the Party proceeds over the next months with its unofficial trial of the men allegedly "responsible for the war," Germany is hardly ever mentioned, England and France are the only suspects on the court's docket, and the verdict in both cases is "guilty." This development has, indeed, been in the cards ever since the Communists set out to prove that the USSR at all times labored for peace, and that the Nazi-Soviet Pact, far from having precipitated the war, would—had it been given half a chance—have prevented it. London and Paris, the Party now declares, were committed to a "so-called reorganization of Europe under Franco-British direction . . . This policy, besides making the war inevitable, caused it to be fought in eastern Europe and, at the same time, distributed the several countries between the two camps that were to fight each other in the interest of imperialist France and Britain." [15] The Communist Party, in other words, takes its stand beside the Nazis on the question of war guilt, and—in this regard as in others—raises the bid on the French political leaders with whom the Germans are doing business. Even in those of the Party's documents that are devoted to problems of Communist theory, the faithful are administered repeated demonstrations of the direct war guilt of the two Western democracies along with the usual attacks on the "capitalist regime."

Not only the war but every other event that involves the foreign policy of the USSR is "interpreted" in this manner: everything is made to contribute to the glory and honor of Russia as it presses forward under the aegis of the Nazi-Soviet Pact—though never, of course, at the risk of giving offense to the Germans. Russia's annexation of eastern Poland in September, 1939, its annexation of Bessarabia and Bukovina in late June, 1940, the "adherence" of the Baltic countries to the Soviet Union in July, 1940—all these are welcome grist for the Party's mill. To call them conquests is to talk foolishness: "All these démarches on the part of the Soviet Government have had the effect of liberating oppressed populations. The soldiers of the Red Army have entered the Ukraine, Byelo-Russia, Bessarabia, Bukovina, not as conquerors but as liberators"; and there has, in none of these instances, been any question of war: "All these démarches have been submitted to peaceful negotiation, and in each case save that of Finland this has resulted in an amicable settlement." In a word, what is in question is an expansion of the "socialist world," and, pari passu with that expansion, a "flowering of the creative energies of the masses of people thus rescued from oppression." [16] "Wherever the Red Army goes, the people takes its own destiny in hand; the barbarous police force controlled by the plutocrats gives way to the workers' militia; the ownership of the large estates is returned to the collectivity; the factories are taken over by the workers." [17] Best of all, the Red Army brings the peoples peace: "Soviet Russia has bestowed upon these peoples not only freedom and independence, but also that most precious of gifts, peace; thanks to the USSR, these peoples are not suffering and will not suffer the horrors of the war—this war into which we have been forced by the scoundrels who were our leaders." [18] Moreover, the Red Army's right hand knows not what its left hand is doing—or at least what its left hand has done. Having emptied its cornucopia, it silently removes itself from the scene: "Look where you will—at Poland, at Lithuania, at Estonia, at Latvia, at Bessarabia, at Bukovina. The Red Army, once it has freed the people from the yoke of capitalism, withdraws, and leaves to the people of each of these countries full freedom and independence." No wonder the peoples in question have welcomed it—to the strains of the "Internationale"—"with an enthusiasm that defies description!" [19] "No wonder millions of Frenchmen, prompted by their deep hatred for the men responsible for the war and for our country's defeat, hail the USSR . . . as the one great hope of the world's workers!" [20]

The Party line on the annexations is laid down in Molotov's August 1, 1940, speech before the Supreme Soviet of the USSR; and the French Communists, along with Communists everywhere else, promptly adopt it. One imagines, however, that they tarry longest over—and think hardest about—those paragraphs of the speech that deal with relations between the USSR and Germany: "Ever since the shift of approximately a year ago," declares Molotov,

our relations with Germany have gone forward as envisaged in the pact. This pact, which the Soviet Government has observed to the letter, has eliminated the very possibility of friction between our two countries—[as witness] the measures now in effect along our western frontier. It therefore provides Germany with assurances against difficulties on its eastern flank. The march of events in Europe, far from weakening the pact, has underlined the importance of keeping it alive and of developing it further still. The foreign press, particularly the press in England and the pro-English press everywhere, has again and again recently indulged in speculation about possible differences between the Soviet Union and Germany. It hopes to frighten us with the supposed consequences of expanded German might. We—and the Germans as well—have on several occasions exposed this scheme, and declared that we would have none of it. Here we can only reiterate our position in the matter, namely, that the relations of friendship and good neighborliness that now obtain between the USSR and Germany do not rest upon chance elements belonging to the immediate situation, but upon deep-rooted interests of state—ours and Germany's.

The speaker also records his satisfaction at the "complete reciprocal understanding" that has lately been worked out between the USSR and Italy, and his lack of confidence in the good relations between the USSR on the one hand and Turkey, England, and the United States on the other.[21]

In view of what we know about the French Communists in their current role of crusaders for national liberation, we might expect them to play these statements down in their propaganda. If we did, we should be wrong. They publish lengthy extracts from the speech in their newspapers, and give the entire text the widest possible circulation by reprinting it both in the *Notebooks of Bolshevism* and in a separate leaflet. Why? Clearly enough, because the Party is still hoping to turn the German-Soviet Pact to its own advantage. At most —perhaps to confuse matters in some minds and ward off certain unfavorable reactions in others—the Party tells its readers, in a note tacked on at the end of the pamphlet, that the German Ambassador has refused to permit "normal" publication of the speech, and that the French Communist Party is accordingly publishing it "illegally." [22]

38, K. French Communist comment on Soviet foreign policy during this phase rings the changes on three basic contentions: (a) the treaties concluded by the Soviet Union are evidence of great strength and prestige; (b) these treaties help keep the war at a safe distance from the Soviet Union; and (c) keeping the war at a safe distance from the Soviet Union is in the interest of the workers of all countries, and of the revolution.

On September 27, 1940, Germany, Italy, and Japan sign their pact, which the Party would certainly have denounced, a little while ago, as an international fascist conspiracy. Since, however, this new agreement underwrites [23] that of August, 1939, *L'Humanité* welcomes it—as "an eloquent testimonial to the prestige, authority, and enhanced power of the country of the Soviets!" [24] In November it reacts in the same manner to the reports of Molotov's negotiations in Berlin: the Soviet Foreign Minister's trip shows "how deeply the leaders of the imperialist countries have been impressed by the power of the USSR," which enables the land of socialism to extend "to its 193 million inhabitants the benefits of peace" while people in capitalist countries are busy cutting each other's throats. "The conflicting imperialisms take turns in insisting that the USSR is on their side. The workers well know, however, that in all circumstances the country of the Soviets acts exclusively in the interest of the Soviet peoples, which interest is identical with that of the peoples of all countries." [25]

In January, 1941, Germany and Russia conclude a new commercial treaty, the major result of which is to be increased trade between the two countries. This also the French Communists greet as a development "of considerable importance —a further achievement of Soviet foreign policy, a genuine triumph." [26] Their press proudly lists the types and quantities of goods that the USSR is to deliver to Germany; [27] and if it takes cognizance of the charge that Germany is, for the moment at least, to be the major beneficiary, it has a ready reply: Look at what the Americans are doing for England [28] —besides which France should imitate Germany's example by concluding its own commercial treaty with the USSR, which is in a position to supply it "millions of tons of food stuffs."

The USSR is soon negotiating with Japan as well, and the

publication *Communist Policy* announces this fact as follows: "The Soviet leaders are negotiating a commercial treaty with Japan. Nobody can dispute the value of such a treaty. For our part, we shall welcome its signature as a further guarantee of peace. It will help to dispel the dreams of conquest that continue to endanger the security of the proletarian state." [29] Mr. Matsuoka, once in Moscow, signs a nonaggression and friendship pact, rather than a commercial treaty. But the French Communists are equally pleased, and easily stretch their current catch phrases to cover the new development: "The USSR of Lenin and Stalin is following an independent peace policy consistent both with the interests of the peoples of the Soviet Union and with those of all other peoples. The USSR has at all times served the cause of peace; and by signing the nonaggression and friendship pact with Japan on April 13 it has shown once more the extent to which its expanding might now inspires caution and respect." [30]

The developments in the Balkans in March and April, 1941, pose far more difficult problems. There are, to begin with, reports of an imminent German invasion of Bulgaria; and the French Communists play for time by denouncing the bad faith of the English radio. The latter wishes its listeners to believe that "present German activities in the Balkans will, as a matter of course, precipitate a crisis in Nazi-Soviet relations, and will lead—why, indeed, should they not?—to a military response from the Soviets." What the English are forgetting, or trying to forget, is Comrade Molotov's statement that German-Soviet relations are based on "deep-rooted interests of state." The Berlin radio, on the other hand, has no business saying that the changes the Germans are about to make in the Balkans will go forward with the approval and even the blessing of the USSR. Everybody knows that the USSR is determined "to prevent any extension of the war, particularly to points so close to home as the Balkans and the Near East." And everyone also knows that the USSR would never associate itself with "any enterprise involving rapine, conquest, or territorial occupation." [31]

Early in March, however, the long-anticipated German

move actually takes place—and, as Hitler's disclosures will show when he declares war on the USSR, without a prior understanding with the USSR. Germany *is* kicking over the traces and *is* choosing to do so in an area whose politics are of special interest to Moscow; and, for all that the final break will not come for some time, here is a clash of interest that calls for something more apposite than talk of bad faith in London. The French Communists accordingly set themselves the two-fold task of (a) getting across the fact that the USSR has at no time approved of the Bulgarian Government's foreign policy, and (b) explaining why the USSR has taken no steps to prevent Bulgaria's being occupied. The first of these points is, of course, easy enough to establish; as for the second, the line is that the USSR has done the next best thing, and the supporting evidence is a few cautious remarks by Comrade Vyshinsky: the USSR's verbal castigation of King Boris and his ministers will "touch the hearts of the Bulgarians and will give great comfort to all peoples whose territory is occupied by foreign troops." If, for the moment, Russia has done nothing more, it is because its policy calls for "determined defense of the peace." [33]

The Yugoslav crisis at the end of March and the beginning of April exposes further points of friction between Moscow and Berlin, and for the first time the Communist press permits itself the luxury of sharply adverse criticism of Germany. "Only a few hours before the Berlin incendiaries were to start a new conflagration by their act of aggression against the people of Yugoslavia," writes *L'Humanité*, "the Soviet Union was signing a treaty of friendship with Yugoslavia for the express purpose of preventing extension of the war," which is further proof that the Soviet Union is "the bastion of peace and civilization." The event does not, of course, lend itself to treatment as a new Soviet "triumph"; but the Communists nevertheless read out of it the same moral they drew from the triumphs canvassed in the preceding paragraphs: the act of aggression against Yugoslavia constitutes a still further reason why France must enter into a pact of friendship with the USSR (it will forward her struggle for independence) and a commercial treaty as well (it will save her from starvation).[34] They have, moreover, a ready answer for anyone who dares to object that Yugoslavia's pact with the USSR has not forwarded its struggle for independence: "Are we, like Yugoslavia, going to wait until the last possible moment, when the story is about over, before we turn to the protector of oppressed peoples?" [35]

Soon, to be sure, Moscow itself is showing signs of alarm at the course of events in the Balkans, and the French Communists must follow suit. *Party Life*, in the very issue in which it welcomes the Japanese-Soviet Pact as a further manifestation of the peace policy of the USSR, thus finds itself using the following unaccustomed language: "The enslaved peoples of Europe are filled with repressed resentment against their masters. Yugoslavia and Greece, losers in a just war of defense against aggression, now take their place on the list of martyred nations which dream only of the day on which they will be liberated." [36] These lines must have been written at the end of May or the beginning of June, when the Party is launching its first drive for a National Front for the independence of France; and the thing we must not overlook is the complete synchronization with the thinking that we now know to have been taking place in Moscow. Rudolf Hess' flight to England on May 12 has aroused sharp suspicions on the part of the Soviet leaders; and these suspicions are enhanced when Berlin suddenly suspends its economic negotiations with the USSR, refuses to say why it is suspending them, and proceeds to avoid all situations in which the question might be reopened. Stalin, sensing imminent danger, is about to inaugurate a new phase in the history of the Communist parties the world over—a phase in which they will move along from social and national liberation to open struggle against Germany. The French Communist Party catches the look in the conductor's eye even while his baton maintains the old tempo, and begins preparations for "a real fight against the oppression to which the

French people are now subjected and against the traitors who are doing the oppressors' work for them." [37]

39, K. What emerges from all the foregoing is that nothing matters to France's Communist leaders except the USSR. They regard France as an expendable pawn on a chessboard—where one of the kings is the Soviet Union and the mate is to come about through world revolution. But for the Soviet Union the Communists, as they well know, would count for nothing in French politics; and if they hope soon to count for even more in French politics, and they do, it is because they are relying upon the Soviet Union's support. Meanwhile the "imperialist" war goes on. The two rival blocs continue to wear each other out. The Communists are confident—still, be it noted, thanks to the Nazi-Soviet Pact—of winning the local engagement in France, or, if not of winning it, at least of preventing a decision until the Soviet Union has had the time it needs to have in order to gain the strength it needs to have before it can intervene effectively in Europe—intervene and, of course, lay down the law. Since they indulge no illusions as to where their strength lies, their task becomes, on one level, that of bringing as many Frenchmen as possible to regard the USSR as indispensable to their future security. This, in turn, can be done only as the Communists keep themselves reminded that the two things that are on their fellow countrymen's minds are independence and food, and make out a convincing case that the road to both passes *through* Moscow and leads *to* Moscow.

The Party, beginning with its mid-August *Manifesto to the People of France,* has persistently demanded a Franco-Soviet pact of friendship, on the grounds that it will guarantee the country's nonbelligerent status and freedom and, at the same time, "complement the Nazi-Soviet Pact." [38] This continuing theme of its propaganda, extended to include a demand for a trade treaty as well, is now stepped up to the point of frenzy. The food problem, what with the approach of winter, is becoming more difficult, and this encourages the Party to redouble its efforts in this direction. Between October, 1940, and April, 1941, it accordingly turns out a veritable flood of tracts,[39] leaflets, and posters[40] calculated to make the proposed trade treaty look more attractive: Russia is the land of abundance; it can supply France with everything it needs:

The USSR is rich in food products. . . . The USSR is the only country in which the people have had no experience of ration tickets, of standing in line, or of unemployment. Its supplies of food products are inexhaustible, and there is no question of a blockade to prevent their reaching France. All we have to do in order to stop going hungry, in order to have enough bread, is sign a commercial treaty with the USSR without further delay.[41]

Let us suppose, for the sake of argument, that the USSR were economically capable of sharing its food supplies with France without restricting its deliveries to Germany (these, as a result of the January, 1941, agreements, are to be increased); it would still remain true that the kind of Franco-Soviet relationship the Communists envisage could go forward only with the blessing of Germany. Foodstuffs from the USSR must travel across territory which the Germans control, and will travel across it only by Hitler's consent. And there is, besides, this equally obvious reply to what the Communists are saying: The occupation authorities are unlikely to suspend their levies upon French crops; and just to the extent that France receives imports from the USSR they will feel safe in demanding ever larger amounts.

The French Communists are taking the Germans' consent for granted; otherwise they would hesitate to say that "there is no question of a blockade to prevent the shipment to France" of Soviet food products.[42] Or—who can say?—they are not taking it for granted, in which case the arguments urged in favor of the pact are conscious falsehoods that we must explain in the following terms: The Party's task is to play upon the dissatisfaction of the French people, to make political capital out of their hardships. The mirage of Soviet plenty lends itself to these purposes because it gives the French people a further reason for looking favorably upon the Party's bid for power. If France is hungry, this is because the Pétain government is deliberately keeping it hungry,[43] which is a state of affairs that the French people will not long endure:

The people are demanding another policy! The people, with nothing to eat but the aching walls of their own stomachs, . . . have stood in line long enough in front of empty stores. . . . They know that the USSR can provide us thousands of tons of food products just as they are providing them to Germany, and that no blockade would stand in the way. They therefore demand an immediate reversal of Vichy's criminal policy. They demand the installation of a government of the people, able to maintain genuine friendly relations with the USSR.[44]

Once in power, this government will have as its first task the conclusion of "a friendship pact with the powerful Soviet Union; this will give us, overnight, the wheat and [thus] the labor and strength we need in order to live in peace."[45]

Here as always the Communists bear in mind the fact that they must hold out to the militants, and to the masses that they promised land that is beyond the horizon but not too far be- hope to carry with them, a hope for the long-term future—a yond it. Every socialist philosophy has—in the absence of a "golden age" to look back on with nostalgia—a utopia that ministers to man's need for something that will fire his im- agination and at the same time make demands upon his specu- lative faculties. Marxism claims to have freed itself from "plan- ning" of this kind, and to have become "the midwife of his- tory." In point of fact, however, it can no more dispense with a utopia than could the revolutionary movements of the past. That utopia is, today, Soviet Russia: it must be glorified world without end, because it is the sine qua non of the messianic spirit without which the Communist church would win no converts.

Russia, of course, is no lost island, undiscoverable on any map. Neither is it a vision relating to the year 2000. It exists *now*, contemporaneously with the very aspirations it must feed. And while this has its dangers, the Party derives from it incalculable advantage over its adversaries. Far from proposing to invent and install a new regime, it is simply pushing back the frontiers of the "one sixth of the globe" in which the utopia has already kept itself alive for a long quarter of a century: "In the Soviet Union, which includes more than a sixth of the world and counts among its friends hundreds and millions of people in other countries, the light of science, democracy, and humanism shines with a purity never seen elsewhere." Never before in history has the destiny of mankind "been reflected with such accuracy in the consciousness of men." [46] The Stalin Constitution of December, 1936, is not only "the most democratic in the world"; it is open to any people that would like to join the Soviet Union, which is Russian today but tomorrow will be European and day after tomorrow world wide. The Red Army of the USSR, now held in reserve and being strengthened every day, is an army of liberation which is "at the service of all oppressed peoples;" and these peoples will give it a grateful welcome—just as the people of the Baltic countries, of eastern Poland, and of Bessarabia have already done. The Russian Revolution is history's first example of a victorious socialist revolution. And because the USSR exists, the fait accompli is for the first time on the side of the working classes.

Two worlds—so the Communists say—stand face to face: one of them a world of war, slavery, and poverty, the other a world of peace, liberty, and abundance. The contrast between the two is driven home on every possible occasion, and always in such fashion as to orient men's hopes and dreams and fancies toward the land upon which the Soviet star "sheds its brilliance and illumination." Because the Bolsheviks were successful in 1917, the French Communists will be successful in 1940 or 1941; the success of the former makes certain the success of the latter:

The Communists offer our people all the benefits of their triumphant experience. Communists today govern one country, and that country has seen nothing of the sufferings brought by the war: its cities are intact; its crops are plentiful; its citizens have known neither the miseries of an armed conflict nor the trials of an invasion. . . . The Communists have already met the test of history. And they have met it triumphantly.[47]

With Russia "pointing the way," the victory of the world revolution is assured—all the more certainly because it is directed by Stalin, "the titan of revolutionary thought and action, the inspired heir of Lenin." If the exploited workers and oppressed peoples of the entire world turn their eyes toward him, it is "because they recognize in him mankind's sure-footed guide along the road to liberation; he is loved by great masses of people whose experience has taught them to see in him the pilot to whom they can entrust their destiny." [48] The French Communist Party is Stalin's own party: Stalin is God, and Maurice Thorez is his prophet; by their combined efforts they will throw open to France the portals of the Soviet Garden of Eden.

The Turning Point: June 22, 1941

40. The Communists' star, as we have seen, rises and falls
with the fortunes of the USSR. When, therefore, on June
22, 1941, Germany attacks Russia, they react in terms of outraged patriotism and trembling anxiety. Their fatherland is
in danger, and these are the appropriate responses.

Through the days and weeks since they received their first
intimations of a possible rupture, they have been constantly
alerted, ready to adopt whatever position circumstances may
dictate. The June 22 issue of *L'Humanité*, published just before the news of the Wehrmacht's offensive reaches Paris, is
still determined to maintain—at all costs—a completely "flexible" point of view. "The English radio," it says,

misses no opportunity to inform its listeners of the imminence of
a Nazi-Soviet conflict. The Moscow radio, level headed as always,
gives the lie to reports of a German ultimatum. Stalin will reply
to any future attempt to force his hand, to any future threat of a
possible deal with the imperialist powers, to any future aggression,
in a manner wholly consistent with the interests of the Soviet
peoples, which interests are inseparable from those of the world
proletariat. The power of the Red Army, its armored divisions,
and its air force enables the leaders of the proletarian state to
adopt with calm serenity whatever decisions the Bolshevik Party
considers appropriate.

These decisions, regardless of their content, will receive the
support of the French Communists, because Stalin is "always
right," and because, even when he is not taking into account
the interests of the French proletariat as such, the objective
and invariable coincidence of those interests with those of
Soviet Russia eliminates all need for critical analysis. If Russia
and Germany come to terms again, the result will be the triumph of the forces making for peace, and the rout of the
Anglo-Saxon "warmongers." If Germany and England gang

up against the USSR, the result will be a new, more imperialistic phase of the war, so that the struggle will have to be waged simultaneously against Berlin and London. If Germany attacks Russia and England takes Russia's side, the result will be a democratic war against fascism. The Communists will fight with the self-same passion, the self-same conviction, no matter which of the "if" clauses proves to be correct.

One might expect the Communists to be disturbed by the sudden removal of the prop upon which they have been leaning most of their weight. Ever since August, 1939, they have been pointing to the Nazi-Soviet accords as guarantees of peace, been telling their fellow countrymen about a glorified socialist USSR that has conferred upon its happy citizens all the benefits of peace, and been insisting upon the contrast between their paradise and the capitalists' hell—where the "damned of the earth" experience all the horrors of war, of famine, and of slavery. Now they can do none of these things, and their critics are sure to ask whether Nazi-Soviet cooperation was not perhaps ill advised to begin with. Stalin himself, speaking over the Moscow radio in July, 1941, anticipates this objection, and makes no attempt to sidestep it:

How was it possible for the Soviet Union to agree to a nonaggression pact with such cannibals as Hitler and von Ribbentrop? Did not the Soviet Government, in concluding the pact, make a mistake? Certainly not. A nonaggression pact is a peace pact between two states. That is precisely the kind of pact that Germany proposed to us. Could the Soviet Union say no to such a proposal? I am of the opinion that no state can refuse an agreement assuring it peaceful relations with a neighboring power. . . . It was precisely such an agreement that we signed.[1]

Stalin's way out of the difficulty, then, is to denounce Germany for its "perfidious" violation of the pact; and the French Communists content themselves with echoing this reproach. They add nothing of their own save an occasional abusive adjective.

Stalin's twofold purpose here is evidently (a) to drive home the fact that Germany started the war, and (b) to shore up the Soviet Union's political and diplomatic position as a belligerent power. Since, however, the future remains obscure, he is careful not to cut himself off from the slogan "defense of the peace"; and this, as far as the French Communists are concerned, is all to the good. It makes it easier for them to cross the gulf that divides the new policy from the ultrapacifism they have been preaching since August 23, 1939. It enables them to renew their accusations against the Anglo-French leaders, who, in 1939, failed to prevent the war by refusing to come to an understanding with the USSR.[2] And, meantime, the fact that the USSR is now at war with Germany yields all the dividends it would have yielded had Stalin spoken otherwise. The Communists can, for instance, now deal once and for all with all the "lies" that have been circulated about them. Whether or not the Kremlin is at war against its will, whether or not it did everything possible to avoid a rupture with Germany—these are questions that are of interest only to the future historian. What matters today is the war itself: the 1939 partners are tearing at each other's throats, and from this it follows that the so-called pact to all intents and purposes never existed. *L'Humanité* will, therefore, soon be straightening the record with such statements as the following: "It is simply not true that the USSR supplied Germany with wheat and oil, since it is precisely because the USSR refused to hand over such supplies that it is today the victim of Hitler's aggression." [3] The past, be it noted, is whatever the present situation requires it to be.

41. The first warnings from Moscow concerning the deterioration of Soviet-German relations prompt the French Communists, as we already know, to launch their cautious and recognizably pacifist May 27 manifesto looking to a National Front for French independence. When the storm breaks, the Party thus has ready for use a political formula appropriate to the new situation, and the task of the Communist militants becomes that of redoubling their efforts to put it across: "An event of the first magnitude"—so read the instructions from the center—

an event capable of revolutionizing our domestic politics and producing international repercussions of the most far-reaching importance, has given us an opportunity to test our cadres' capacity for getting things done. We refer to the necessity of organizing a vast National Front that will bring together all Frenchmen who think like Frenchmen and wish to act like Frenchmen —which means, in the present situation, helping the USSR defeat Hitler, since victory for the land of the Soviets is a precondition of France's liberation.[4]

The Communists are, in a word, free until further notice to be as patriotic as the next fellow—the more since, in the present situation, any discord they can sow between the French and the occupation authorities, any difficulties they can create for the latter, must redound to the advantage of the USSR. "In the present circumstances," a later instruction sheet says, "no distinction can be drawn between the behavior of the Communist and that of any other patriot." [5]

The Communists were, of course, insisting upon the identity of interest and destiny between France and the USSR long before June 22, but in terms such as the following: The USSR, as Germany's friend, can use the August, 1939, pact as a means of exerting pressure in Berlin on France's behalf. It can get France better terms, assure it peace, and save it from want— this last by sending foodstuffs drawn from its own abundant supplies. The militants must now learn a new set of supporting reasons: The USSR is the enemy of Hitler Germany, which is France's enemy. "The liberation of France depends upon the victory of the USSR; let us, therefore, do everything in our power to hasten that victory." [6] The USSR is performing, on the level of world politics, the same liberating mission the French Revolution performed in Europe, so that the axis of French history now passes through Moscow.[7] We shall encounter further arguments of this type in the following chapters.

42. The National Front is intended to include everyone who is prepared to use "all available means" in achieving the following "common" objectives:

1. Prevent the German war machine from drawing on French resources;

2. See to it that no French factories work for Hitler, and at the same time back up the workers in their day-to-day struggles over grievances (the workers, in fighting for their own bread and for that of their children, are serving the cause of France);

3. See to it that France's railroads shall not carry its national wealth and the products of its industry into Germany;

4. Organize peasant resistance against delivery of agricultural products to France's oppressors;

5. Organize the struggle against Hitler-Vichy repression (every National Front militant, atheist or believer, Radical or Communist, must enjoy the benefits accruing from our common solidarity);

6. Assure wide distribution for such books and pamphlets, manifestos, and other documents as the National Front may wish to circulate, and at the same time systematically expose the lies of the enemy;

7. Stimulate and extend—in the teeth of the invader and his henchmen—the sentiment of patriotism and the will to fight for the liberation of France.[8]

The reader will notice that this program contains no slogans that are "political" in the strict sense of this term. The Party, determined to win the confidence and, if possible, the active support of certain conservative elements, avoids all mention of the future residence of power lest it estrange some potential ally. This does not mean, to be sure, that it says nothing at all about politics, but rather that it confines itself to formulations that call for no prior commitments. Here is a typical example: What France needs is "a government of the people," a "genuine national liberation government," which "would assume leadership in the struggle against the nation's oppressors and would be capable, because it would act with an iron hand and because it would base itself upon the people, of purging France of its traitors and defeatists and of creating the necessary conditions for the resurgence of a free and independent France." So much at least is safe, and can therefore be said—along with such variants as the following: "In order to save itself, France must have a government of the people. Such a government is the solution that the people will impose in the days ahead. On this point the Party is sure that it is speaking the mind of the entire French nation." [9] There are, however, some patriots who do not yet share the Party's views on this matter, and an attempt is made to allay their suspicions by reviving, for the purposes of the new National Front, the formula prepared in connection with the first such front at the beginning of May: The Party will support anyone who means business about fighting the Germans. [10] (With regard to the programs of the local sections of the National Front, however, the Party follows a somewhat different course. It writes into them, wherever possible, its own long-standing political demands.)

The Party's major emphasis for the moment, then, is on "national liberation," which means that it has quietly jettisoned the first of the two adjectives in its old slogan, "social and national liberation." [11] A while ago, to be sure, it was insisting that the one kind of liberation could not go forward without the other and, in a pinch, that "social emancipation will clear the way for national liberation"—as in Russia, which "was able to solve the national problem because it had solved the social problem." [12] Today, when maximum aid to Russia is the Party's top priority, it needs the support of each and every one of France's social classes; and since it believes this can be achieved most easily by appealing to national sentiment, national sentiment becomes the watchword.

New Forms of Struggle

43. The program of the second National Front sets forth, in broad outline, the forms of struggle that the Communist Party considers appropriate to the new situation, that is, the types of anti-German activity it believes most likely to assist the Soviet Union. This program calls for: (a) restriction of industrial production by means of the slowdown and sabotage; (b) pressing demands vis-à-vis the authorities; (c) agitation against Vichy's Labor Charter; (d) restriction of agricultural production (or, failing this, refusal by the peasants to make deliveries to Germans or collaborators); (e) exploitation of the food shortage as a weapon against German requisitioning. The program also calls for the continuance of certain types of activity into which the Party has been channeling its energies through the last months, with, of course, such modifications as the new situation demands: (f) agitation among the nation's young people; (g) all-out effort to win over the intellectuals and the middle classes. All this, however, is to be accompanied by an important change of emphasis in the Party's internal training program: the cadres are to be schooled in the techniques of "direct action," for example, (h) patriotic demonstrations, and (i) terrorism, and increasing attention is to be given to (j) improved methods of defense against the repression.

This shift of gears is accomplished with a minimum loss of time; and the Party's new mood expresses itself in such phrases as the following: "Not one man, not one grain of wheat, not one hour of work for the assassins of the French people, the plunderers of our country, the executioners of French prisoners of war!" [1] "We must press forward with the struggle for better wages, with the drive against German requisitions, and with the campaign for reducing the production of goods intended for the occupying power. We must demand more bread, more meat, more soap. . . . We must harass the Vichy government, in order finally to drive it out of office." [2] "What helps Hitler hurts France, and what hurts Hitler helps France and the USSR as well." [3] "Nothing for Hitler, everything for freedom." [4]

The chief points the Party must get across to other people are (a) that the struggle for the liberation of France can, at the present time, go forward only as it takes the form of effort on behalf of the Soviet Union, and (b) that the Nazi-Soviet war, by forcing Hitler to reduce the size of the army of occupation, has created a situation highly favorable to such effort. "Workers, peasants, intellectuals of France," says the June 22 *Manifesto to the French People*, "the hour of our liberation is drawing near. Let us prepare to squeeze the fullest advantage out of the opportunity afforded us by the weakening of Hitler's forces within our frontiers." [5] Relative power relations within the country are manifestly much less "favorable" than these words imply and are likely to remain so throughout the predictable future; but for the Communist leaders, whose single and besetting preoccupation is to lighten the burden on the Soviet Army "by whatever means possible," that is a small matter. The Red Army's situation has become increasingly difficult through the month of July: The Germans enter Riga on July 2, then occupy the whole of Latvia. They surround several powerful Soviet units at Bialystok, sweep through Minsk, occupy the Lvov region. About July 20 (Stalin asserts as early as July 3 that "the country is in danger") the Germans force the "Stalin line," cross the Dniester, advance beyond Smolensk, and gain access to the road to Moscow. Soon Kiev is threatened, and Rumanian forces have, meantime, broken through into Bessarabia. Russia's fighting units, in short, must have help—at once and at any cost; and for France's Communist leaders that is reason enough for organizing the people of France as guerrillas and hurling them against the German rear. Germany, which has attacked the USSR, will then be caught "between two lines of fire."

The underlying logic, it will be noticed, is unabashedly military; the Communists do not say so in so many words, but they are evidently putting aside the politically oriented thinking characteristic of the preceding period. Politics is henceforth to be the handmaiden of strategic necessity.

44, A. Through the days just following the outbreak of hostilities on the Russian front, the Communist Party is evidently assuming that events will move slowly and that there will be time for adequate planning and preparation with respect to each item of the above agenda. It does not, for example, ask French workers engaged in production for Germany to give up their jobs. Most of them, as a matter of fact, must keep their jobs or go hungry, so that—purely aside from the Party's wrong guess about the immediate military future—telling them to walk out would be highly unrealistic. However that may be, the Party considers sabotage its best bet for the moment and urges it precisely on the grounds that it is the halfway point between a man's duty to withhold assistance from the enemy of the USSR and of France and a man's need to accept what employment happens to be available. The *Manifesto to All the Workers* puts this point as follows:

Undoubtedly the problem of finding our daily bread is a terrible one for us. . . . Undoubtedly we can survive only by trading the work we do with hand and brain for food. We are caught in the grip of grim necessity. . . . We can nevertheless bend necessity to our will, comrade. In the present situation, for instance, to work is one thing, to produce another thing, and to do good work still another. As matters now stand, "to work" can and should mean to produce defective products in a craftsmanlike manner. Work and sabotage should be one and the same thing.[6]

When, however, things go badly for the Red Army sooner than the Communists have had reason to expect, they are obliged to speak more forcefully: "In order to hasten Hitler's defeat we must, by whatever means we have at our disposal, sabotage his war plants and his transportation of men, matériel, and provisions."[7] All categories of workers are included, at least by implication; but the Party singles out some for special notice: "Railroad workers, refuse to run the trains; dockers, refuse to load them; metal workers, insist that the iron you produce remain inside France; miners, refuse to mine any iron that is to be delivered to the occupying power." [8]

What leaps to the eye here is the importance the Communists attach to communications. The railroad workers, among whom they have numerous followers (in large part because they have thought forward to just such a moment as this, and have diligently sought members among them), are to gain time for the USSR by creating confusion within the nation's railway system: "When a munitions train heading for Germany goes astray, or ends up on a siding somewhere, we can chalk up a point for our side in the struggle for the liberation of France." [9] The railroad worker who is a patriot will, if possible, see to it that trains bound for Germany never begin their journey,[10] and to this end—note the escalator technique of the appeals—"destroy communications apparatus and sabotage equipment." [11] The *Tribune of the Railroad Workers* for August-September is still more specific:

Our job now is to sabotage the transportation of German arms, provisions, and troops. The trains must not even begin their runs; the locomotives must be put out of commission; the freight cars must be burned, war matériel and all; the switches must be blocked. The German bandits must never again feel safe on our railroads for a moment's time; they must be made to tremble with every click of the wheels. If we act together for this purpose, the Germans will never be able to make available enough Gestapo gangsters to police our railway system.[12]

Even the Party newspapers intended for general circulation pick up the theme and tell in glowing terms of cases of successful sabotage of key installations of one kind or another. The man who wants to serve the cause of France, says a Party pamphlet, will choose such targets as "dams, power plants, transmission lines . . . As for the factories producing for the Germans, there we must do all we can to slow down production and turn out defective material. We must shoot the works on the slowdown and bad workmanship, so that the product will be small in quantity and inferior in quality." [13]

Hundreds of newspapers, tracts, and handbills are devoted to the various forms of sabotage, which range all the way from the slowdown through the deliberate production of defective pieces to the destruction of machines and factories. As the weeks pass, indications of a broad general character give way to specific recommendations, and before long the Party has created a special organization to assume responsibility for planning sabotage and other terrorist activities.[14] Before long, also, it has assembled the materials for a "handbook" for the "accomplished saboteur," the broad outlines of which are set forth in a pamphlet published in September, 1941:

We have no time to waste on cutting telegraph wires. What we must now do is organize for sabotage on a much larger scale, especially in the factories that are actually producing for the Germans and the Italians. But for that we must have real specialists, since this job, which yields such marvelous dividends, is a difficult one to perform. We must also maintain good relations with our comrades in the stone quarries and the mines, so that we shall never lack for explosives. Actual operations should be organized, if possible, on an individual basis.[15]

45, B. The Communists have, ever since the Armistice, made it their business to ferret out "grievances" and espouse "demands"; this has, indeed, been their major tactical weapon. After June 22, 1941, they use it on an even larger scale—not so much to win supporters (though they are glad to have them) as to create difficulties for the occupation authorities. To press demands, they tell themselves, is to weaken the enemy, that is, the German Army. (Yesterday's enemy, the Vichy government, is now of secondary and merely derivative importance, and the Party's attacks upon it will henceforth run in terms of its complicity in the "anti-Soviet war," its having broken off diplomatic relations with the USSR, and its alleged determination to get France into the war "on Hitler's side and to Hitler's advantage." [16])

The grand target, in short, is now German military power, and the grand problem that of discovering—and using—the most effective means of weakening that power. Sabotage strikes at it directly, espousing demands strikes at it indirectly; but since, in the long run, the indirect blows may be the more hurtful, may, for that matter, transform themselves into direct blows, the distinction is less important than it might seem. As grievances and demands snowball, the factories will become centers of profound discontent. This will have its day-to-day effect upon production totals, and will also hasten the day when the Party will be able to inflict upon the Germans the highest form of sabotage, namely, the strike, for which read the complete stoppage of production. Meanwhile, it can have it both ways in its propaganda: (a) "to fight for wages is to fight against Hitler," [17] while at the same time (b) the workers can, "through the slowdown and sabotage," speed the day of liberation and "obtain better living conditions and higher wages." [18]

As we have already noticed, the Party's best bet in this connection is the metal workers in the Paris region. Most of them are employed in factories whose production is earmarked for Germany,[19] and many of them are already sympathetic— besides which the Party has easy access to them, for organizational purposes, through the committees of the people. The following "Letter from the Committee of the People" in a certain metal works, published in *Workers' Life*, gives a lucid picture—all the more lucid, no doubt, for having been written in a Party propaganda office—of what is expected of them:

Our Committee of the People has been operating for some time now, and no major blow has yet been struck at it. We are, to be sure, careful to observe all the rules for underground activity. But this has not prevented us from becoming a mass organization known to the workers and able to put its slogans across to them. We have a finger in everything. We publish our own pamphlets, and a shop newspaper as well. Here are some things we have done to forward the fight on behalf of the people's demands: We have adopted and circulated the notebook of demands brought out by the Metal Workers' Central Committee of the People, including the demand for a 50 per cent increase in wages. We have also drawn up our own notebook of demands, based on grievances that relate specifically to our factory. On several occasions we have demanded wage increases running from one franc, 25 centimes, up to two francs, and got at least part of what we were asking for. We have forced the management to install a canteen, and, more recently, we have forced it to lower the canteen's food prices.[20]

The letter adds that since all these demands have been presented to the management by large delegations, they have given rise to no retaliatory measures; and it points out that several of the delegations have been backed up by unanimous work stoppages.

The major demands always relate to "higher wages and more food"; [21] but what the Party really has its eye on is the resultant restlessness in the factories, which it will one day translate into Communist-led strikes.

Action on the Trade-union Front:
The Labor Charter

46, C. The Communists' campaign on behalf of the workers' demands can produce the desired results only if it is backed up by a genuine mass organization. That is why the Party now renews its appeal to its militants and sympathizers to join the existing trade-unions,[1] even those led by "reformists" and "traitors," and it is also why the Party gives careful attention to the new "Labor Charter" promised by Vichy.

For a long while its information concerning the Charter's stipulations is brief and fragmentary. As of October, 1940, for example, it knows only that the central theme is to be "compulsory" corporations and trade-unions; and this it interprets, optimistically of course, as a further reason for urging upon it sympathizers "immediate adherence to the unions"—on the theory that strength in the basic organizational units upon which the new structure is to be built may enable it to control the latter.[2] Pending further information, it contents itself with needling Vichy about the repeated postponement of the Charter's publication.[3]

When the text is finally published in the *Official Journal* on October 26 the Party finds that, in one sense at least, the Charter is made to order for its own purposes. *Workers' Life*, with every show of reason, exposes it as an import from Germany and Italy, "designed to enslave the workers."[4] The *Miners' Tribune* denounces it as "an iron collar placed around the neck of the working class."[5] But this is mere name calling; and it remains for the special November issue of *Workers' Life* to adopt the most effective possible device for discrediting Vichy's handiwork: it patiently details the Charter's shortcomings as seen from the standpoint of traditional French trade-unionism, and stresses particularly (1) the prohibition on strikes, which "places the working class at the mercy of its exploiters," (2) the absence of arrangements for the direct and uncontrolled representation of interested parties, (3) the fact that the "bosses" will as a matter of course dominate the so-called social committees, and (4) the provision for state intervention in all labor disputes.[6]

The chief weapon upon which the Party seizes for its struggle against the Charter is the slogan of "working-class unity," though with new overtones. Through the months preceding the German-Soviet war it was bent upon "conquering" the trade-unions as a means of establishing contact with the masses;[7] and it interpreted "unity" rather narrowly—so as to exclude, for example, most of the leadership of the CGT. Now, however, it is thinking mostly of the strikes with which it intends to disrupt French war production for Germany, and "unity" can and must be interpreted more broadly. *Workers' Life* states the new policy as follows: "Many trade-unionists who do not share our philosophy of unionism are opposed to the Charter. . . . Only the big bosses, the native fascists, and the Hitlerites are pleased with the Charter, their reason being that they expect it to strengthen their hand against the people." All the trade-unionists and all the workers must be brought together in a united front "against this reactionary maffia."[8]

47, C. Even on the most optimistic showing, France's trade-union organization is in no condition at this time to serve as an effective fighting force in the long and sustained struggle now beginning. The Party is, of course, willing to make use of the unions when and where it can; but for the major engagements it places its reliance upon combat units of a more flexible and dependable character, that is, the Party cells, and even where it does use the unions (e.g., for harassing the rear of the German Army) it will see to it that they remain completely subordinated to its own political and military objectives. The Party thinks of France as "allied" with the USSR, and of itself as, quite simply, the nation's clandestine government, charged with responsibility for winning the war: for it to let the initiative pass into the hands of the trade-unions, entangled as they are in the struggle over economic issues and led as they are by "traitors," is out of the question. On the other hand it does not wish, at this time, to "capture" the unions, since this might frighten off those of the unions' members who fight shy of Communism. The middle course it adopts is that of accelerating the creation of committees of the people (for each shop, for each category of workers, for each locality, for the nation as a whole) which, though speaking the mind of the Communists, will *appear* to be speaking that of the working class. Most of these committees, in point of fact, will exist only on paper, that is, they will be the present Communist cells under another name. As illegal organizations they will, unlike the unions, be beyond control by the government; and they will be able, in addressing themselves to the workers or speaking for the workers, to claim a wider mass base than the unions themselves; for they can boast the support of the unorganized workers as well as the organized, and no one is in a position to prove that they do not have it. Best of all, flesh can be added to the committees' bones as and when circumstances (for example, a "revolutionary situation" in France) may call for it. For the committees of the people are to be, as we have said above, a rough outline of the future Soviets; as R-day approaches they will, as the Party's own units within the factories, outflank the generally more cautious and conservative trade-unions.

No one can say whether the framers of the Charter, as they planned their "social committees," expected them to be a lasting guarantee against the workers' demands and other manifestations of the so-called class struggle. If so, they should have looked further into the history of the working class. Employers in the United States have, perhaps, had some success in using "company unions" to forestall industry-wide unions and, in a pinch, to break strikes. But American experience is, in this regard, exceptional. The Bolsheviks, on the eve of the October Revolution, met their bitterest opposition in the

Socialist-dominated National Union of Railway Workers, but had the shop councils on their side. In Italy throughout the period 1919–20 the shop councils in such industrial centers as Milan and Turin were Communist strongholds, as witness their role in the occupation of the factories. There is, in short, no a priori reason to expect workers' organizations on the shop level to be more amenable to capitalist influence than those on a regional or national level; sometimes, indeed, they are easy marks for extremist (e.g., Communist) infiltrators. The French Communists know this, and their policy regarding the committees of the people on the factory level shows how well they know it. They instruct their militants, as we have seen, to join the unions; but at the same time they are busy explaining that "the committees of the people must be kept alive and strengthened," since they "will organize and lead the struggle of the masses." They will, for example, take the initiative by demanding "general assemblies" of union members and by insisting upon the "free election" of union officials. They will exert continuous pressure on union headquarters and on the worker members of the social committees.[9] And, most important of all, they will assume leadership in the struggle on behalf of the workers' demands, which now more than ever must be oriented in the direction of the strike.

The Rural Areas and the Food Problem

48, D. Even as early as its June 22 program, the Party is pressing upon the peasants the idea of withholding agricultural products from the market.[1] When it moves to build the National Front, one of the latter's tasks thus becomes the organizing of "peasant resistance" to prevent "further deliveries of agricultural products to the country's oppressors."[2] And this is to be, for a long while, the dominant note in the Communists' propaganda in the rural areas of the two zones of France.

One might easily get the impression that only deliveries to the occupying power itself are in question—the more since the supporting argument runs as follows: "any reduction in the amount of food consigned to the invader of France is a boon to the French consumer."[3] The Party's real intention, however, is to bring *all* agricultural production to a stop—to paralyze the rural activities of France and leave the occupying forces and the Vichy government with a lifeless country on their hands. What it wants, in short, is the nearest approach to a "scorched earth" policy that is possible in the circumstances.

A pamphlet issued in July, 1941, to be sure, shows the Party still saying to the peasants the same things it has been saying through the preceding months, and repeating the same slogans: down with the trusts; the plunder of the fields for the sake of the invader must cease; the gap between agricultural prices on the farm and in the stores must be closed; an end to inflation; justice for the small property holders; and so forth.[4] There is the usual appeal for unity with the working class, for aid to the Communists, and for adherence to the National Front; and there is the inevitable plea for the creation of a "people's government." But this means merely that the Party is biding its time; soon it must move to bridge the gap between the old forms of action and those appropriate to the period that has just begun. The precarious situation on the Russian front, for which read the necessity of giving immediate support to the Red Army, calls for prompt action calculated to disrupt the entire machinery of requisitioning and food distribution. Soon, therefore, the Communists will be attempting to line the peasants up against any state intervention whatever in the rural economy—that is, to plunge the country into chaos, so that the Germans shall be able to draw from it no further resources for their war in the east.

The details of what the peasants are expected to do are set forth in a pamphlet distributed in the autumn of 1941:

Peasants of France!

There is much that you can do in the struggle against fascism. You must pit your capacity to act, your capacity to withhold action, and your cunning against the edicts of the Nazi bosses and their French satellites.

As you make your declarations, as you answer the questions put by the production census takers, as you fill out the blanks sent to you, remember that your duty as Frenchmen—and your interests as well—oblige you not to comply with these inquisitorial measures and, if need be, to make false statements.

When you gather in your crops remember that you can cache part of your supply at the homes of friends and neighbors, and that if you don't that part will be taken from you.

When you are compelled to furnish livestock or commodities to the requisitioning authorities, don't give them anything but low-grade cattle or inferior products.

When you sell on the open market, avoid selling to firms which may be doing business with the Germans.

With all the means at your disposal, fight back against the bureaucracy that is serving the oppressor, against those who are ravaging your villages.

We are aware that you are already getting around the law in numerous ways, despite the regulations and despite the threats. That is all to the good, and we congratulate you for it. Keep it up! [5]

We find approximately the same emphases in a pamphlet aimed at the wheat producers, who, following a brief reminder that the "Boches" are responsible for the inadequacy of the bread rations, are instructed as follows:

Grain growers of France! In the midst of this kind of plunder there is nothing to do but keep on resisting. Grind your own grain, making do with whatever instruments you have at hand. Bake your own bread—taking care of course that nobody sees you. Feed your friends. Demand increased bread rations. Cache your crops where the requisitioners can't touch them. Falsify your returns to the census takers! [6]

This advice is repeated in the *Manifesto to the Peasants of France:*

The interest of the peasants is clear, and it goes hand in hand with their duty to the nation. . . . Cache your crops, using your heads about where to cache them. No Vichy inspectors, no Gestapo brutes, can match wits with you. Slaughter your livestock if anyone tries to force you to turn it over to the occupying power. Sell only to Frenchmen who make deliveries to Frenchmen. Prove your shrewdness and skill by sidestepping the requisitions. [7]

Since the French and German authorities are in position to use force to put a stop to this kind of thing, only meager results can be expected from it. The authors of the manifesto we have just cited therefore include a summons to active resistance as well, and evoke the memory of the peasant uprisings during the Great Revolution:

We call upon our peasant friends to be resolute. Stop at nothing in your determination to deliver nothing to the invader. When the Vichy inspectors or the Germans come to search your farms, your stables, your barns, your haylofts, and find you united and ready to use your pitchforks, they will think twice before plundering your villages. Jacques Bonhomme made his rallying cry heard in every hovel in the land. That cry should be heard again tomorrow and should be carried from village to village throughout France, because you also are determined to defend your property, to send the thieves packing, to become once again masters of your own households, and to remain Frenchmen. [8]

The Communist Party is, in short, asking the peasants to rebel—or is at least talking as if the conflict between the peasants and authorities might conceivably assume the character of a pitched battle. This is, in the premises, romantic foolishness. Most of the peasants have long since surrendered their rifles; and for all their resentments they are not going to seek an engagement in which they will fight with pitchforks and the enemy with efficient modern weapons. For this and other reasons, some of which are hardly flattering, all but a very few of them are going to sell their products as dearly as possible and no questions asked. The way to their hearts, as anyone knows who has actually lived with them, lies through their conservative instincts and their commitment to the religion of inherited property; which is to say that you waste your time when you summon them to heroism and self-sacrifice. As time passes the Communists recognize this, and when, for the first time after June 22, 1941, they revise the demands they offer to the peasants they seek, in the main, to mobilize their self-regarding instincts against the organization responsible for the supply of food. These refurbished demands are as follows:

Peasants, you must demand:

Higher prices for your products, so as to close the gap between agricultural and industrial prices;

The right to sell your products freely, to whomever you please, without going through a middleman;

Lower taxes, and reimbursement for damages caused by the war;

An end to inquisitorial procedures in the rural districts of France (the production census, forms to be filled out, etc.);

An end to the new bureaucracy which these inquisitorial procedures render necessary.[9]

These slogans, though put forward under the guise of reserving French agricultural produce for Frenchmen and Frenchmen only, will—in so far as they are effective—necessarily paralyze the machinery upon which all Frenchmen except the peasants depend for their daily bread. Their appeal, be it noted, is to the peasants' deep-rooted "conservatism": to their love of peace, independence, liberty, and land; and since there is no necessary connection between the individualism thus encouraged and resistance to the invader, the results are not easy to predict. The peasants may, that is to say, end up looking all the harder for the highest bidder, and that highest bidder may very well *not* be a Frenchman.

The Party seeks to seal off the possibility just mentioned by undermining the peasants' confidence in the value of money. The peasants must be taught that the franc is "monkey money": for, once they have been so taught, they will produce only for household consumption and for barter. Exchange between town and country will thus be brought to a stop.

The *Manifesto to the Peasants of France*, the most important vehicle of Communist propaganda in the rural areas, thus puts increasing emphasis on the alleged dangers of inflation:

We urge our peasant friends not to be fooled by the high prices the Germans are able to offer. Don't forget that they are paying you in monkey money, that is, in money which tomorrow will be worthless. Germany is making France pay tribute in the shocking amount of 400 million francs a day. This calls for the issuance of billions of francs in paper money without backing of any kind. The result of all this is going to be the downfall of the franc and one of the greatest bankruptcies history has ever seen. How sure are you that it is smart to save up bank notes which tomorrow, in all probability, will be barely worth the paper they are printed on? It makes far more sense to save up something that has intrinsic value.[10]

A printed pamphlet—printed because intended for wide circulation—relates the history of the German inflation in the 'twenties, and tells how the German peasants defended themselves against the falling value of the mark: "They sold just what they had to sell in order to procure the funds they needed for immediate outlays, because they knew full well that the products of the land retain their value whatever happens, while bank notes would only lose value with each passing day." [11]

The Communists eagerly seize upon every symptom of peasant resistance, and before long are attempting to exploit the communal governments as rallying points for it. "The resistance on the part of the peasants," declares *Party Life*, has reached a point of such intensity that the mayors of many rural communes are standing up against prefectorial ordinances contrary to the interests of the peasants. We need hardly add that where a mayor does stand up against a prefect, however timidly, the Communists' task is to rally the peasants of that commune behind the mayor, and thus encourage him in his rebellious attitude toward the prefecture. The result will be such a wave of public opinion that nobody in the commune will be willing to take over the mayor's functions if and when the prefect removes him. . . . The rural communes can play a crucial role in the French people's resistance to the Nazi oppressors and their errand boys in Vichy.

Even in its passive phase, resistance of this kind will tie the hands of the government and make for chaos out over the country—besides which it will not, it is believed, remain in its passive phase: as the situation develops, that is to say, the struggle will "take on an entirely different character." [12]

49, E. The peasants are urged, mostly by indirection to be sure, to keep what they produce. At the same time, however, the population is urged to demand more calories. "Producers! See to it, always and at whatever cost, that your bins are empty when the requisitioners come around. . . . Consumers! Join us in demanding more generous bread rations." [13] Does this mean that the Communists are working at cross purposes with themselves? Not at all. The contradiction disappears when we remember that it is no part of the Communists' purpose to feed France—that, since France is producing for Germany, the reverse is true. The real target of the propaganda to the peasants, in short, is the French food supply —as anyone can see who asks himself what would happen if the peasants obeyed the Communists' instructions. The Germans are to be caught between a diminishing supply of food in the countryside and a rising tide of demands in the towns and cities. The gainer will be the Red Army. France may starve a little; but it will do so in a good cause.

The Mobilization of Youth

50, F. The Party, as we have pointed out above, attaches great importance to the recruitment of young men and women, especially students.

Work among young people is primarily, but by no means exclusively, the task of the Federation of Communist Youth: "The winning over of the nation's youth, the mobilization of a patriotic Youth Front against the invader, is the responsibility not only of the FCY but of the Party as a whole." [1] Inter alia, the Party must lend the FCY a helping hand when, as happens now and then, it needs one; it must not so burden FCY leaders with other Party tasks as to limit their effectiveness in their own milieu; it must teach the youth the importance of the Party's rules for underground activity, but must at the same time be careful not to undermine their spirit of initiative. [2] It must, in overseeing the FCY's activities, see to it that energies are wisely distributed among the various categories of young people (workers, peasants, those interested in sports, those in the armed services, etc.), none of which is to be neglected. [3]

Large numbers of youth committees are accordingly included in the new National Front; and steps are taken to have them adopt the following program, easily recognizable as a mere adaptation of the Front's own:

1. The liberation of France, and the expulsion of the invader; . . . the suppression of the line of demarcation between zones; the repatriation of the prisoners of war.
2. The triumph of the USSR and England over Hitler's Germany, which means: creating an impossible situation for the occupying power; seeing to it that Hitler gets from France not a single grain of wheat, not a single weapon, not a single freight car, not a single telephone wire.

3. Support for the victims of Pétain's secret police and of the Gestapo, and for all who have been jailed or persecuted for participating in the struggle for national liberation.

4. Freedom for the youth of France, which means: no jumping them through the hoop in the Nazi manner.

5. Refusal to send the French Army and Navy into the war on the side of Germany. France's young soldiers and sailors . . . will refuse to fire on their brothers from the Soviet Union and England. They will, rather, turn their weapons against Hitler's troops.

6. Disorganization of the occupant's rear as a first step toward the liberation of our nation's territory.[4]

These are not idle words: the intention is, just as this document states, to send the nation's youth into direct action against the forces of the occupying power. "It is not enough," proclaims the FCY, "for us to have an unshakable faith in the triumph of the Red Army and to await that triumph with folded hands. We must lead the youth of France into battle; we must make our own contribution to the USSR's victory; we must achieve our own victory over our own oppressors."[5] No student of the documents of the period will, moreover, fail to notice that the FCY is here merely echoing the early October manifesto from the "young men and women of the Soviet Union" to the "young men and women of the occupied countries": "Do not give the barbarians who are our enemies a moment's peace. Cut the telephone wires. Derail the trains. Learn the skills of the sniper. Sabotage production. Wreck the factories."[6]

In so far as the program is stated in the language of French patriotism, however, it conveys a quite inadequate picture of the FCY's propaganda, which normally makes no attempt to conceal the fact that the true fatherland is the Soviet Union and the true leader Stalin. The Soviet Union is, to be sure, no longer the "country of peace"; but it continues to be the Garden of Eden—and the hope of the world. In all the countries oppressed by Hitler, declares *Notre jeunesse*, "the name of Stalin is the symbol of the most sacred aspirations of the

popular masses and of the young." Stalin "has transformed the
Soviet Union into the land of plenty," and "has made its
young men and women the happiest young men and women
in the world." He is the captain on the bridge, "sure of himself in the midst of the storm"; he is "the best friend the world's
young people have." The last line of the litany is, of course,
a gloria: "Glory to Stalin, architect of victory." [7]

Beginning in June, as we already know, the Communists
shift their attention from the political to the military level.
Naturally enough, therefore, they intensify their propaganda
among the younger men in the armed forces; and the Party's
old antimilitarist slogans, which urged the soldiers and sailors
to turn their weapons upon their own officers rather than fire
upon the "proletarians" and "colonial cousins" in the opposing
army, are now put to work on behalf of Communist neo-
patriotism: "Soldiers, airmen, and sailors of France"—so reads
the *Manifesto to the French People* of June, 1941—"if you
are ordered to fire upon the soldiers of the USSR, you must
refuse to obey. Turn your weapons against the traitors who,
in giving you such orders, will be acting as accomplices of
Hitler, the oppressor of our country." [8]

The Party, recognizing the need for a separate publication
in which to develop this phase of its propaganda, creates *Vive
la France*, which describes itself as the "organ of all enlisted
men, noncommissioned officers, and officers who think like
Frenchmen and are determined to act like Frenchmen." The
masthead conveys no hint of the newspaper's Communist
origins. Rather it affirms that its sole purpose is to establish
contact among "those members of the Armistice Army who
are resolved to work for the liberation of France" [9]—an idea
which assumes clearer outlines in the pamphlet *To the Frenchmen of the Armistice Army:* "Any army, however small, can
and should play an important role in the decisive battle that
is now under way—provided all its members are tied together
by the fraternal bonds of true patriotism." [10] Only a few
months ago, to be sure, a Party pamphlet with a similar title,
To the Enlisted Men in the Armistice Army, was urging upon

these same readers a fundamentally pacifist determination to keep France out of the war at all costs: they must refuse "to take any further part in this struggle between rival imperialisms, whether on the side of the plutocrats in Germany or that of the plutocrats in England." [11] Now it is a struggle between imperialism on the one side and liberty on the other, Churchill's "hirelings of British finance capital" have become crusaders for democracy, and the soldiers of France must, come what may, show themselves "faithful allies of the Soviet and English peoples." [12]

The following paragraphs throw still further light on what the Communists expect to accomplish with this phase of their propaganda:

We must bring together all members of the armed forces, of whatever rank, who are anti-German and desire the liberation of France. We must, in their presence, denounce the Pétain-Darlan government as a Boche government, and those of their officers who have betrayed France as despicable agents of Vichy and Germany.

One thing must be made clear to every soldier and every sailor, namely, Germany is France's enemy. We must arouse their patriotic sentiments, and do everything else that needs to be done in order to prevent our army and navy from entering the service of Hitler, who is France's enemy.

We must tell the soldiers and sailors about the heroism of the Red Army, and make them feel that it is their duty, whatever happens, to be the faithful allies of the Soviet and British peoples.

Our militants—alike in our youth organizations and in the Party itself—will in performing this mission need all the organizational capacity they can muster. They must create a National Front Committee in each unit. They must lead these committees into action on behalf of an armistice army that will be truly democratic and truly national. To this end they must demand liberty of expression and the right to organize for every enlisted man, noncommissioned officer, and officer who thinks like a Frenchman and is determined to act like a Frenchman. They must, above all, remember to support any demands the soldiers and sailors may be making, for example, for better rations, periodic leaves, etc.

We must, at the same time, continue our propaganda among the soldiers' and sailors' families, so that they also will explain to their loved ones in the armed forces that they must never shirk their duties as Frenchmen. We should seize every opportunity to raise the level of patriotic morale in the Armistice Army.[13]

This preoccupation with "patriotic morale" is, be it noted, precisely what we should expect in the light of what we know about the Communists and about the recent changes in the objective situation. A while ago, certainly, the Party was speaking quite another language. But at that time the Soviet Union, far from being at war, was the *tertium gaudens* of a conflict which it had itself helped to unleash. Now Hitler's attack on the Soviet Union has turned the tables; and the workers' fatherland is fighting for its very life. The Communists know that bad blood between Frenchmen and Germans means, as matters now stand, reduced pressure on the Red Army—which is another way of saying that, for the moment, the interests of the Soviet Union coincide with those of French patriotism and, at one remove, with those of morale in the armed forces. A similar logic of course underlies the sudden cessation of Communist propaganda addressed to the enlisted men to the exclusion of their officers and noncommissioned officers: Today's mission calls for patriotic unity against Berlin and Vichy. And the differences in class and rank that the Party yesterday had reason to exaggerate it today has reason to ignore.

The Mobilization of the Intellectuals

51, G. The Party, after June 22 as before, proceeds on the assumption that its propaganda for each social class should be "specialized" with an eye to the outlook and intellectual level of that class, and its relative importance as a potential ally. Its major propaganda efforts are therefore directed at the industrial workers, whom it needs because they are in position to sabotage war production, and at the peasants, whom it needs because they are in position to restrict agricultural output. And we have seen in the preceding chapters what themes the Party regards as appropriate to these efforts.

Propaganda for the intellectuals clearly calls for different and highly specialized handling, and for several reasons. They are, for one thing, susceptible to certain themes that would be of only marginal interest to other people; and the Party, because of its shift of emphasis from "social emancipation" to "national emancipation," is now able to drop certain other themes that they are likely to find objectionable—most particularly its class warfare and revolutionary slogans. They are, for another thing, allies that the Party is somewhat less concerned to win for itself than to take away from someone else; which is to say that the Gaullists' strongest support is to be found in such minority groups of intellectuals as the teachers and the students. They are finally, in the light of the Party's experience over the past months, considered easy marks as compared with, say, the workers and the peasants, and thus make less urgent demands upon the Party's propaganda skills.

Along with the emphasis on class warfare the Party has, as we know, dropped that upon the purely imperialist character of the war—in favor of slogans reminiscent of those used by the Allies through the years 1914–18: beginning with June

22, 1941, the war is a war between civilization and barbarism, democracy and fascism, the spirit of reason and the spirit of violence. This is fortunate; for, though it is of course open to the Gaullists to do the same thing, the Party can now approach the intellectuals in terms of a crusade that follows thoroughly familiar lines. The pamphlet *The Spirit of Europe*, distributed in the occupied zone in July, 1941, is thus built mainly around the theme: "The forces pitted against the Axis are the guardians of culture and of the rights of the conscience of mankind." [1] But it contains one motif, which we have cited briefly above, that merits careful study as an indication of where the intellectuals are going to find themselves if they agree to come along:

It is to the Catholic Church that we are indebted for the earliest formulation of the idea of Europe. Through the centuries during which it held sway, Europe and Catholicism were one and the same thing; and when Rome entered upon its period of decadence Leibnitz, the eighteenth century, Voltaire, and the Encyclopedists took the place of the great Christian thinkers. From that time forward the consciousness of Europe took on a philosophical and literary form deriving from France. There resulted a European humanism whose roots were in France, and it commanded the scene until the rise of nationalities. The French Revolution, together with the myth of the nation which that revolution had inscribed upon the banners under which it fought its wars, produced—as a reaction against it—the compartmentalization of Europe. Then came the nineteenth century with its blind antagonisms and its partitions. The moment soon arrived when Europe was a mere mosaic, and when the minds of Europe were striving for a unity that was no longer possible.

1914: catastrophe supervenes and aggravates the situation. The spirit of Europe, and this means the spirit of man, sinks to its lowest level.

During the postwar period we have seen three rivals step forward to claim the succession to the old spirit of Europe: (1) the American and European carriers of old-fashioned liberal humanism; (2) Communist internationalism; (3) Hitlerite Pan-Germanism. [2]

Let us pause to examine the concluding lines of this some-what oversimplified summary of the intellectual history of Europe. The author of the pamphlet clearly regards the first of these rivals as now out of the running. There remain, there-fore, only two; and it is between these two that the intellectu-als, nolens volens, must choose. And they must make their choice in the knowledge that Hitlerite Pan-Germanism is going to be destroyed in the present war, so that—we are now thinking somewhat ahead of the pamphlet's manifest content—there will remain only Communist internationalism.

If Europe is to be "unified"—so the Communists' argument runs—the job must be done either by Hitler or by Stalin; and, this being the case, it becomes the duty of every Frenchman to take his place among the forces led by Stalin. Grant the premise, and the conclusion no doubt follows; but meantime we begin to see why the Communists in their propaganda di-rected at the intellectuals insist so stubbornly upon the need for restoring the rule of "reason" in Europe. They wish, for one thing, to identify themselves with that mainstream of "rationalism" which, on their showing, dates back to Des-cartes and the Encyclopedists, and which, again on their show-ing, is one of the forces that have made the spirit of France what it is. (This identification is necessary because it is to the rationalist thinkers that the Communists are going for argu-ments to use against the neoromanticism of the doctrinaire Nazis.) They wish, for another thing, to accustom the intel-lectuals to thinking, like the intellectuals of other days, in universalist terms—in terms, that is to say, inimical to dividing lines between nations. The rule of reason plays, in their formu-lations, the same role as the *Seele* in the formulations of the National Socialists. It is a shorthand expression for the Pan-Sovietism which is the Communist counterpart of Nazi Pan-Germanism.

The Party, then, tells the intellectuals that they should support it because their commitment to "reason" makes it im-possible for them to do otherwise. And it is careful, in choosing day-to-day issues for them to go to work on, not to belie this claim. It needs their assistance, it assures them, in its struggle against the repression in general,[3] and in its campaign against the continuing arrests of scholars and teachers. It calls upon the rector and the deans of the University of Paris to resign in protest, and it summons the nation's teachers to withdraw from all committees and councils of which they are members, to pass up offers of appointment to the jobs of their arrested colleagues, and to refuse to swear allegiance to the existing authorities.[4] And a so-called "group of French intellectuals who are friends of the Soviet Union" lays down, in an *Appeal to the French Intellectuals*, the following over-all program:

We will refuse to speak, to write, or to act on behalf of the aggressor. But we will also refuse to remain silent and passive. Since we cannot speak out in public, we will keep up a steady flow of . . . pamphlets, posters, and caricatures. Those of us who are teachers will get across to our pupils what the greatness and strength of the USSR means today, and thus awaken in them a love for Russian history, Russian art, and Russian literature. Those of us who are technicians will make it our business to see to it that nothing is produced in our factories that can be useful to Hitler.[5]

The Party regards the universities as potential allies of great importance in the struggle against Vichy. University teachers and officials are accordingly singled out in its propaganda for special handling—of which the keynotes are adulation and pie-in-the-sky. The Communists, the university folk are reminded at every turn, will be in power tomorrow, and will do wonders for the educational system and for science. "The French working class,"—so reads the pamphlet *Homage to the University of Paris*, which the Party distributes in December—

the toilers of France and the nation as a whole are today proud of the University of Paris, and of its teachers and students who, faithful to the traditions of honor and courage common to the people of France and the great minds of France, are fighting back against the enemy, and thus defending science against obscurantism, our national culture against Germanization, civilization against Nazi barbarism. . . . In the new Europe we are going to build everything possible will be done to spread knowledge of science on a scale never seen before, to bring science into the homes of the workers in the industrial capitals and into the remotest hamlets in the countryside. . . . That is the program that the Communist Party pledges itself to achieve at all costs.[6]

Mass Demonstrations and "Terrorist" Activity

52, H. The step from passive resistance and the slowdown on the one hand to open revolt on the other is a long one, and can be taken only in a congenial—which is to say overheated —atmosphere. The Party's purpose in organizing its demonstrations and in setting aside its special days to celebrate the great events of French history is to generate such an atmosphere.

Even before June 22, 1941, the Party was, as we know, exploiting the tradition and imitating the methods of the revolutionaries of 1789; it now does both on a far more ambitious scale. Why not? Has not the Vichy government, by trying to play down Bastille Day, invited the Communists to take over everything it represents? and first of all the day itself?

A special Bastille Day of *L'Humanité* sets the tone of the Communists' demonstration on July 14:

Men and women of the working class, stay away from work on Bastille Day. Go out on strike, and then insist on full pay for the hours you miss from work. Frenchmen and Frenchwomen of all classes, of all shades of opinion, celebrate the national holiday of France by putting out your tricolor flags. . . . We shall see whether Pétain's and Darlan's police are so impudent as to do Hitler's bidding. . . . Organize demonstrations in every city and town. Display tricolor flags. Sing the "Marseillaise."

Numerous specially prepared pamphlets and handbills printed with tricolor borders dwell upon the historic dates 1789, 1792, and 1793, and reproduce quotations from Robespierre, Saint-Just, and even Lafayette. The quotations are, of course, selected with an eye to their accidental relevance to the existing situation,[1] and the points are driven home by endless reiteration of the Party's current propaganda themes: resisting the oppressor, the present-day tyrant; building a National Front; aiding the USSR; creating a "government of the people." These themes are, be it noted, themselves essentially patriotic; and, save for a few items published either by the youth organizations or by some of the local headquarters,[2] the pamphlets and handbills preserve a discreet silence about all matters that have no direct bearing upon the war—that is to say, about the slogans of the period before June 22. The words "French Communist Party" appear modestly, as a kind of signature, at the end of the text; and nothing is said about, for example, the Party's ideology or its dreams of power. When *L'Humanité*, on August 3, 1941, refers to the Bastille Day demonstration as a real "victory," what it means is that the demonstration has helped the Communists make the transition, in the eyes of the general public, from the old line to the new one. The August 12–13 demonstrations at the Porte de Saint Denis are made to serve the same purpose.

We have spoken of an atmosphere that the Communists would like to create by means of these demonstrations, and the following two excerpts from the accounts of the events of August 12–13 published in the Party press show what they have in mind:

On August 13, twenty-four hours after Pétain's speech [suspending the activity of all political parties], the area about the Porte de Saint Denis was the scene of a demonstration by men and women shouting "Long live the USSR!.," "Long live England," "Down with Hitler!," "France for the French!" "Long live France!" The police . . . tried unsuccessfully to stop the demonstration, whereupon the Hitlerite gangsters aimed their weapons into the midst of the crowd and fired. . . . Some of them paid dearly for their intervention in this matter, because *the demonstrators defended themselves with courage and skill.*[3]

"French blood has been spilled in the streets of Paris. [But] the French people will never knuckle under to fascist rule. *Tomorrow all of France, responding to this summons from Paris, will rise in arms. . . . The resistance will become a tidal wave."*[4] The Communists, in a word, are hoping for re-

enactments of the Porte de Saint Denis tragedy all over France, and for the mood of exasperation and combativeness which, as it believes, must result from them. If (as proves to be the case) they are thinking much too fast, what will be called for is redoubled effort to evoke nationwide demonstrations on occasions like Bastille Day, which will little by little get people accustomed to moving and acting against the wishes of the authorities. Half a loaf is better than no bread at all—as we may see from the energy with which the Communists, oblivious of their attitude on the same date last year, make their preparations for the celebration of November 11.

A "National Committee for November 11, 1941," which is in point of fact nonexistent, "signs" the following instructions:

(1). Everywhere—even if the illegal Vichy government decides otherwise, even if the occupying authorities intend to erase this national holiday from our calendar—Armistice Day, 1941, must be a day of celebration. Nothing shall prevent the French people from fêting the anniversary of their 1918 victory.

(2). Employees should insist that each and every firm in each and every town and city be shut down on Armistice Day. They should also insist on being paid in full for this day of nationwide celebration. If any employers, obeying the orders of the occupying power, make an issue of this matter, and require their employees to work on the 11th, those employees, in order to fulfill their duty as Frenchmen, must unanimously desert their jobs, that is, go out on strike.

(3). In every village, in every city, in every neighborhood, the entire population will file silently past a selected memorial to the dead, and each person will deem it his duty to place a wreath at the foot of the monument or at least a flower—a flower of remembrance, a flower of hope.

(4). The parades in the arrondissements of Paris and in all the communes in the suburbs will take place during the morning hours. In the afternoon, the people of Paris—men, women, and children—will proceed en masse to the Place de l'Etoile, and will march past the tomb of the Unknown Soldier, where they will deposit their flowers.

(5). Everywhere the Armistice Day demonstrators will bear, along with their flowers, the colors of the fatherland." [5]

Arrangements "in each city, in each quarter, in each village" are to be in charge of "local committees," which are, however, as much a fiction as the National Committee.

It is in Paris that the Party expects to make the greatest showing. The demonstration of November 11 follows the same lines as the demonstration of Popular Front days: long lines of marchers move from specified points at the edge of the city, and meet finally at the Etoile, so that the center of Paris is inundated by great waves of people rolling in from the "Red Belt." The only difference is in the place chosen for the demonstration: the Place de la Republique and the Place de la Nation are abandoned in favor of the "sacred tomb" of the Unknown Soldier. The propaganda which prepares the way for the demonstration turns on the theme of "victory": November 11 recalls the French victory of 1918, and thus presages a new victory over the Germans. The Communists call attention to the fact that "the French people know in their hearts that they were betrayed, not defeated. Their spirit is not broken; they feel that the hour of liberation is at hand, and they retain their national pride in spite of their misfortunes." [6]

On this occasion also the Communists appeal to tradition and to patriotic feeling. "We shall show the world that the France of Joan of Arc, daughter of the people, the France of Hoche and of Marceau, the France of the Marne and of the soldiers of Verdun, the France of liberty and of the Rights of Man, lives on; it is proud of its past and sure of its destiny." [7] A pamphlet addressed especially to war veterans says: "Never will the descendants of the ancient Gauls consent to live the life of a vanquished people." [8]

Appeals are addressed to different categories of the population, with carefully chosen arguments calculated to draw them into the demonstration. Those intended for veterans of the first World War remind them of its triumphs, and stress Vichy's downward adjustments in veterans' benefits and pensions. Those addressed to students remind them of their comrades who fell at the Etoile on November 11, 1940. Those addressed to workers hold out to them the prospect of a holiday with pay. All refer in exultant terms to the USSR, which has just celebrated the twenty-fourth anniversary of the Revolution.

The demonstration of November 11 fits easily into the campaign for "unity" which the Communist Party has been conducting since June 22, and serves to publicize the National Front and its program. This unity is to be built upon a twofold hatred—against the Vichy government, which is reviled for its attempt to "do away with" Armistice Day, and against the Nazis, in whose honor on this occasion the slogans of antifascism are dropped in favor of slogans calculated to mobilize and aggravate traditional anti-German hatreds.

53, I. For a while the Party believes that its mass demonstrations will both yield dividends in spontaneous terrorist action on the part of the participants and observers, and serve as a "cover" for terrorist action in general—that is, make the terrorists harder to identify. Neither of these expectations is, in point of fact, fulfilled; but the Party's own terrorist efforts go forward, on an ever-broader front, in the hands of small specialized groups, each operating on its own and at its own risk. Other resistance movements had of course created such groups—and put them to work—long before June 22, 1941; but the Communists are still early enough to make a decisive contribution to this phase of the war.

The activities of these specialized groups enjoy, if not the active support for which the Communists have hoped, at least the passive approval of the broad masses of the people; and for this the Communists are indebted in large part to the Germans' own savage behavior. What with the repression and the measures of retaliation, that is to say, popular resentment against the occupation authorities rises from week to week quite independently of the Communists' propaganda efforts.

The partisans of Vichy, both "collaborators" and "noncollaborators," pose a more difficult propaganda problem, and as time passes the Communists try increasingly to drive a wedge between them and the rest of the population. The slogan "Run the traitors out of the country!," the threats of immediate vengeance or inescapable punishment in the future, are soon on the tip of every Communist tongue: "They will be punished," declares a Party newspaper, "all those among us who have caused the shedding of so much blood and so many tears, all those among us who are responsible for our short rations and thus for the physical deficiencies of our children, all those among us who, on top of crying 'Bravo!' to Hitler, would now like to rush the country along the path of adventure, in a word, all the traitors at Vichy."[9] One could cite countless statements of similar character. Sometimes the threats single out particular categories of "traitors" (e.g., the magistrates, the policemen); sometimes the culprits are warned that no individual need flatter himself that he will be able to escape the day of reckoning: a clause of the future armistice will guarantee the repatriation of those who have fled the country[10]—besides which each and every one of them is to be under constant surveillance until the end of the war.[11] Sometimes the message is conveyed by means of a sticker pasted on the door of the offender's home: "The inhabitant of this house is a Pétainist, thus an agent of Hitler, thus a traitor to France." On the level of action, as contrasted with propaganda, there are at least enough "measures of self-defense," ranging all the way from shadowing known police spies to exposing or even executing them, to keep the constantly reiterated threats from sounding like idle talk. In some localities there are "patriots' tribunals," organized by this or that branch of the resistance movement or by a local committee of the National Front, which try and sentence suspects in absentia. Their verdicts are regarded as final, and are promptly executed.[12]

These activities, even if they accomplish nothing else, tend to hold in check the abundant flow of (usually anonymous) "denunciations" to the offices of the French police and to the Kommandatura. They by no means dominate the situation; but they do establish themselves as an additional factor which the potential collaborator must take into account before making himself useful to the repression. They are, so to speak, bits of steel filing that the Communists are able to toss into the machinery of the repression.

Given the situation on the eastern front, however, steel filings are not enough. The Party must bring pressure to bear upon the occupying power in such fashion as to hold in the French theater large numbers of German soldiers who might otherwise take part in the drive toward Moscow. This calls for a "partisan" state of mind on the part of the masses of the French people, for, in a word, a resistance movement in France of the same character, and on the same scale, as that in the occupied portions of Russia; and the Communist press reproduces over and over again Stalin's numerous calls to the peoples of the occupied countries:

We must strike at the rear of Hitler's army as well as its vanguard. Our great leader Stalin has, in a historic declaration, called attention to the crucial importance of the rear in the present war. We must blow up bridges, destroy highways and telephone lines, and set fire to fuel tanks. We must make the situation in the occupied countries intolerable for the enemy; we must harass him at every turn, strike him down at every opportunity, abort his every plan.[13]

Obviously, however, the Communists cannot represent the struggle within France as a mere phase of Soviet strategy and let it go at that—for all that the connection between a Soviet victory and the liberation of France is no longer open to dispute. The obvious out, the one they in fact adopt, relates current guerrilla action against the occupying power to other glorious episodes in French history: Joan of Arc's crusade against the English, the Great Revolution, the francs-tireurs of 1814, the resistance to the Prussians in 1870. The heroism of the snipers of 1870, declares a Party instruction-sheet, "has for many decades been held up as an example to the boys and girls in our primary schools. Their tradition is still alive in the hearts of the French people, who accordingly swear a vow of deadly hatred when they see the men who are making a good thing out of the fall of France, the men who earn their living by treason, that is, by groveling before the Boches."[14]

Neither Communist theory nor Communist practice has ever, in the past, conceded much importance to action by individuals or small groups. Both have placed their major emphasis, for tactical purposes, upon action by the masses—in part, of course, because it affords excellent "cover" for the movement's underground organization. Now, however, the Party is willing to neglect no possibility that may serve to weaken the occupying power, and this means that it must write off its prejudice against direct action by individuals. It is, for the rest, all the more ready to do this since in this unprecedented context no one can predict what this or that isolated individual example, plus the retaliatory action it may bring in its train, will produce in the way of large-scale results. In this atmosphere of tension and frayed nerves, that is to say, a single revolver shot may one day precipitate the event that will modify the course of the war—and who, in such a situation, is to think ill of revolver shots? When, on August 27, 1941, Paul Colette fires on Laval and Déat at Versailles, the Party at first adopts, to be sure, a position which echoes its traditional views:

The Communist Party, which is engaged in a struggle for national liberation and has taken its place in the ranks of the National Front, . . . recognizes that the well-being of France will be assured by action on the part of the masses, and not by the gesture of some individual. It nevertheless pays tribute, as all France does today, to Paul Colette . . . , who has given his life in order to strike a blow at France's traitors.[15]

But when the Paris press chooses to describe young Colette as a Communist, the Party recognizes its opportunity, sets out to create a new Communist martyr-hero, and withdraws its reservations on the question of individual action.[16] Is it acting wisely? The answer depends on what data we examine: A single RAF raid on the Renault factory hurts production for the war effort more than any four months' of Communist sabotage throughout France; so that if we are looking for concrete results we must declare this phase of Communist strategy unsuccessful. But there is every reason to suppose that the

Communists have discounted this, and have been thinking from the very first in terms of the psychological effects of sporadic violence. And here, if we look at the rising tide of discontent, at the increasing willingness of large numbers of people to welcome political action along new and ambitious lines—and these are the areas in which the Communists are always most at home—we must say to them: "Well done!"

The Defense against the Repression

54, J. If we plotted on a graph a line measuring the intensity of the repression, it would fall away toward zero at the point corresponding to the Armistice, would waver within narrow limits just above zero at the point corresponding to late September, 1940 (it cannot rise because of the attitude adopted by the occupation authorities), would move gradually upward between the points corresponding to October 1 and June 22 (Vichy is organizing in preparation for the green light it expects from the Germans), then rises sharply to a level not noticeably lower than that of pre-Armistice days. The German authorities are, by this time, quite as eager as Vichy itself to press the campaign against the domestic Communists, whom they correctly regard as a menace to the security of the occupation forces. The mere possession of a weapon becomes, overnight, a crime punishable by death; [1] new regulations, backed up by unprecedently severe sanctions, go into effect against demonstrations in the streets; acts of terrorism, whether against persons or things, are treated as capital offenses. And before long hostages are being executed in lieu of the terrorists themselves when the latter cannot be apprehended. [2]

The first victim is executed on July 19, 1941, the second five days later. "The French worker André Masseron has been assassinated by the Gestapo," writes a Party pamphleteer, "for having demonstrated his faith in the liberation of France by singing the 'Marseillaise.' " [3] There are further executions following some demonstrations on August 15 and 16, and events move with increasing swiftness over the next weeks: On August 23 Vichy promulgates a law establishing so-called special tribunals for the trial of persons guilty of "Communist or anarchist" activities; and only four days later one of these tribunals, sitting in Paris, sentences three Communists to death and a fourth, a former general secretary of *L'Humanité*, to life imprisonment at hard labor. On September 6, three French hostages are executed following an attempt on the life of a member of the German armed forces. This is the first evidence the French have had that the Germans are really prepared to execute hostages; but when the attacks on Germans continue further confirmation is not long wanting: Ten hostages are shot on September 16, and twelve on September 20. This infernal tit-for-tat continues through the rest of September and on into October—to lead finally to the massacres at Nantes and Bordeaux, each of which claims fifty hostages.

At first the Communists are unclear as to what attitude to adopt toward these developments. A tract published early in September implies that the Party has had nothing to do with the recent attacks on Germans, which are, for the rest, merely being used by the authorities and the "kept press" as a means of justifying the monstrous measures being adopted "against the people and the Party." [4] Soon after, however, some Party spokesmen begin to take the logical next step: the authors of the attacks are police agents, provocateurs.[5] But this line also is promptly abandoned—in favor of patriotic appeals to outraged national sentiment: the victims are martyrs to France, and must be avenged.[6] How? By giving the Germans a dose of their own medicine, i.e., the *lex talionis* multiplied by ten. "If a Communist or any other Free Frenchman should be shot down by the Germans or by any person in their employ, ten German enlisted men or officers, or ten of their creatures who still call themselves Frenchmen, will be executed immediately, unhesitatingly, without regard to the consequences." [7] The "exchange rate" of ten to one becomes overnight a Party slogan, and finds its way into countless Party publications.[8] One looks in vain, furthermore, for any note of skepticism as to the feasibility of the course of action thus envisaged—that is, as to whether or not the Party has at its disposal the resources it will need in order to impose this emphasis of its will upon the occupying power. "Some of your officers and enlisted men," the pamphlet *Patriotes français* tells General Stülpnagel, "have already paid their lives in return for those of certain Frenchmen. . . . Vengeance is a sacred thing in the eyes of an oppressed people; and we are telling you in the simplest manner we know how that vengeance, a terrible vengeance, will be exacted for every Frenchman condemned to death." [9] But by mid-September, still more clearly by mid-October, talk of thus retaliating on the Germans has largely disappeared from the Party's publications, which have retreated to the less extravagant position that the dead will be avenged one day in the future. The reason, of course, is that the rate of exchange has moved in the opposite direction: instead of ten Germans being "struck down" for every Frenchman executed, twenty, fifty, sometimes one hundred Frenchmen are being executed for every attempt on the lives of German officers and enlisted men. From the German point of view, in short, the atrocious hostages system has proved successful—and, since the Germans control the market in which the rate of exchange is determined, there has never been any reason to expect it to fail. This the Communists now realize.

There are, henceforth, few cases of individual "direct action" against the Germans, and the Party's struggle against the repression is in the main conducted by other means. The most effective of these, perhaps, is the preparation and distribution of pamphlets designed to enlist popular sympathies on behalf of the "patriots"—[10] mostly, of course, Communists— who have suffered at the hands of the enemy, for example, the Communist deputies who are in jail or concentration camps.[11] (The Party's campaign for the liberation of Jean Catelas and Gabriel Péri is of especial interest because some of the relevant pamphlets, written of course before June 22, still make use of the argument that the Germans should release them because of their having adopted a correct attitude toward the war.) The Party makes notably skillful use here of executions by the German authorities: the pamphlets record in excruciating detail the final moments of the condemned men's lives, emphasize their courage and defiance, and tell what they had done for France—all in a hagiographical vein that produces much more telling effects than the Party ever had any reason to expect from yesterday's irresponsible threats of vengeance. The eye-witness account of the execution of twenty-eight hostages on October 22, 1941, written by an inmate of the Châteaubriant camp who will himself be shot in December, is a masterpiece in its genre. But the Party's editors do not permit sentiment to blind them to possible political dividends: the pamphlet in which the account just mentioned appears ends with the words: "Frenchmen: join the Communist Party, the party of the hostages of Châteaubriant." [12]

The Party's purpose in this phase of activities is, we must remember, twofold: to defeat—or at least counteract—the repression; and to forward the grand purpose to which all else is now subordinate, namely, immediate and effective aid for the Soviet Union. This leads to some curious results—for example, to repeated insistence upon the strike as a means of combating the repression. "The way to save the lives of the hostages," says a November pamphlet addressed to the workers, "is to make it clear to everybody that you are prepared to make use of your most dependable weapon, the strike." [13] Since the writer of these lines knows perfectly well by this time that the Germans do not react to aggressive tactics of this kind by sparing lives, it is easy to see that his real target is the output of the factories in which the strikes are to occur. He also knows, and the center knows too, that successful strikes are out of the question at this stage of the game, and the Party accordingly contents itself most of the time with proposals for brief though usually nationwide work stoppages —or even "moments of silence" in memory of this or that fallen comrade. Late in October, for instance, it issues the following call to the metallurgical workers in Paris (Jean Timbaut, former secretary of the Metal-workers Union of the Seine, has just been executed): "Make arrangements in

each shop for observing a few minutes' silence in honor of
. . . Jean Timbaut." [14] The basic strategy, which is to tie
together in the workers' minds strikes, sabotage, and the
struggle against the repression, emerges clearly in what follows: "Show your firm resolve not to keep on producing for
the assassins of our most valuable militant. Slow up production." [15]

55, J. We must notice one other aspect of the Communists'
response to the new wave of repression, namely, their treatment of the French magistrates and policemen who are the
(willing or unwilling) administrators of the repressive measures. This treatment swings back and forth between the two
poles—threats of retaliation at some future date, and appeals
to patriotic sentiment. When "special courts" are created to
handle Communist cases, the Party press publishes the names
of the Paris judges who are to sit on them, and appends the
following comment: "The people of France, who know that
the special court is a Gestapo court, will not forget these
names. The Germans are not going to be in Paris forever." [16]
A month later, however, the Communist-inspired pamphlet
Judges of France, published over the signature Association
for the Defense of the French Legal System, reveals the pendulum at the other end of the arc:

The special courts are—as regards both the authority under
which they operate and the procedures they employ—*illegal*.
. . . What the enemy has hoped is that the judges of France will,
by participating in them, give the appearance of legality to a piece
of arbitrary terrorism.

Judges of France, do not perform this service for the enemy.
Refuse to hand down judgments in the name of German bayonets
and in contravention of the rights and interests of the fatherland.
Take the side of France against the enemy and his lackeys.

All French judges for whom patriotism still has meaning will
choose to aid their people against the enemy—never the enemy
against their people. They are in a position to do a great deal;
they can earn the gratitude of the fatherland by solemnly de-
claring, on every possible occasion, that the current persecution

of patriots is against the law, as also by taking a firm stand against treason—that is, by demanding the full penalty of the law for the traitors who have made deals with the enemy.

As for the special court: it is plain that there is only one thing for a judge of France to do, namely, resign.[17]

The judges, however, are of small importance to the Communists as compared to the police, with whom they must reckon in the course of each day's work. It is the police who are called upon to disrupt the Party machine, arrest its militants, and seize its literature; and it is the individual policeman who, in actual practice, decides how energetically these things shall be done. Any wedge that the Party can drive between them and the Germans will, thus, pay immediate dividends.

At an early moment, therefore, long before June 22, the Party sets out to convince the individual policeman and gendarme that the existing regime is doomed, and that the only safe thing for him to do is come to an understanding with the men who will govern France tomorrow, that is, the Communists:

Bear in mind the fact that none of the things you are doing will be forgotten in the days ahead, and that we are fully informed concerning the *attitude of each and every one of you.* . . . Bear in mind also the fact that Pétain has to find jobs for his legionnaires and his young fascists. And don't forget that your superiors would like to have incriminating evidence against you, so as to get rid of you at some future moment. If you are ordered to keep on the lookout for Communists distributing their newspapers and handbills, which is to say the only genuinely French reading matter now available, keep your eyes shut, or betake yourself to the other side of the street from that on which the distribution is taking place. You will then proceed on your way with the satisfaction of having done your duty, the satisfaction of having acted like a Frenchman. If you are ordered to arrest Communists, use all the means at your disposal to warn the persons concerned, so that they may take whatever steps are necessary to escape the repression.[18]

The propaganda addressed to the policemen after the outbreak of the Nazi-Soviet war is in this same vein, save for one
new emphasis: their duty to contribute to "national liberation." Certainly there is no change in the major supporting
argument: "Do not forget . . . that the hour of liberation is
drawing near, and that the French people are soon going to
call upon you to account for your conduct. Don't take ship
on a vessel that is sinking." [19]

The policemen, like the other groups the Party would like
to win over, are interested in higher wages and better working
conditions. The Party makes it its business to translate these
interests into "demands," and misses no opportunity to insist
upon their satisfaction.

The New "National Front"

56. Up to June 22, 1941, the Party had a single task: to work for the triumph of world revolution. Its thinking in connection with that task revolved, as we have seen, around three "basic" factors: the USSR, the oppressed countries, and the colonies. On June 22 that task disappears, and its place is taken by another: to fight Germany; and the Party must rethink its tableau of basic factors. One of yesterday's three, the colonial peoples (and their future revolt) goes by the board. The other two are retained but transformed. The USSR, formerly the "country of peace" waxing stronger against the backdrop of a "capitalist" world in an advanced stage of disintegration, becomes the USSR at war, its very existence endangered by the onslaught of the Wehrmacht. The peoples of the occupied countries, for whom the appropriate slogan has been "Neither London nor Berlin," now become "elements" to be mobilized against the German enemy. And England, yesterday "plutocratic" and "imperialist," must henceforth be regarded as a member of the democratic Popular Front which can stop Hitler only by going to the aid of Russia.

No part of this penance can, even for face-saving purposes, be waived or even postponed. Stalin, speaking on July 3, 1941, announces that "the peoples' front for the struggle for liberty is about to become a reality," and describes as "historic" Churchill's and Roosevelt's statements on aid to Soviet Russia.[1] Soon afterward he is able to announce an Anglo-Soviet "pact," which at least puts the party propagandists on familiar ground.[2] The Party press forthwith holds up Anglo-Soviet cooperation as an example for the French people to copy even in their internal affairs: "Hand in hand, the Union of Soviet Socialist Republics and democratic England wage the war against

fascism. French anti-fascists, unite in a National Front!" [3]
Stalin, speaking again on November 6, 1941, establishes the
new vocabulary once and for all by referring to "a coalition,
a united front, among Great Britain, the United States, and
ourselves." [4]

At first, the Communist press is hard put to it to explain the
new situation to its sympathizers. It makes much of the fact
that the present alliance is the one that *should* have been concluded before August, 1939, and would have but for British
perversity. "The England of Winston Churchill, matured
by unhappy experience, has finally done in the midst of war
what the reactionaries Chamberlain and Daladier refused to
do for the sake of saving the peace, that is, reach an agreement
with Soviet Russia." [5] Or it explains that political and ideological differences do not matter where there are genuine common
interests:

Without doubt, those who are fighting against the hegemony of
Hitler have no shared ideology. The English Conservatives do
not think like the Russian Communists or like the American Democrats. It has nevertheless proved possible for them to act together
because interests beyond the merely political have been at stake.
All peoples now fighting in self-defense must, as a matter of course,
unite their efforts in this way against their common enemy. This
is the major explanation for the alliance between the USSR and
the Anglo-Saxon democracies, which some people find so strange. [6]

In general, however, the propaganda machine leaves people
to work out their own explanation and hastens on to other
matters.

Everything that emphasizes the far-reaching character of
the rapprochement is seized upon and praised. *L'Humanité*
lauds the creation of an Anglo-Soviet trade-union committee,
sponsored at a Trades-Union Congress by Sir Walter Citrine,
and conveniently forgets [7] the book on Russia, *I Search for
Truth in Russia*, [8] that had once made his name anathema in
the Communist press of all countries. It honors the exploits
of the RAF, and, in the *Manifesto of the National Front* in-

vites the French to pool their efforts with those of "the Soviet soldiers and the British aviators." [9]

The British air raids in France pose a real problem, but the Party quickly decides to welcome them—and to fit them, for propaganda purposes, into its plan for paralyzing production. On July 4, after the bombardments in the north, the Party issues its leaflet, *Don't Die for the Nazi Machine,* which clearly reveals this phase of its strategy:

British aircraft have begun to strike at French factories working for German imperialism.

These bombardments have already resulted in numerous casualties among the workers and townspeople in Fives-Lille, Comines, Hazebrouck, and elsewhere.

Women and children living in the districts surrounding these plants have lost their lives.

It is going to be like this everywhere.

Neither the prefecture of the north nor the German authorities have taken any steps whatsoever to protect the population.

Workers in these industries, you are inexorably sentenced to death. Don't stand for this. Don't make widows of your wives and orphans of your children.

Your safety demands that you stop work at once.

Pull yourselves together. Leave your workshops, present yourselves to the municipal authorities, and demand your unemployment insurance.

Let the people living near the factories get together and force the authorities to evacuate them and house them in less dangerous areas.[10]

This document sets the tone for many others that will be published in similar circumstances over the next months.[11] The careful reader will not miss the explicit justification of the bombardments in the phrase "working for German imperialism"; but the central idea is to terrorize the workers into stopping production, into striking, by holding out to them the prospect of certain death if they continue to report for work. As for the proposed evacuations, they will help slow down production and will disorganize the transportation system as well. The Party has clearly come a long way from the position adopted barely two months earlier, toward the end of May, 1941, in the manifesto of the first National Front. The USSR was not then at war, and the line was "absolute neutrality": we must prevent "our cities" and "our factories" from being exposed to air bombardment.

The Party press now extends its a priori approval to every expression of Anglo-Soviet cooperation, whether military or diplomatic or, as in the case of Iran, both. Let us stop for a moment to examine the Iranian developments, since they are a perfect illustration of the ease and unconcern with which the Party reverses its position. The Anglo-Russian intervention at Teheran closely parallels the earlier British intervention in Iraq: the motives, the methods, even the consequences are recognizably similar. In the spring, however, Britain was not Russia's ally, and the events in Iraq were presented as an episode in the "war of plunder" being conducted by the "British imperialist clique," which had "designs on the oil wells." [12] In the present case England is acting in concert with the USSR and the Communist press is enthusiastic because "the plans of Hitler are being blocked." [13] Nor is that all. British action in Iraq is now, so to speak, entitled to blessing a posteriori. So is the attack on Syria in May-June, 1941, which the Party press had treated as a "colonial adventure" in which French soldiers should in no circumstances participate.[14] "The mission of the traitor General Dentz," the instructions to the militants read, "was to promote Nazi infiltration of Syria in order to pave the way for operations against the Middle East, and for a drive toward the oil wells of Iraq, Iran, and the Caucasus. The entry of British and Free French forces into Syria, the liquidation of the pro-Nazi Government of Iraq, the penetration of Anglo-Soviet troops into Iran, the expulsion of the Germans and the Italians from Afghanistan—all these constitute just so many setbacks for German policy." [15]

57. The terminology and arguments associated with the "second imperialist war" have, then, disappeared. France now faces only one problem—that of "national liberation." The

Vichy government is the ally, the "valet" of Hitler, and Hitler is the "enemy" of France—the *absolute* enemy, who must be destroyed. The Party republishes ad nauseam the anti-French passages in *Mein Kampf*.[16] Russia's entry into the war has, in a word, transformed the meaning of the war itself, and consequently the attitude France should adopt toward it. A few weeks ago, the Party was addressing itself to the peasants in such terms as these: "Whoever wins, Germany or England, France will be conquered, despoiled, enslaved." [17] Today it tells the peasants: "There is no salvation for our country except in a definitive victory over the Axis Powers." [18]

This reversal forces the Party to modify its attitude toward the Gaullist movement. We have already remarked on the asperity of its attacks upon that movement, which were still being pushed as recently as May, 1941—when the Party was launching the first version of the National Front. Listen to it after June 22: "All Frenchmen salute the soldiers of de Gaulle as fighters against Hitler . . ." [19] The rival has become an ally, the "domestic front" is now only an extension of the "distant front" on which the soldiers of de Gaulle are waging war. To take one other example, the Party was yesterday tarring "the traitors of Vichy" and the "provocateurs in London" with one and the same brush. "The traitors of Vichy send Frenchmen to their deaths in Syria at the behest of Germany as de Gaulle and Catroux send other Frenchmen to their deaths at the bidding of England." [20] Now, however, the Party welcomes "the entry of British and Free French forces into Syria" [21] and proudly affirms that de Gaulle, in the course of his journey through that country, has been "the object of enthusiastic demonstrations on the part of the population" [22]—the same population with whom, before June 22, the soldiers of the "Armistice Army" were being urged to "fraternize" against France and the other "imperialist" powers.

Formerly de Gaulle was a "traitor," a "felon," an "aristocrat," an "adventurer," a "mercenary"; now the *Student Patriot* points to him as an example of uprightness and fortitude for French school children to imitate.[23] Henceforth nothing must divide the Communists and the Gaullists, who have a single "rallying cry: France," a single "word of command: expel the invader." This is the easier to do, incidentally, because political considerations have been adjourned in favor of military considerations; more than any other French movement, that of the Gaullists is ready to use the sabotage and guerrilla tactics advocated by the Communists—the more ready, of course, because it did not wait until June 22 to begin using them.

If the Communists have any lingering doubts about their rapprochement with de Gaulle, these will soon be dispelled by clear indications of Moscow's attitude in the matter. The *Manifesto of the National Front*, distributed in the unoccupied zone in November, "salutes as a gage of battle and of unity the recognition extended by M. Maiski, Soviet Ambassador in London, to the 'National Council of Free French' under the leadership of General de Gaulle." [24] Even the most squeamish orthodoxy thus no longer has anything to fear: de Gaulle bears the Kremlin's seal of approval. Cooperation with the Gaullists forthwith becomes the order of the day, and the Gaullist symbols—the "V," the Cross of Lorraine—are adopted by the Communists, and are used interchangeably or in conjunction with the hammer and sickle. Certain "orders" from General de Gaulle, that for a five-minute work stoppage on October 31 for instance, are relayed by the Party's press and obeyed by its followers.[25]

The Communists also align themselves with the Gaullists on North Africa, and issue no more calls to the "Algerian people" to revolt against France. It is no longer a question—pending a further shift in the Party line—of "oppressed colonial masses," but rather of strategic positions to be defended against Axis designs.

58. The National Front sponsored by the Communists must be as "broad" as possible, which is to say that it must include all French "patriots," of the Left or of the Right, whatever their political affiliation, their social position, or their

religious creed. The manifesto distributed in the occupied zone
in July lists in detail the categories of persons who have allegedly participated in the creation of the National Front, or
at least attended the initial rally: "(1) authorized leaders of
workers' organizations and political groups; (2) authorized
agents of peasant groups from the several regions of France;
(3) delegates of the middle classes (merchants and artisans);
(4) distinguished representatives of the educational, artistic,
and scientific worlds." The manifesto goes on to say that the
participants included "freethinkers, well-known Catholic dig-
nitaries, members of the Protestant church, and members of
the clergy, as well as Communists." [26] The November manifesto in the unoccupied zone offers a similar list, which includes "Catholics, Protestants, freethinkers, republicans, syndicalists, Gaullists, Communists, technicians, workers with
hand and brain, men of the liberal professions, and the military." [27] This is, of course, merely a roll call of the political
and social "forces" that the Party intends to have represented
on the "National Committee" of the new organization; and
it shows that the Party, in the context of the program adopted
after June 22, is thinking more optimistically than ever in
terms of a coalition that will embrace peasants, women, young
people, soldiers, industrial workers, intellectuals, and the middle classes.

The Party now makes a great effort to disarm the suspicions
of the Catholics, and win them over to its scheme. The propaganda it addresses to them gradually becomes more adroit: all
allusions to the USSR are omitted, and emphasis is placed upon
Nazi persecutions of the Church and upon "the fate of Austria." The Communists even attempt to discover a patch of
ideological ground common to the Catholics and themselves.
A pamphlet of the Federation of Communist Youth, addressed
to a "young Christian worker," reminds him that "Nazism is
the negation of all morality and of the ideal of human brotherhood, which is yours as well as ours." [28] Another pamphlet,
sent by mail to the nation's priests, uses more curious language
still: "It is not for us," it says,

to argue with you on the level of exegesis, but it is inconceivable to us that Christianity, born as it was in the struggle against the temporal power of Caesar, born as it was of the sufferings of martyrs delivered up to wild beasts and to the stake, born as it was in a great upsurge of human brotherhood—it is inconceivable to us that Christianity can, without betraying its origins, acquiesce in the destruction of civilized humanity, when that destruction proceeds under the infernal sign of the hooked cross, the sign of the Black Mass and of nothingness.

Alluding to "the influence that the priest has over the faithful," the tract invites him to use that influence to rally a "broad front of Frenchmen," and points out that this activity will enable him to keep in closer touch with his fellow countrymen through the days ahead! [29] The pamphlet also urges Catholics to listen in to a clandestine station (Radio Christian) which offers broadcasts especially prepared for them. And an appeal addressed to Catholics on Armistice Day adds this fillip: "Say a prayer for the repose of the victims of two wars and for the martyrs of national liberation. Lay flowers on the tomb of the Unknown Soldier. Go down on your knees and pray for the resurrection of the fatherland." [30]

The lists of political "forces" that belong or are to belong to the National Front almost never include the Socialists, save for an occasional reference to "former members" of the Socialist Party.[31] Indeed the Party goes out of its way to reassure the "Rightists of former days"; it does not even insist that adherents shall be anti-fascists,[32] and apparently sees no reason why employers and workers should not work within the front side by side.[33] Certainly no one could ask for a "broader" National Front.

This does not mean, however, that the Party renounces control. Now, as before June 22, "the National Front, if it is to fulfill its liberating mission, must have as its driving force the French working class, with the Communist Party at its head." [34] Statements of this kind entirely to one side, the National Front (to the extent that it exists at all) goes forward under virtually complete domination by the Party. It is, and must be, an underground organization; once it takes shape, it will provide a network that will greatly increase the Party's capacity for maneuver, initiative, and control.

Actually, the National Front remains primarily a piece of political camouflage, under cover of which the Party enlarges its sphere of action and recruits new members. The Party nevertheless attaches great importance to it—as may be seen from the following urgent instructions to its militants:

All our groups must make it a point of honor to bring into the National Front the village teacher, the elected official who has been removed from office by Vichy, the worker who used to belong to the Socialist Party, the peasant who used to belong to the Radical Party, the young Frenchman who ardently desires the liberation of his country, the true patriot, the Catholic who wants his country liberated, the former member of the Croix de Feu who has been disillusioned by fascist dictatorship in action, in short, every Frenchman who wishes to act like a Frenchman. It is the Communists' glorious mission to rally a great fighting force for the independence of France.[35]

The Party proposes to acquire, in this way, a highly varied following, and place itself at the very heart of a patriotic drive against the occupying power.

"Organization Is What Counts"

59. The Party must get today's job done today, and at the same time keep an eye on tomorrow. This means that it must have a "correct" policy, which includes, inter alia, squaring off promptly to new situations, seeing far enough into the future to ward off surprises, and keeping itself in position to change its tactics as circumstances require. The watchwords, in short, are firmness *and* flexibility, unlimited patience *and* quick decisions; and it is a proper balance between these apparently conflicting elements that the Party calls "political capacity," or "political resourcefulness."

No amount of "correct" policy will make the Party effective unless it is supplemented by good, sound organization. The Communists, alike on the level of theory and on that of practice, have a clear grasp of this truth. Lenin, for example, insists upon nothing so strongly as that the decisive role in the struggle for the dictatorship of the proletariat shall be played not by the proletariat itself but by the Party, that the Party shall have higher echelons whose every member is a "professional revolutionary," and that it shall cope with the obstacles in its path precisely by dint of its organizational efficiency. The Bolsheviks' victory in the October Revolution was, again, in large part an organizational victory, as also was that achieved by Stalin a few years later—that is, Stalin was able to crush his rivals one after another, and to achieve his absolute monopoly of power, only because he had first captured the Party's organizational apparatus. Nor—as the Socialists in several countries can testify—is the record different outside Russia: again and again the Communists, though at a great disadvantage from the standpoint of numbers and strategic position, have won out because of their greater capacity for sustained and methodical effort, and their skill at forging the appropriate organizational forms. "Organization is what counts," the Communists say; [1] though here as elsewhere they fight shy of all attitudes that might be described as conservative, or might involve their clinging too long to established procedures or modes of thought. They combine a lively awareness of the importance of organization—an awareness that contributes to and yet feeds upon the Party's *mystique*—with a deep appreciation of the need for adapting methods and structure to an objective situation that is constantly changing.

60. Between September, 1939, and the Armistice the French Communist Party was, as we have seen, illegal. It was able to continue its activities through that period, the period of action against the "imperialist war," only because it sentenced to death the local and shop cells upon which it had relied in the past, and replaced them with "groups of three," conceived in terms reminiscent of the secret societies of the Restoration period, the July monarchy, and the Empire. By the end of June, 1940, or perhaps the beginning of July, the situation has changed again—which is to say, the future suddenly looks bright and promising, and the Party's leaders, influenced no doubt by Moscow, convince themselves that their moment has come. The defeat is going to destroy the established order; and the Communists, thanks to the indulgence of the German authorities and to assistance from the Soviet Union, are to inherit its responsibilities.

New situations, new organizational forms—so reads the first instruction sheet the Party distributes following the Armistice. [2] French imperialism is stretched full length upon the ground; the Party's task is to deliver the *coup de grâce* that will keep it there; and the Party must, to this end, make the most of the overlap between its own interests and those of the German invader—first of all by wheedling out of this "accidental ally" the concessions it needs in order to regain its freedom of action. One such concession, indeed, has already been won: "The Communist Party is no longer wholly illegal. It is now semilegal." Other concessions will follow in due time: "Our immediate concern is the struggle for full legality

. . . The slogan, for the moment, is not 'power for the people,' but rather 'lift the ban upon the people's organizations . . . ' " [3] The September-October instructions repeat this theme: "We must dare to do what needs to be done in order to regain our status as a legal party . . ." [4] And since an organizational structure based upon groups of three is inappropriate to the daring type of action here envisaged the groups of three must go. But even the June-July instructions are categorical on the central point: "We must write off our groups of three, and resume the organizational structure we were using before we created them: the cells, but with a narrower base—at most eight persons, with Party members of long standing assuming the positions of leadership." [5]

So confident are the Party's leaders that the situation is shifting rapidly in their favor,[6] so confident are they that the German authorities will view favorably their bid for legal status, that they do not hesitate, on the crucial level of organizational planning, to jump the gun. And this is not merely a matter of resuming the *forms* associated with the Party's period of legality: the old base units are not only to be revived, but also to be increased in number and thrown open to new applicants for membership.

We need no longer be afraid to invite the thousands of sympathizers who are now supporting the Party's activities to join our ranks. We must not of course jeopardize the Party's security; we must keep in force certain indispensable precautions; but within the limits set by these considerations we must organize the Party in such fashion as increasingly to facilitate recruitment by the base units, and to encourage each Party member to get the Party's slogans and policies across to the people about him.[7]

In short the Party is to slough off, little by little, the organizational forms it has maintained underground; and it is to move, through gradual modification of its structure and its activities, in the direction of the legal, "mass" Party of the future.

61. In order to accomplish the major tasks it has set itself for the immediate future, the Party must—as it puts it—"set

the masses in motion." It must, therefore, in adapting its organizational forms to the present period of "semilegality," look ahead to more remote goals. This, says the June-July instruction sheet, it will succeed in doing "to the extent that we keep in touch with the masses," and, above all, to the extent that "[we are able to] create organs of representation that will be recognized by the authorities, and thus get ourselves into a position, during this period of confusion and bewilderment, to take over the conduct of public affairs." [8] By August *Party Life* is speaking of a "drive for new recruits" and explaining the need for such a drive in terms of expanding the Party's activities "among the masses." [9] (The chief instrument upon which the Party will rely for this purpose is, as we have seen, its committees of the people.)

When, somewhat later, the situation begins to look less favorable, and the Party cadres are beginning to feel the effects of a new wave of repression, the Communists still cling to the notion that they are going to be able to continue, and even intensify, their activities among the masses. "Both our own experience and that of the glorious Bolshevik Party," says a December (1940) instruction sheet, "show that all our energies should be channeled into organizing the masses of the people throughout the country." [10] And one of the Party's brochures, anticipating the objection that these activities cannot go forward without infringement of the Party's "rules for underground activity," upon which it has again become necessary to insist, makes this reply: "Our major strength in our struggle against the provocateurs is the mass character of our revolutionary organization." [11]

62. The dreams of the Communist leaders, alike in Moscow and Paris, have thus lasted hardly longer than a morning's sunlight. What has happened is that the German authorities, after playing along with the Communists through the summer, have suddenly (October, 1940) decided to give Vichy a free hand as regards the repression of the Communists; and this means that one of the foundation stones for the building projected in June, namely, the blessing of the occupying power.

is now unavailable. And once it is clear that this has happened the Party in fact has no choice but to retreat in the direction of the program and organizational structure of the period before it began to indulge its hopes. It must, that is to say, abandon its more exposed positions; and if it does not at once recognize that such a retreat is necessary, this can be explained in terms of an all-too-human reluctance to write off a brilliant future that has been taken too much for granted. (For a time, moreover, the Party is entitled to ask itself whether the new honeymoon between Vichy and the occupying power will last—whether, if you like, the Nazis are tacking to the wind or actually changing their course.) However this may be, the moment comes when the strategic retreat can no longer be postponed, so that the Communists' *Organizational Plan for a Cell*, which apparently belongs to late September, lays down the principle that "a cell should include at most six members" [12] —as against the maximum of eight stipulated in the June-July instruction sheet. An October instruction sheet (not the September-October sheet referred to a moment ago) rolls the figure back to five: "Back in the days before the ban on our Party," it explains,

we had cells of fifteen, twenty, or even thirty members. This type of organization is, however, quite out of the question at the present time, because it would jeopardize our security. Following an interval during which the Party's organization was based on cells of three members each, we increased the size of the cells to eight, or even twelve. This is too large a figure by far . . . That is why, as matters now stand, we must see to it that no cell includes more than five members. We shall, in this way, make it easier to ward off the blows aimed at us by our class enemy . . .[13]

In December they repeat this directive, and set forth a detailed plan for carrying out the reduction without prejudicing the Party's activities among the masses (the excluded members are to be organized in new neighborhood, block, or shop cells).[14]

Toward the end of December and even more noticeably after the turn of the year, the shift back to groups of three

becomes increasingly imperative. The following excerpt from
a pamphlet distributed around the first of the year is a clear
statement of the principles of the new structure, as these are
understood by the Party leaders:

The organizational unit of our Party is the group of three, and
no Party meetings may be held with more than three comrades
present . . . The connecting link that joins the groups of three
to one another is an official of the neighborhood or shop headquarters, whose identity should, if possible, be known only to
the group leaders in his neighborhood or shop (whom he deals
with individually) and to the section leaders from whom he receives directives. Each of the sections is divided into neighborhoods in such fashion that no neighborhood leader is responsible
for more than four or five group leaders. Each region similarly
is divided into sectors in such fashion that no sector comprises
more than four or five sections. The regional leaders are thus able
by communicating with at most four or five persons to make their
control effective throughout the territory assigned to them. The
headquarters of each region, sector, section, and neighborhood
has a maximum complement of three members, each of whom is
assigned a specific function.[15]

Centralized leadership; an organizational structure based
upon watertight groups of three; vertical communications—
these are the major emphases of the organizational plan the
Party adopts at the end of 1940, and this plan will remain in
effect without substantial modifications throughout the period
covered by this book. As the months pass, the Party will insist
with increasing stubbornness upon its being followed to the
letter—the more since some of the peripheral organizations,
after several months' habituation to the more easy-going methods of the period of "semilegality," show a certain reluctance
to adopt it. They are, of course, brought promptly back into
line by directives from central and regional headquarters.[16]

As Vichy steps up the pace of the repression, violations of
the Party's "rules for underground activity" become increasingly dangerous. The Party leaders accordingly direct attention to these violations in ever-sharper language, reiterate the

rules themselves, and remind the militants that no one, however important or unimportant the post he occupies, is to make his own decision as to whether or not to obey them:

Any attempt by a base unit of three members to establish contact with another such group will be viewed with suspicion, and appropriate sanctions will be applied. Communications between organizations on the same echelon are strictly forbidden. (There should be no liaison whatever among the base units. There should be no liaison whatever among the cells. There should be no horizontal communications of any kind.) No meetings are to be held with more than three comrades present. The groups of three are [now] the Party's base units, or cells. Any attempt to organize groups comprising more than three members will be dealt with as an infringement of Party discipline . . . Existing groups comprising more than three members must be decentralized at once.[17]

63. The Party, then, is highly centralized as regards political direction and control, highly decentralized as regards organizational structure. On the highest echelon we find the Central Committee and its Bureau, from which instructions radiate downward through the leaders on the lower echelons, which are as follows: the region, the sector, the section, the locality, the shop, the neighborhood or shop cell, and the base unit (i.e., the group of three). The leadership on each echelon is designated and controlled by the echelon just above it; the base units are wholly isolated from one another and, at least in theory, ignorant of one another's existence; each of the base units relies for all its communications with the cell to which it is assigned upon a single member, whom it designates for this purpose. This same pattern is repeated on the other echelons: the several regional and sectional headquarters are likewise unaware of each other's existence, so that communications move either upward or downward, never horizontally. This arrangement, be it noted, confers two great advantages: security risks are enormously reduced; and at the same time a surprisingly high percentage of Party members are called upon to act, in one context or another, as *leaders*.

Let us take, as an example, Section X, which has just been organized in compliance with instructions recently received by a sector headquarters from a regional headquarters.[18] Section X now becomes a distinct locality on the Communist map; and this new locality contains, let us say, two "neighborhoods" and one reasonably important shop. Now the new section headquarters is in touch with only four headquarters—above it, that of the sector; below it, two neighborhood headquarters and one shop headquarters. Let us suppose further that the first of the two neighborhoods contains three cells, the second two, and the shop, which performs two distinct operations in two separate buildings, two more. Each of the neighborhood headquarters maintains liaison only with section headquarters on the one hand and the leaders of the cells under its control on the other. These leaders, in turn, are in touch only with a single member of each of the base units assigned to their headquarters. And all this, restated in terms of the second of the two advantages we have just claimed for these arrangements, means that if the section has a total membership of ninety, thirty-three militants are learning daily lessons in the responsibilities of leadership—or, if we are willing to count the spokesmen of the nineteen base units as leaders (as I think we should), the number rises to fifty-two. We shall direct attention below to what this implies as regards the struggle against the repression [19] and the development and promotion of promising militants.[20]

The Rules for Underground Activity

64. If it is to get on with its job and make good use of the cadres and resources at its disposal the Party must make itself as secure as possible against measures of repression and provocation.

"We must make the Party inviolable" [1]—this becomes the theme of countless directives handed down from on high to the militants. The Vichy government and the occupying power, as one Party publication puts it, are engaged in a savage repression, the object of which is the physical destruction of the Communist Party. To this end, these enemies propose (1) to take advantage of every imprudent action, every carelessly spoken word, every organizational blunder, that might deliver Party militants into their hands, and (2) to demoralize or, failing that, kill off the thousands of militant Communists now in prison, jail, or concentration camp.[2] If it is to cope with this new offensive, the Party must discover new political techniques, reform its organizational structure, and impose upon its members new rules and procedures calculated (a) to give it increased control over its cadres and their activities, (b) to bring about more strict observance of the principles of underground activity, (c) to assure maximum protection against agents provocateurs, and (d) to maintain morale. We devote a section to each of these four points.

(a). A constant check must be kept upon the Party's cadres and upon each of the Party's activities. Otherwise there will be organizational kinks, which are incompatible with maximum efficiency. Nor is that all. The Party wishes to know the facts about each militant's family situation, his activities, and his political connections both now and in the past. All the relevant data must accordingly be forwarded to the Party's Personnel Commission, which provides for this purpose a "biographical questionnaire" and a set of instructions which reads as follows:

The purpose of the following biographical questionnaire is to permit the Party leadership to get better acquainted with their comrades. This will enable them to take into account each militant's personal relations and present activities, and thus assign him a task in which he can work for the Party's best interests. Each comrade who receives this questionnaire will be expected to complete his return within forty-eight hours. The questions are to be answered in the clearest manner possible. Yes and No replies are to be avoided, so that the Party can obtain an accurate picture of the comrade making the return. Any comrade who attempts to mislead the Party, or to hide something from it, will be tried before the Party's Control Commission; and any comrade who fails to make a return will be relieved of his responsibilities. Each comrade's reply, together with his copy of the questionnaire, is to be placed in a sealed envelope, which will be stamped "Confidential" and forwarded to the Personnel Commission. Only members of this commission will have access to the returns.

The questionnaire itself is as follows:

Autobiographical Data

1. Date (year only) and place of birth. (Do not include name and address.)
2. How much education have you had? Where did you attend school?
3. What is your occupation? List your places of employment since leaving school.
4. List the occupations of your parents, your brothers and sisters, your uncles and aunts. State whether or not they are active politically. To what organizations do they belong?
5. Are you married? What is your wife's occupation? What is her nationality? List the occupation and nationality of each member of her family. What are her political opinions?
6. How many children have you? What are their ages? Of what organizations are they members?
7. Are there members of the Socialist Party in your family? in your wife's family? Are there any Trotskyites?
8. Are there policemen, gendarmes, or police informers in your

family? in your wife's family? Are there persons in either family whose means of livelihood is obscure? If so, what is the character of your own relations with these persons?

Training and Political Activity

9. When and how did you become a Communist?

10. Were you ever a member of any other party or organization?

11. Were you ever a Free Mason? When and why did you withdraw from the Masonic organization of which you were a member?

12. List, in chronological order, the various posts you have held in the Party. What is the nature of your present work for the Party?

13. Were you on active duty [with one of the armed services] during the war? Where?

14. Have there been periods during which you were not active in the Party? in your trade-union? When? Why?

15. What Party schools have you attended? What books have you read by Marx, Engels, Lenin, or Stalin? Have you mastered the *History of the Communist Party of the Soviet Union (Bolsheviks)*? Do you read the Party's pamphlets and books?

16. Have you ever been connected with the Trotskyites? With the Barbé-Célor group? * Have you ever maintained relations of any kind with Doriot? . . . with any other person who has been expelled from the Party? Do you know anyone who maintains relations with such persons? How well?

17. Have you ever been disciplined by the Party? By any other organization? When? For what?

18. Have you ever been picked up by the police? Have you ever been found guilty of a common law offense? When? What offense?

19. Have you been in any respect a victim of the repression? Were you arrested? sentenced? For how long? In what circumstances were you set free?

20. Have you ever been in the colonies? abroad? When? For what purpose?

21. Is this the first time you have filled out a biographical questionnaire?

* "Barbé-Célor group" is the catch-all term applied to the pre-Thorez Communist leaders whom the Party expelled in 1931. W.K.

> Do not keep a copy of this return.
> Do not sign your name.[3]

The meaning and purpose of this questionnaire, which calls to mind the so-called "job inquiries" the Bolsheviks use in connection with their purges, of course leaps to the eye. It is intended to place the militant's entire life under a magnifying glass: every shortcoming, every suspicious circumstance, becomes immediately a subject for detailed study and investigation; and when these supplementary inquiries are completed every possible entree for provocateurs will have been sealed off, every nascent ideological deviation nipped in the bud. Each member's private life is, in a word, brought completely within the orbit of the Party.

Nor, from this point of view, do the Party's numerous organizational units enjoy a more privileged position. Each is required to submit its weekly report to the Central Committee. Each must use for this purpose, each week, the same invariable form. Each must adopt certain specified precautions, whose purpose is to keep the report from proving useful to the police should it fall in their hands.[4]

The form provided for these reports is as follows:

MODEL WEEKLY REPORT

Situation Report

Marked discontent among the workers of this or that factory, and for such and such reasons. Drive launched at such and such a place to press such and such demands. Women's delegations organized for such and such purposes.

The following remarks overheard in the streets:

Propaganda Report

The following publications have been distributed in the amounts specified:

L'Humanité, No. 10:

Workers' Life:

L'Humanité (women's supplement):

Russia Today:

Pamphlets:

Comment: two new duplicating machines put into service, etc.

Organizational Report

New units organized in such and such factories, and x number clubs opened at such and such addresses. Contributions easier to collect. Headquarters or groups of three organized at such and such places, etc.

Mass Activities Report

Notebooks of demands set up in such and such factories.

Women's groups organized, as follows:

Successful penetration of the following bourgeois organizations:

Repression Report

X number comrades arrested on suspicion (x number at home, x number during working hours); x number leaders arrested. Such and such a trial has been held, resulting in such and such a sentence. The accused behaved in the following manner:

Solidarity Report

The following sums have been collected, the following families visited, the following relations maintained with such and such prisoners, camps, prisons, etc.[5]

This kind of report, abstracting as it does from all useless detail, enables the center to maintain a continuous check on the activities of all units on all levels, and keep itself informed with regard to the results being achieved. Requiring it is tantamount to an uninterrupted on-the-spot investigation—which is, for the rest, precisely what will follow if and when the center suspects that the returns are being falsified.

65, B. The Party's "rules for underground activity" merit careful attention because they tell us much about what it means to be a militant—that is, about the terms on which one is admitted to Party membership, the habits one is expected to acquire and those one is expected to get rid of, and, most important of all, the implications of the resultant discipline for one's personal development.

Let us notice, to begin with, that the mere fact of operating on two levels, of engaging simultaneously in legal and underground activities, involves hazards that the Party could largely

avoid by projecting its efforts on one of the two levels to the
exclusion of the other. But it also involves great gains: "The
influence the Party acquires through its underground activities," writes *Party Life*, "is so much working capital for its
legal activities"; [6] and, what is equally important, the legal
activities often provide excellent cover for what the Party is
doing underground. For the rest, the hazards can be greatly
reduced through strict observance of this simple rule: Never
use a known Communist in legal activities, and never include
one in, for example, a delegation that is to negotiate with the
public authorities, or with an employer.[7] The known Communist, to be sure, presents a difficult problem for the Party's
underground activities as well, and the general rule here is as
follows: "No militant who was known to be a Communist
before the war should think of taking part in any underground
activity without first adopting certain indispensable precautions."[8] For instance, "he must never, for any reason whatever, go near any address that is known to the police in connection with him, since any such address is sure to be under surveillance."[9] Another rule, applicable to any militant living at
a known address and about to participate in an underground
mission, states that he must not only change his address, but
also sever his relations with his family. "The militant called
upon to choose between his family life and work for the
Party," declares a Party pamphlet, "has an easy choice."[10]
Another rule, intended especially for the leadership, warns
Party members against disclosing their identity to strangers,
forbids their indulging such frailties as vanity and curiosity,
and instructs them to preserve the most complete secrecy
about their work when talking with persons outside the movement.[11] Even co-workers and subordinates, the rule continues,
are to be told only what they need to know in order to perform their tasks.[12] Yet another rule instructs the militants to
ask no unnecessary or indiscreet questions, even of one another.[13] And the rule makers invariably add: Anyone who
violates these rules is to be regarded with suspicion. The
Party has no use for "the nosy and the talkative."[14]

The very structure of the Party, its "atomization" into water-tight groups of three, is of course a device for holding losses to a minimum if and when the enemy penetrates the defenses. Several of the rules here in question are likewise addressed to this end: no meetings may be held at which more than three comrades are present; [15] no meetings may last longer than sixty minutes; [16] militants are expected to arrive at rendezvous precisely on time ("arriving early attracts attention to you, arriving late exposes the comrade who is waiting for you"); [17] meeting places that might conceivably be under surveillance (restaurants, the homes of known Communists, etc.) are to be avoided in favor of those the police are not likely to think of (theater lobbies, spots out in the country or along the sea-shore, etc.); [18] no meeting place is to be used for successive meetings of the same group; [19] plans for meetings should never be discussed by mail or in the presence of third parties, and should be discussed over the telephone only in emergencies. [20] A militant who is on his way to a meeting must make sure that he is not being followed, [21] since the police like nothing better than to postpone an actual arrest until the suspect leads them to his co-workers. [22] The militant who has gone underground must never reveal his address, even to other Party members; [23] and printing and duplicating materials must never be stored at an address known to more than two comrades. [24] If, despite these precautions, a militant's domicile becomes known to the police, it will be of no use to them for any purpose other than that of placing him under arrest, since the well-trained militant stores nothing of value at his place of abode; [25] for him to keep a list of Party members there, for example, is unthinkable. [26] The militant whose mission requires him to make use of a Party document, or to serve as a courier, will first of all make sure that all information that might prove useful to the police is written in code; and if, in performing the mission, he runs afoul of the police, he will make every effort to destroy the papers he is carrying before he is actually taken into custody —if necessary, by chewing them up and swallowing them. [27] Underground workers, underground leaders especially, must make frequent changes in their mode of dress, their way of combing their hair, their gait and carriage; and they should not hesitate to adopt outright disguises when the circumstances seem to call for them.[28] They must avoid all forms of routinized behavior, and must, above all, keep a cool head.[29] But they must be careful, at the same time, not to surround themselves with an atmosphere of mystery, and not to give anyone the impression that they think they are being followed.[30] They must cultivate an air of naturalness, and must remember that "the surest way to go unnoticed is to look like everybody else." [31] The Party, for the rest, repeatedly warns them that all this is by no means easy to do: it is a matter of developing, gradually and over a long period of time, a set of reflexes that comes to be one's second nature, and that does not, even when it is fully developed, excuse one from the necessity of keeping oneself under constant observation.[32]

66, C. In all countries, and under all forms of government, the police endeavor to get at the facts about revolutionary movements by using informers and provocateurs. In France this practice can be traced back at least as far as the days of the Equals; * we have, from a former police prefect himself, an account of its employment (for the financing of anarchist newspapers) as recently as the days of the Third Republic.[33] Its methods are sufficiently an open secret to admit of at least this generalization: the more extremist the character of the revolutionary movement, the more it lends itself to penetration by provocateurs. Naturally therefore the Communists see a provocateur behind every tree; naturally also they give careful thought to the problem of defense against his activities. "The Party's entire apparatus," declares a writer in *Party Life*, "from the Central Committee all the way down to the cells, should make it its business to see that no act of provocation goes unpunished. This calls for careful investigation and analysis of the causes of every untoward event, every pointless

* The Société des Egaux, organized by Babeuf (1760–97), was outlawed by the Directoire in 1796. It was the "Conspiracy of the Equals" that resulted in Babeuf's execution. W.K.

debate that has the effect of slowing up the Party's activities, every arrest of a Party member." [34] The struggle against provocateurs is not, in other words, to be left up to the leadership. The rank and file also must take part in it; and the general rule is that the provocateur, once apprehended, shall be publicly denounced—and, as the Party press always adds, "given the treatment that an enemy of the Party deserves from the working class." [35]

A Party pamphlet published early in 1941 discusses the "several forms" provocation takes, and attributes them to three major causes: (a) divided counsels within the Party organization (i.e., indiscipline); (b) "corruption"; and (c) bad morale among the militants. The police, it points out, prefer to use persons already inside the movement. To this end they seek hungrily for information concerning the individual militant's weaknesses, his needs, and his resentments, since it is upon these that they must capitalize if they are to turn him into a collaborator. [36] The problem, in short, is only marginally that of the police agent who bores his way into the Party organization from outside; and it follows from this that for most cases of provocation the Party has only itself to blame. Here the crucial point is (a) in the foregoing list of causes: the Party regards itself as peculiarly vulnerable where discipline breaks down because of ideological differences, or disagreements concerning policy or tactics. Why? Because this can bring into play against the Party something infinitely more dangerous than the chicanery of the police and the reluctant revelations of militants who have played into their hands, namely, the disinterested purposefulness and sense of outrage of the sincere dissident. If the Party is ever to be brought low by provocateurs, it is this kind of thing that will create the relevant opportunity. From its own point of view, therefore, the Party speaks with strict accuracy when it denounces as provocateurs those who dare to challenge any emphasis of the Party line, or react to shifts in that line in terms other than those of unquestioning obedience. The Party, that is to say, knows what it is doing when it teaches its militants to regard the ideological recalcitrant as a criminal whom the organization must liquidate without delay.

This frame of mind results, of course, in a regime of ideological terror within the Party; and this, in turn, is the surest possible guarantee that every attempt to criticize the official line, or to think independently about doctrinal or even tactical problems, shall be nipped in the bud. In September, 1939, for example, Paul Nizan, foreign affairs editor of *Ce Soir*, conceives and publicly defends the notion of a "national communism." The Party promptly disavows him as an "agent of the police." [37] Sometimes, indeed, the dissident is discredited *before the fact* of his dissidence, that is, in anticipation of heresies that the leadership merely regard as *possible*—as when, late in 1941, there is reason to expect "patriotic" resistance to the new shift in the Party line. *Party Life* gives the potential dissidents the following foretaste of what is in store for them: "We must adopt a firm policy with those amongst us—if there are any such persons amongst us—who may try to hide their opportunism or cowardice behind so-called theoretical affirmations tending to discredit the activities of French patriots. Our Party would in no circumstances tolerate such affirmations." [38]

Provocation arising from bad habits, frailties, and corruption on the part of the militants is, as we have already indicated, another matter. Party members are duly warned against "pretty women who are generous with their favors": likely as not, they are seeking information about the Party's underground apparatus which they can include in reports to their employers.[39] In general, the Party tends to look askance at anyone who reveals a fondness for riotous living; most provocateurs, it believes, are men who have at some time been picked up by the police, and can be picked up again—perhaps for theft, perhaps on a "morals" charge, perhaps even for drunkenness. "That is why we must give a wide berth to young men and women who have formed bad habits. We recruit no gamblers, no hell raisers, no chronic offenders." [40]

The police know how to recognize and exploit both venality

and disillusionment—each of which, for the rest, tends to produce the other; and the Party does not need to be told that the Party member who has, for example, felt the heavy hand of the repression (or whose family has suffered because of it), is an easy prey to fatigue and discouragement. The moment comes, that is to say, when he asks himself: Why bother? Why not get back to normal living? But the first thing he must do in order to get back to normal living—or so he is likely to believe—is to regularize his relations with the police; and he soon learns that if he is to accomplish this he must first make himself useful to them. Just what the police will require him to do depends upon a number of variables, most particularly on how much evidence they have against him and how much they think he knows. The main point, in any case, is that once he has begun to do business with them he finds himself increasingly at their mercy. This is why the Party tends to hold at arm's length the militant who has just been released from a prison or a concentration camp. Since it has no way of knowing whether he has made a deal with the authorities, it must— even if he can prove that he "escaped"—make a complete investigation before it entrusts him with any responsibilities whatever. This investigation must "take into account, first of all, the militant's political position before his arrest, his present attitude toward the Party's policies and leadership, and his views on the Soviet Union, which is the avant-garde of the proletarian revolution. He must be required to submit a detailed report concerning his past activities, the circumstances in which he was arrested, his trial and imprisonment, and his release. This report must then be checked against the data supplied by his acquaintances or on file in the Party's archives." [41] For, even if the police have not attempted to enlist him as an informer, even if they have attempted and failed, they may have put him back into circulation merely as a means of identifying the persons with whom he proceeds to establish contact. In a word: "as a general proposition, the police let a man go either because they are using him, or because they hope he will lead them to militants on higher echelons." [42]

67, D. For the Party to fail to keep a watchful eye on points of contact between its militants and the machinery of law enforcement would be, quite simply, to invite disaster. Party members are accordingly lectured and coached concerning the attitude they are to adopt in case of arrest, and what they are to say and do from the moment they are taken into custody until the moment they are released. They are, moreover, brought to understand that the slightest departure from the course of action thus laid down for them will be regarded as treason to the Party.

The good militant can be counted on to keep a cool head when the police come to pick him up. "The militant does not lose his nerve. He is fully aware that he may, one day, be arrested; and when this finally happens it comes as no surprise." [43] Once in custody, he tells the police absolutely nothing about the Party's organization and activities, and, at the same time, laughs at the suggestion that he should disavow his Communist affiliation. "What we are saying here does not mean at all that the arrested militant should deny that he is a Communist. On the contrary. But he will regard it as a sacred duty to divulge no information relating to the Party's activities and organization—no information whatever. He will yield neither to intimidation, nor to flattery, nor to threats, nor to blows." The Party will, moreover, take cognizance of any indiscretions of which the militant may be guilty during such a testing time, and it makes no secret of the fact that it has a long memory: the author of such an indiscretion will one day "answer for it, both to his own conscience and to the working class." [44]

The good militant holds his tongue at the police station, and does his talking only when he is brought into court and is provided with counsel. [45] If he is sure that the police have no evidence against him that will stand up in court, he is free to deny his Communist sympathies and connections: he can and should profess complete ignorance both of the Party's activities and of its teachings.[46] The instructions for known Party leaders, as also for militants who have been caught *flagrante delicto*, run to the opposite extreme: they are to set a lock upon their lips as regards the Party's organization and activities, and are to take full advantage of the courtroom as a platform from which to "defend the Party's policies," i.e., they are to imitate the example of George Dimitrov, who "when he was tried at Leipzig called world-wide reaction into the stand as the defendant; he used the proceedings as a means of mobilizing the masses in all countries and of getting across to them the program and objectives of Communism; he thus made himself the accuser of his own jailers, and left them no alternative but to set him free." [47] Militants belonging to these two categories must, then, never remain on the defensive in the courtroom; rather they must seize the opportunity to "enter an all-out indictment against the capitalist system." [48] One difficulty here, of course, is that the militant's lawyer may insist upon his abandoning this posture, may even base the defense upon the alleged responsibility of "the Party's high-level leadership and its policies." [49] This must be avoided at all costs; and the militants are accordingly taught that they must never permit such a plea in their behalf—and, what is more to the point, that they must retain only counsel approved by the Party organization. In any case, counsel is to be entrusted only with the strictly legal aspects of the defense. The accused will himself assume responsibility for its "political" aspects.[50]

The Party regards renunciation of one's Communist convictions, whether at the police station or in a court of law, as a crime no less unpardonable than that of revealing information concerning its organization. "You must refuse to sign any statement condemning or disavowing the Party, its youth organizations, or the USSR." [51] The militant who has run afoul of the law must, above all, not permit himself to be persuaded that signing such a statement is an idle gesture which can itself be disavowed when the appropriate moment comes

—the more since the law-enforcement officers, in the hope of putting further pressure on him, will be telling his family that he will be freed if only "he agrees to sign a simple little statement disavowing the policies of the Communist Party." The police are interested in disavowals, the Party argues, merely as a means of undermining the morale of the militants they hold in their power. "We must not mince words on this point. If any political prisoner disavows the Party's policies, he will be publicly denounced for having made a deal with the enemy— that is, with the architects of France's hunger and oppression. This must be made clear to the prisoners' families, whom we shall always keep reminded of our active solidarity." [52]

The Party has, be it noted, good reason to concern itself about the morale of those of its militants and sympathizers who are in jail. For one thing, every prisoner whose morale gives way is a potential provocateur. For another thing, the political prisoners are, from the Party's point of view, an enormous store of accumulated capital, whose "maintenance" is a matter of prime importance. If the Communist press is to be believed, there are—between Party members and fellow travelers—no less than 100,000 potentially useful men and women in the prisons and concentration camps of the two zones; and even if—as seems probable—this figure is a bit large, the Party is fully entitled to regard them as a valuable reserve against the future in so far as it can keep alive their faith and their confidence in its own ultimate success. All this is no doubt in the leaders' minds as they write their *Letter to Communist Militants Who Have Been Jailed, Interned, or Deported:* "Take heart, comrades. The struggle will be a hard one. But the people will be victorious, and the red flag with the hammer and sickle will tomorrow wave triumphantly over France, and other countries as well. A world-wide victory for Communism is what the future holds in store." [53]

Political and Military Organization

68. From June, 1941, onward new tasks impose themselves: the Party, in order to give effective support to the war effort of the Soviet Union, must stir up a maximum of trouble for the occupation army and its "accomplice," the government at Vichy. The Party therefore redoubles its agitational activities, whose principal aim becomes, as we have seen, the instigation of a series of strikes designed to restrict and disorganize war production. It launches an intensive campaign for sabotage and the production of defective matériel. It attempts, under the banner of French unity, to organize mass demonstrations on such occasions as May Day, Bastille Day, and Armistice Day, and takes yet other steps to create an atmosphere of frenzied patriotism. During what we may call the "Soviet" phase of its aspirations and activities, the Party used as its mouthpiece a particular type of mass organization—the committees of the people; now during its "patriotic" phase it employs a new and notably more effective device—the National Front. But the most far-reaching of its adjustments to the changed situation is none of these things we have been mentioning, but rather this: the Party finds itself drawn increasingly into activities of a primarily military character, the aim of which, as we have seen, is to catch the German Army between two lines of fire. France, it decides, must have francs-tireurs who will fight with the same weapons and with the same determination as the "partisans" in the occupied territories in the east. *Terrorism* thus becomes, overnight, an important branch of the Party's activities.

This is not to say that the Party organization as such is mobilized for terrorist activity. Terrorist activity calls for units with highly specialized training, both psychological and technical; it can therefore not be entrusted to the undifferentiated mass of the Party's members. We must distinguish here, once more, between the two levels of Party activity. On the one the Party conducts its continuing campaign against the occupying army, foments latent resentments and channels them against that army, incites people to strike and to sabotage, and so on. The Party will be pleased in so far as all this bears fruit in the form of spontaneous action against the Germans; but the chief purpose is, clearly, to create an atmosphere favorable to deeds of daring on the second of the two levels—that is, to the recruitment and maintenance in being of a fighting force which, acting under orders, will execute specific, carefully planned missions. This fighting force is to consist of specialized elements, capable of extremely rapid action and brought together in an entirely separate and distinct organization. No documents containing reliable information on this organization are available—and this is hardly surprising, since the leadership are careful not to do anything that might betray its existence to the authorities. I have, however, had access to a classified circular of the Vichy Ministry of the Interior which is based on information about it gathered toward the end of 1941. It offers the following account:

Recent raids by the police have made it possible to identify and arrest several persons who have taken part in sabotaging factories, railroads, and French or German matériel within the occupied zone, or have made attacks on members of the German Army.

The documents seized and other information obtained in the course of these raids establish the existence of a terrorist organization, called the "Special" or "Secret Organization" (SO). The organization seems to comprise units on four levels:

(1). A central directing body. This body lays down directives regarding the choice and supervision of leaders on the other three levels, bearing in mind the fact that the latter *may soon be called upon to assume political and military responsibilities in the popular army that the course of events may call for at an early date.*

(2). *Regions.* Each regional organization consists of the following units:

(a) a personnel office;

(b) an information and intelligence office; the goal is to create a second bureau each of whose members will have a network of contacts in factories, cities, neighborhoods, etc.;

(c) an office of supplies;

(d) an office of operations under the direct supervision of the chief of the SO;

(e) a health office.

A political commissar and a military commissar is to be designated for each region; liaison with the Central Committee is, however, to be maintained by a single chief.

(3). *Sections. The section is an organ for controlling and coordinating the various groups (see 4). The section leader is alone empowered to determine the maximum number of groups which he is to lead. He integrates the various projects undertaken into a single plan.*

(4) *Groups.* Groups "made up of francs-tireurs" seem to be responsible for the carrying out of the various missions assigned. As a rule two units are assigned to each task; each of them comes to the place of operation at the appointed hour, but by a different route. One of them carries out the act of sabotage itself, while the other unit keeps watch and does not intervene except where absolutely necessary. If there are any wounded this second unit removes them in order to prevent their being identified by the police.

It has been found that all persons who have been convicted of acts of sabotage have connections with the Communist Party. The persons who are assigned important missions in the SO are, it appears, members of that party, and are thus in a position to use the underground network of the Communist Party in organizing the aforementioned "regions," "sections," and "groups." [1]

There is nothing improbable about the data contained in this circular. In so far as we are prepared to take their authenticity for granted, we are entitled to draw at least these two conclusions: (1) The Communist Party's terrorist activity is carried on by a special organization. (2) The structure of this organization parallels that of the Party itself.

The history of revolutionary activity (especially in Russia) over the past fifty or sixty years indicates that any political movement that undertakes military or terrorist action necessarily creates special organs and cadres for that purpose. These organs as a rule enjoy a wide range of operational autonomy, but at the same time are kept under the over-all control of the Party—or rather, since this kind of control is effected at the top levels only, the Party leaders. Thus the Narodniki and their successors, the Social Revolutionaries, created a special "fighting organization," and the Bolsheviks in the period preceding 1914 put special teams of "expropriators" in charge of gathering the funds needed for Party purposes. The same conspiratorial tradition pervaded the Communist parties of the Third International, where certain functions of defense, intelligence, and armament, in so far as they were undertaken at all, were carried on by separate organizations.

The situation here is much the same—though the reasons are different in the two cases—for a "legal" Communist Party and one that has been outlawed. The legal Party, if it entrusts forbidden activities to its own units, will find it difficult to disavow them when they are apprehended, and thus uses special units for such activities as a matter of course. But so does the outlawed Communist Party, i.e., it distinguishes between those of its underground units that engage in "normal" activities (agitation, propaganda, etc.) and those that perform missions involving obviously great risks (sabotage, espionage, assassination, etc.). For security reasons the members of the special organizations created for these latter purposes cease to maintain connections with the basic units of the Party: even the existence of such units is, in theory at least, unknown to most Party members. Within the special organization itself, contacts are minimized, so that the arrest of a single member will not give the police clues that will lead to further arrests. The members of the special units are of course almost invariably recruited from the general Party membership; but as soon as a member is taken into the fighting organization he must discontinue all contact with former comrades and move to another part of town or to another locality.

The Press

69. All Communist parties, whatever their status in the eyes of the law, engage to some extent in underground activity. Even, that is to say, where the law does nothing to prevent the Party's operating completely out in the open, the underground activities still go forward in an atmosphere of closely guarded secrecy—and, since they are regarded as indispensable to the conquest of power, must go forward in such an atmosphere. They are, in the main, activities relating to the Party's established technique for capturing power in a revolutionary situation that may present itself at some time in the future: shock units must be trained, strategic points must be identified and plans elaborated for occupying them, and so forth. They are, that is to say, activities which if brought out into the open would become pointless and self-defeating.

Lenin and his disciples were very clear about the need for combining legal and underground activity, and explained it in terms of the Party's commitment to destruction of the existing legal order as an ultimate goal. The Party may, where it feels that this goal can for the moment best be pursued by creating an appearance of respectability, adopt slogans and tactics appropriate to such an appearance; but this never means that it has ceased to plan the destruction of the existing legal order.

Misconceptions on the point we have just been emphasizing lead to serious errors of judgment on the part of many sincere and otherwise clearheaded anti-Communists. It is on the other hand equally wrong—and equally dangerous—to think of the Communist Party as *merely* a league of conspirators. A certain type of anti-Communist becomes obsessed with the doings of the secret branch of the Party, and tends to devote the major portion of his time and energies to ferreting out its actual or supposed "operations." The thing to remember here is that while the Party's secret branch enjoys a certain—usually very great—measure of *tactical* autonomy, its strategy is a part of the over-all strategy of the Party as a whole, is strictly subordinated to it, and is ultimately only as effective as it is. The Communist Party is a "mass" organization, and it succeeds or fails according as it does or does not win over and organize the masses. The road along which it makes the march to power is, that is to say, a road whose rule is the law of large numbers (from this it follows of course that the way to prevent that march to power is to block off its access to that road). The Party can rely upon its hard core of convinced militants only for its *existence;* for its *success* it must depend upon the support or at least the good-will of millions. Where the millions remain indifferent, the secret branch can accomplish nothing. That is why the French Communist Party, like all sections of the Comintern, values *political agitation* and *political propaganda* above all other types of activity.

"Propaganda," writes *Party Life,* "must occupy a prominent place in the activities of all Party organizations." [1] There is, for one thing, the spoken word, which however is of limited usefulness while the Party is illegal (as it is through most of the period covered by this book); also there is the written word, which, paradoxically, is the easier of the two with which to defeat the vigilance of authorities. During the period of illegality, therefore, the Party's printing, mimeographing, and duplicating equipment is its major treasure. It reserves the printing equipment for the special editions of its newspapers, for occasional leaflets to whose message it attaches exceptional importance, and for such of its pamphlets as are to be given wide circulation. But even this limited program overtaxes the secret presses at the disposal of the Central Committee and the major regional organizations, and constant use is made of the facilities of regular printing shops (by connivance with the owner or—more commonly of course—with the typographical workers) and material printed in Belgium or Switzerland through the good offices of the Communist organizations in those countries, then smuggled into France.

The police are constantly on the lookout for mimeographing machines, and of course confiscate any they find—besides which the supply of paper for mimeographing is strictly regulated by the government. The local organizations therefore reproduce most of their propaganda on duplicating machines, which can be improvised at home out of ingredients purchasable at any drug store; and the leadership directs attention to their virtues in terms reminiscent of capitalist advertising: they "take up little space, make no noise, and are easy to hide." [2] The center's major preoccupation, however, is with the paper shortage, which is acute even for individuals and organizations able to make open purchases. It urges the sections to do everything in their power to maintain reserves against the dreaded day when paper may become absolutely unobtainable.[3] It invites the militants to levy upon the paper supply of "the office, firm, or agency" in which they are employed.[4] And when this expedient proves inadequate, it proceeds to organize nocturnal raids on storage cabinets in city halls and other public offices. Increasingly, however, the Party and its organizations are obliged to employ propaganda techniques that make a little paper go a long way or, better still, use no paper at all: stickers, posters, slogans painted or scribbled on walls and billboards.[5]

Even after the paper and printing problem has been solved . for today's propaganda output, there remains the problem of getting it distributed; and the Party is always torn between two conflicting desires: to reach the widest possible audience; and to see to it that the police shall make no large hauls. As late as August, 1940, the normal procedure is still "open, large-scale" distribution of newspapers and leaflets in "the densely populated neighborhoods and along the approaches to the factories and railroad stations" [6]—that is, a large edition is distributed all at once to a large group of Party workers, some of whom do the actual job while the others look to their safety; where this is impossible, smaller groups are sent out under cover of the black-out. As the suppression of illegal propaganda becomes better organized, and the curfew and police patrols make it dangerous to be abroad at night, the Party is obliged to invent still less conspicuous methods of getting its propaganda into its readers' hands and to stiffen its security precautions. The instructions call for simultaneous printing of relatively small quantities at widely separated points (which not only reduces the maximum loss from any single police raid, but also holds down transportation problems), and for use of the largest possible number of distributors —which, besides cutting risks, "will make for wider and more rapid circulation." [7] Increasing amounts of material are sent, *faute de mieux*, by mail; and the center repeatedly emphasizes the need for constantly varying and improving the techniques employed.[8]

70. The Party Central Office cannot achieve its political goals unless it keeps the cadres well in hand, and maintains a close check both on their work and on their private lives. The Party, having enriched their minds with a doctrine and their hearts with a mystique, assigns to them clearly defined tasks which both train them in the skills it requires and test their claims to advancement. The Party may, from this point of view, be thought of as a blast furnace which either melts or hardens whatever is pushed into it. The heat in this furnace is controlled from the Central Committee, whose directives to the branches—on all subjects, including therefore propaganda and agitation, organization, and terrorist activity—are the Party's nearest approach to law. The leadership's principal channel both to Party members and to the masses is the Party press: *L'Humanité* for the general reader, *L'Avant-garde* for young people, *La Vie ouvrière* for the working class. These three papers—of which there are sometimes special local editions—keep up an uninterrupted flow of comment on current events, and it is to them that members and sympathizers, as also those responsible for minor propaganda functions, natu-

rally look for the Party line. There are, besides, numerous regional and local newspapers. (I counted thirty-eight between the end of June, 1940, and December, 1941.)

In general, however, the organization channels scant energies into these lesser publishing ventures: even those in the great industrial communities or in localities with solid Communist cadres (e.g., the Nantes *Avenir normand*, the St. Etienne *Cri du peuple*, the Lille-Roubaix *Enchaîné*, the Marseille *Rouge-Midi*, the Clermont-Ferrand *Voix du peuple*, and the Lyon *Voix du peuple*) appear only from time to time; the others are suspended after the first two or three issues. For reasons that are not always entirely clear, some of the Party's organs are revived now and then for a single issue, and are immediately suspended.

As we have often had occasion to notice in the foregoing pages, there are also publications, sometimes short lived, for this or that class or social grouping, and yet others devoted to some specific problem. *Worker's Life* is the nucleus of a whole cluster of trade-union papers. The Communist Youth publishes, besides *L'Avant-garde*, the theoretical organ *Notre jeunesse* and three newspapers for particular groups: *Jeunes filles de France* for young women, *La Caserne* for youths in the army, *La Relève* for students. There is a special Party newspaper for teachers, *L'Université libre*, which by December, 1941, is in its fortieth issue; and there are yet others for the peasants, the unemployed workers, the families of prisoners of war, the housewives.

71. The above data tend to convey a somewhat exaggerated idea of the imaginativeness with which the Party adapts its messages to various clienteles. The major impression one carries away from an examination of a representative sample for, say, any particular week, is one of unrelieved monotony: everything appears to have been written by the same pen; and the same tricks of phrase, the same arguments are made to do service indiscriminately for all purposes. When there is a change in the line, all the papers execute the change at a given moment, offer the same explanations, cite the same evidence,

reproduce the same quotes. This, be it noted, is one aspect of the rigid control from the center that we have noticed in other contexts. The center maintains the publication *Notre propagande* for the precise purpose of handing down model leaflets and handbills which are to be reproduced everywhere with at most minor variations for "local color." If the housewives of Sète and the housewives of Châlons-sur-Marne seem to talk much alike in their propaganda output, this is because both are copying from a model leaflet that their betters at Party headquarters have distilled out of their own wisdom. The farther away one goes from the center, moreover, the more one is struck by the resultant inflexibility: the organizations at the periphery must, above all, not be caught violating or misrepresenting the Party line, and they insure themselves against this by merely parroting the center's handouts.

XXIII

Party Finances

72. Numerous activities, large permanent staffs—these require abundant funds, only part of which are raised by the Party itself, the rest being supplied by the Comintern. A Budget Committee, attached to the Secretariat of the Comintern, each year examines requests for subsidies presented by the member parties on the basis of their respective plans and financial estimates. The Secretariat itself however here plays the role of a mere intermediary, as it does not have any resources at its disposal: the subsidies, which vary with the importance of the parties and the roles that they have been assigned within the framework of Soviet policy, are furnished by the Bolshevik Party of the USSR, that is to say, by the Soviet state. In principle, allocations are fixed for a year in advance, but supplementary allocations can be made later in certain circumstances, such as the establishment of a newspaper, an electoral campaign, a political drive of particular interest to the USSR, etc. The parties also receive financial aid through other channels: the Profintern (International Council of Red Trade-unions), the MOPR (International Association for Assistance to Revolutionaries in Other Countries), etc. Sometimes the Soviet state intervenes directly, without working through the Comintern, where the Communist movement of a country—for example, China in recent years—is an immediate instrument of Soviet diplomatic and political activity. None of the Communist parties created since 1919 has been able to get along without Soviet subsidies, even when there has been no ban on its activities. Some of them have been supported by these subsidies almost exclusively from the beginning, as is the case with the Communist Party of Great Britain.

When one of the parties is forced to go underground, as the French Party was after September, 1939, it must rely even more heavily on financial aid from Moscow, which accordingly tends to increase. Operating underground is costly and limits a party's opportunities for seeking public subscriptions. The militants of an illegal party must, if they are to elude the police and hold security risks to a minimum, be highly mobile: they must be prepared, at the slightest warning, to move to another address or even to another city; and they must not at such times be obliged to consult their pocketbooks. The costs of the printing and distribution of printed matter increase greatly: equipment must be replaced as often as it is seized by the police. The technique of illegal activity demands greater specialization, a greater number of "professional revolutionaries"; one can rely much less on amateur or part-time assistance from fellow travelers or militants who are gainfully employed. Finally, clandestine activity is a great "consumer" of manpower: the police take into custody large numbers of militants who, along with their families, must not be abandoned. In short, outlays increase, and local resources diminish.

The above considerations weigh heavily on the French Communist Party during the period here in question. A while ago, when it was operating out in the open on a basis of "semi-legality," the Party could expect to procure at the very least some supplementary resources through assessments and drives conducted by the local organizations: "Although a high percentage of workers are unemployed," writes *Party Life* in August, 1940, "it remains necessary to collect dues, though always with an eye to capacity to pay. . . . The sums collected must be carefully allocated, *bearing in mind always that one fourth of the total receipts should be forwarded to the central organization.*" The repression soon renders such questions academic, and the Party, toward the end of 1940 and the beginning of 1941, goes through a financial crisis.

In a circular distributed early in 1941 this problem is posed in the following terms:

Our expenses must be reduced. This reduction must not restrict either our means of propaganda (purchase of equipment, etc.) or our travel and communications; without these our organi-

zation simply cannot exist. Thus the entire weight of the re-
ductions must fall upon salaries. The rule by which our budgets
must henceforth be balanced, on all echelons, is the following:
one half devoted to propaganda outlays (purchase of equipment,
etc.), the other half to administrative outlays (salaries, miscel-
laneous expenses, travel, rent, etc.). As for our expenditures under
the general heading of solidarity [with the victims of the war and
the repression], the cuts we must make here are especially regrettable, for everyone knows that we have been expending our
funds carefully. . . . Draw up for us your proposed budget,
taking these observations into account, and we shall let you know,
by the next courier, what subsidy it will be possible to give you.[1]

We do not know to what extent this economy drive was
successful: the administration of the Communist Party, for
all of its authoritarian character, must reckon with the sort of
resistance that budget cuts encounter in all administrative
setups.

The Party supplied, along with the circular just cited, a
model monthly account to which the local offices must henceforth conform. According to this specimen account, for what
it is worth, the sum of local Party resources (dues, subscriptions, etc.) amounts to scarcely one third of the receipts and
covers but one fourth of the expenses incurred during the
month. Two thirds at least, perhaps three fourths of the expenses, must thus be covered by subsidies from the central
organization of the Party—that is to say, from Moscow.
After June 22, 1941, as the repression and the miltary and
terrorist character of Party activity begins to require greater
resources, this disproportion between the funds it finds at
home and those that come to it from abroad is necessarily
accentuated.

The necessary money can get to France through various
channels, even when the Soviet Embassy and certain obliging
banking institutions are closed. The frontiers are not water-
tight, besides which the Party's good relations with the Gaullists, plus the Anglo-Soviet alliance, allow it to maintain its
liaison with the USSR even in this field with no insurmount-
able difficulties.

XXIV

Personnel

73. An organization is as good as its membership: if its membership is inadequate, whether in number or in quality, neither good policy nor ingenious tactics will rescue it from impotence.

The Communist Party, which above all things wishes to affect the course of events, surpasses all other parties in the importance it attaches to the problem of personnel policy. It regards the problem, in the first place, as *political*—that is, as a problem with which the Party leaders must continue to concern themselves even when they delegate the routine functions connected with it to subordinates, and for which they therefore remain responsible. The following criticism, addressed by indirection to a regional secretary, puts the basic principle here as clearly as possible:

We are sorry to hear the secretary of a large region saying anything like this: "Since I have put someone in charge of personnel, I no longer wish to know who the comrades are who do the work; when I need a man or a woman for some job, I turn to the official I have put in charge of personnel." Can anyone possibly believe that the mere fact of having named a personnel officer—this is, of course, indispensable—discharges one's responsibility in connection with this problem? Not at all: the personnel problem is infinitely broader than that. *It is a problem for the whole Party.* Everybody in a responsible position must get to know the comrades who work directly under him. . . . A man in charge of a region must be familiar with the political capacities of his collaborators on the sector and section levels. He must have ready the "alternate" who is to replace him when he becomes a casualty or is ill; he must help his lieutenants to do likewise. The man in charge of personnel merely assists him in this task, and performs the many tasks relating to personal investigations and checks.[1]

The advantage that the Communists enjoy over the Socialists and, in general, over all other parties—an advantage that is sometimes able to offset their weaknesses in other respects—is in large part a matter of their peculiar handling of this problem.

74. The defeat and the exodus have, over several weeks, kept the Party's network in a state of complete disorganization.[2] "Little by little, however," says an official document, "the country dresses its wounds, evacuees are sent home, and life begins to get back to normal. The Communist Party resumes its activities pari passu with the general recovery."[3] "First of all reorganize the Party" is the watchword of the first instructions, those for June and July, 1940; and this means, primarily, finding and putting back to work the Communists being mustered out of the armed forces:

Each day witnesses the return of comrades who have for several months been in the army. They come back with the conviction—because of what they have seen—that the ruling classes have betrayed and sold out the country. They come back after having been cut off from the Party for some time, and in at least partial ignorance of its activities. We must, on all echelons, welcome these comrades as brothers, talk with them, explain to them the positions adopted and the tasks performed by the Party in the course of the events we have lived through since September, 1939. We must enable them to get acquainted with our propaganda material and other Party documents. Finally we must enlist these comrades for work as soon as possible, and see to it that they have no trouble locating the Party organization.[4]

The Party must, at the same time, intensify its recruitment of new members: it is primarily with this purpose in mind that it moves to a more "open" type of organization.[5]

75. "The needs of our Party for members," writes *Party Life*, "are limitless. . . . New organizations are being founded in which our movement must be represented. The National Front calls for a vast number of members."[6] There is, as it happens, no reason to think that the desired new members cannot be found: even at the height of the repression, the

Party has had no trouble picking up recruits. And, given a proper mixture of audacity and caution, it can continue to pick them up and, with a little time, make leaders of them:

A Communist leader worthy of the name must single out the best of the active members. He must help them in their development. He must adopt toward them an attitude at once critical and comradely, devoid of favoritism. . . . We need many members today; we shall need still more tomorrow; but we can always discover a trustworthy comrade qualified to fill this or that responsible post and capable of further development. . . .[7]

An organizational structure based on groups of three lends itself to the selection and training of new leaders, if only because it multiplies posts of responsibility. The decentralization which characterizes the new structure of the Party will "permit tens, hundreds of active members to rise to positions of responsibility after earning their spurs in the game of political leadership at the head of a group of three."[8] The essential things are to distribute and graduate the various tasks in such fashion as to utilize and develop all available capacities, and to avoid the "catapulting" of active members into "positions of too great responsibility." The Party is an army in which promotions are made on the basis of performance. "We need daring in our personnel policy," says the *Notebooks of Bolshevism*,

we need a bold policy of promotion, but, naturally, one that takes account of the members' present aptitudes and of their potentialities for development. We must not, in the hope of advancing them, give them responsibilities too heavy for their shoulders; still less should we prevent their being given a practical test in combat conditions by letting them jump over intermediate grades. To move a member up does not mean to pile task after task on his back, but rather to advance him from a task that he has discharged well to some more important post.[9]

There is only one way to reconcile these diverse requirements: keep an eye on each and every member as he goes about his work, and get to know him through and through. The Party must, then, maintain a simultaneous check on jobs and men, and measure the one against the other. Let us listen once again to *Party Life:*

Every man in his place, according to his merits, his capacities; bringing about this state of affairs must be the central preoccupation of all regional and cell leaders. . . . Each Party member must be put where he can yield the maximum return, and each Party member must be evaluated by all the others. . . . The only things that count are personal courage, political constancy, unshakable confidence in the Party and its leaders, personal initiative, enthusiasm for work, and ability to resolve problems. The minute scrutiny of the comrades who best fulfill these conditions must never cease.[10]

And yet again:

We must watch each post, and see whether the man in charge is up to his task—whether, that is to say, the comrade next to him is not more capable and bold, does not have greater ability for leadership. If such is the case, we must make the necessary change. All organizational work will thus be stepped up to a higher level of efficiency, and the man hitherto in charge will continue to do his best in some other position. As we demote members who show themselves incapable of performing their tasks, we will be advancing a multitude of young people who will display more initiative and enthusiasm. . . . There are responsibilities for every comrade. We have posts commensurate with every level of talent. We need talents commensurate with each of our posts. It is up to us to learn how to discover them, how to aid them in their development, and how to place them where they ought to be.[11]

Party Training and Party Mystique

76. The principle of "centralism" that dominates all the Party's activities is in no way inconsistent with the decentralization of Party structure to which we have repeatedly directed the reader's attention. Decentralization is the organizational expression of the Party's determination to make its presence felt in all spheres of the nation's life and in all the social groupings in which it is even remotely interested; which is to say that the Party is willing to multiply its groups and cells and committees because, purely aside from the increased security it thus achieves, it is able in this way to be in many places at the same time. But, as we shall see repeatedly in what follows, it keeps all the groups well in hand, so that wherever the Party's presence is felt the influence of the center is felt also. (The tendency toward structural decentralization is intensified during periods of illegality; but this is primarily for security reasons, and it is precisely during these periods that the Party tends to drop the term "democratic centralism" in favor of "centralism" tout court.)

The totalitarian movements of recent years have taught us, among other things, how easy it is for the leadership of a political party to place itself beyond control by the membership through the skillful use of mass rallies in conjunction with the seemingly contrary technique of "atomization." The leadership sees to it, on the one hand, that the members of the party are brought together now and then in great public demonstrations, where everything that is to happen is arranged beforehand, where reports turn automatically into harangues, and where the only possible audience reaction is unanimous applause. The individual, on such occasions, is simply absorbed into the mass: what *it* thinks and feels *he* thinks and feels. At the same time, lest these individuals come together elsewhere for purposes of collective thought and action, the leadership breaks the party up into numerous small and separate units. This, once it is accomplished, creates a situation in which no proposal can have greater impact upon the organization as a whole than the leadership wishes it to have.

The French Communist Party, imitating the example of the Bolshevik Party through the years since Stalin's accession to power, has developed the two techniques just described to a high degree of perfection, so that the position of the individual Party member vis-à-vis the leadership is, through the period covered by the present book, one of complete impotence. Some misguided militant may, to be sure, permit himself on some occasion the luxury of a doubt. He may even go so far as to work out in his mind a criticism that he would like to put forward. He may, if he is daring, even venture to utter this criticism to the other two members of his group of three. But the moment he begins to seek some means of communicating his criticism to comrades who are not members of his group he finds himself up against a blank wall. He is, furthermore, in no better position if the other members of his group agree with him: the group as a whole can communicate with other groups only through the headquarters just above it, which can be counted upon to sound the alarm. The all-powerful center then goes into action: it calls the dissident on the carpet, and either convinces or expels him. The Party can tolerate no opinions in conflict with those currently in vogue at the center, which accordingly itself defines the authority of all officeholders on all echelons, and sees to it that they command, in its behalf, all the channels of communication. The result, viewed from the standpoint of those at the center, is the virtual elimination of the element of surprise: the moment an infection sets in in some part of the Party's anatomy the center learns about it, and puts the Party's surgeons to work. The latter's instructions always are to amputate at a point well above the affected area.

Over against all this we must, to be sure, set the fact that the Party constantly calls upon its militants to develop "initi-

ative" and "responsibility," [1] and sermonizes them about the
virtue of "independent thinking." In both cases, however,
the militant is being asked to pack a suitcase for a trip he must
never make—for, to carry the metaphor just a little further,
travel is permitted within such narrow limits that what he
needs is an overnight bag containing a toothbrush and an extra
shirt. And the Party is likewise talking through its hat when it
inveighs against "bureaucratic methods of leadership" and
summons its officers to surround the militants with an atmosphere of "fraternal vigilance"; [2] for, however fraternal,
the vigilance with which the militants are in fact surrounded
is inquisitorial in the extreme, and takes the form of a relentless purge the moment there is any suspicion of heresy.

The Party in short assigns top priority to homogeneity and
cohesion, and thus exacts—over a certain area—automatic
obedience. On the other hand it does *not* wish to destroy the
militants' will to act—or the intelligence by which that will
must be guided; and it knows that too much automatic obedience will destroy both. The leadership, and under its tutelage
the militants themselves, must therefore strike a nice balance:
automatic obedience where automatic obedience is called for,
plus the intelligence and awareness that the Party's purposes
require; or, if you like, automatic obedience that subordinates
the higher faculties of the man and yet within certain narrow
limits develops them—though only to subordinate them the
more completely. The perfectly trained militant can be
counted on for this kind of automatic obedience; and the
task of the Party's psychologists and teachers is to produce him.

77. The skilled railway engineer knows which levers he
must move and how far he must move them in order to stop or
start, speed up or slow down his locomotive. The Party leaders
tend to conceive the ideal relation between themselves and
the militants in much these terms, i.e., in so far as the militants
are less than completely manageable, this reflects on their
skill, and sooner or later must pose the question whether their
jobs should be turned over to someone else. They therefore
strive constantly to bring about that ideal situation—partly by

prescribing, ever more minutely, the character and method of each militant's work, and partly by trying to synchronize simultaneous operations within the Party as simultaneous operations are synchronized in an up-to-date factory. Let anyone who doubts this pause to consider the following *Plan for the Organization and Activities of a Cell*, which is drawn up by the Central Committee in September, 1940 (thus during the period of "semilegality," when the Party is about to initiate its retreat from the "open" cells to the groups of three):

The cell is the Party's basic organizational unit. It is therefore imperative that each cell obey the following instructions to the letter:

A. The cell should have a maximum of six members. The resulting decentralization facilitates the holding of meetings. It also makes for improved division of labor and enables the Party to maintain a close check on each militant's performance.

B. Each cell is required to hold weekly meetings. The time and place of these meetings will be changed each week, and those who are to attend will be notified at the latest possible moment. Each meeting will adjourn at the end of 60 or at most 90 minutes.

C. The agenda for each of these meetings will be as follows: (1) questions relating to finances; (2) questions relating to the cell's operations; (3) questions relating to training and policy.

The secretary of the cell will work out a detailed agenda based on this outline, and will explain it to the comrades present at the meeting in clear and precise language.

Example: questions relating to finances (15 minutes). This will be the first item on the agenda. The treasurer must not fail to explain how important funds are to the Party, or to remind the comrades of their duty both to contribute to these funds and to collect contributions from the Party's numerous sympathizers. Everything relating to money should be taken up under this item.

Questions relating to operations (20–30 minutes). During this important phase of the meeting the cell leader, bearing in mind the Party's security regulations, should assign the members their respective tasks, and make all necessary explanations. Pamphlets; posters; slogans on walls and sidewalks. Display of map of surrounding neighborhoods; assignment of stations and streets to each member. Decision on the most favorable hour for performing each mission, *to be based on recommendations by the comrades.*

Questions relating to training and to Party policies (30 minutes). We must never forget that the cell is the Party's classroom, and that the comrades are expected to make a genuine intellectual effort to understand Party policy and Party tactics. The meeting should, to this end, discuss the Party's circulars, pamphlets, and newspapers. One of the comrades will offer a brief talk on current problems. Continuous study of the *History of the Communist Party of the Soviet Union (Bolsheviks)* and *Left-wing Communism: and Infantile Disorder.*

Comrades, the present situation—beyond any in the Party's history—calls for order, discipline, courage, caution. You must seek these qualities in yourselves.

Forward, comrades—to become the true élite of the people and the guarantors of the final victory.

Note: This note is to be read aloud at the cell meeting.[3]

Questions relating to training and Party policies, it will be noticed, fill from one third to one half of the time devoted to the meeting, which is further proof of the importance the Party attaches to this phase of its activities. But the phrase "understand Party *policy* and Party tactics" is highly significant. The Party wishes its members to possess a sense of the continuity and meaning of Party *policy*—as distinguished from the day-to-day *policies* dictated by tactical necessity. They are, however, to achieve this sense through a process of *assimilation;* and the words "talk," "study," and "discuss" should be read in that light.[4]

78. Let us look for a moment at France's other political parties of recent date. Their "militants" subscribe to a program, pay dues, subordinate themselves—to a greater or lesser extent, to be sure—to party discipline. Their relations with the party are, however, projected exclusively on the political level: they are expected to support the party's candidates at election time; they are called upon now and then to take part in a demonstration or a parade; but so long as they perform these clearly defined chores their other activities go forward without inter-

ference by the party organization. The party's influence, in short, does not extend beyond the threshold of their private lives.

It is quite otherwise with the Communist Party, whose militants are tied to it by bonds of a much more intimate character. The Party asserts control over every department of their lives, and recognizes no dividing line between the political and the personal. The militant, therefore, either subordinates himself and all his interests to the Party, or invites certain consequences that are sure to give him pause. The Party is a movement to which he belongs, a community in which he lives, and a way of life in which he participates. It is the supreme reality in whose presence all else fades into insignificance. His personal interests and his personal feelings count for nothing in so far as they conflict with the duties that attach to his Party membership.

The Party is, on this showing, less a party in the ordinary acceptation of the term than an ecclesia. Or, to put the same thing in another way, it possesses certain characteristics which Georges Sorel, when he found them in the socialist and working-class movements in their early days, regarded as repetitions of the mores and tendencies of the early Christian communities. The Party, like the "evangelical" socialism of which Sorel wrote, ministers to certain deep-seated needs—both of the masses and of their élites—which the socialist movement in its contemporary bourgeois phase neglects as a matter of course. Like Sorel's evangelical socialism, the Communism of the Communist Party is a *societas perfecta,* with its own values, its own hierarchy, its own structure, and its own mores—a society-within-a-society which regards itself as destined to destroy the society it is within. Your true Communist thinks of himself as already a citizen of another polity, as subordinated to its laws even as he awaits the time when he can impose them upon others. The Party is the model-in-miniature of the new society, and it is all the easier to recognize as such because that new society already lives and has its being over a sixth of the earth's surface.

The man who joins a French political party other than the Communist Party simply withdraws when that party's program takes a turn that he dislikes; and in later years he looks back upon his period of membership as a mere episode in a lifetime that would have taken approximately the same course if he had never joined at all. It is quite otherwise with the man who joins the Communist Party. His period of membership puts an imprint upon him that will never wear off, as one can see by studying the personalities and careers of both the bitter-enders and the renegades. (Alone among French non-Communist parties the Action Française appears to have had a similar effect on its members and sympathizers.) The Party comes to be at once the militant's family, his way of life, and his fatherland; and Party "spirit" comes to be his supreme value, which he must cultivate and nourish incessantly.[5]

While, therefore, the Party's documents frequently insist upon the "need for the fullest possible development of a spirit of initiative and responsibility on the part of each member," [6] they always hasten to identify initiative and responsibility with "Party spirit." Nor could they do otherwise without violating the basic tenets of "Marxism-Leninism": The proletariat is what matters, because its historical mission is to represent the general interest. The Communist Party, as the party of the proletariat, is the unique bearer of the proletariat's mission, as the proletariat is the unique bearer of the nation's mission and thus, ultimately, of the mission of all mankind; so that the Party, at the apex of the pyramid, speaks and acts for them all.[7] No further demonstration is needed, furthermore, to establish the Party's claim to pre-eminence: the lines of authority have been inked in on the chart, and are there for all to see. "The spirit of initiative and responsibility," observes *Party Life*, "that is to say *Party spirit*, is the distinctive quality of the Communist. He places the higher interests of the Party —that is, in the last analysis, the higher interests of the working class and of the toiling masses as a whole—above everything, including life itself." [8]

In the Communists' hierarchy of values, then, the Party

stands above class and still further above the nation. Party spirit may well coincide with national spirit, i.e., with patriotism; but when it does it is because the conditions under which the Party is fighting have taken this turn rather than that. Or, to put the same thing in another way, where Party spirit clashes with patriotism, the latter must give way; but there are some situations in which Party spirit *includes patriotism within it for the time being;* and at such times patriotism becomes one of the elements in Communist strategy. Devotion to the Party is the sine qua non of the Communist, and the man who is devoted to the Party is devoted to the Party's leaders, to whom he owes a "debt" that can be paid only with faith and obedience. The spirit of initiative and responsibility is, therefore, also identified with "unshakable faith in the Party and its leaders." [9]

The Role of Doctrine

79. The main emphasis, as we know, is upon the continuous selection of leaders under conditions of actual combat. Even this principle, however, is not absolute: the purpose, at any particular moment, is to create precisely and exclusively the leadership needed for the achievement of some specific objective, so that the leadership principle is itself a relative truth —a truth whose claims are measured from moment to moment by the yardstick of usefulness to the Party. This is the one yardstick from which there is no possible appeal.

The above considerations apply also to "doctrine" in the Communist scheme of things. It occupies a place of high honor in the Party's scale of priorities. But the claims of any particular doctrine to such a place are always highly provisional, and may be canceled at a moment's notice because the objective has changed.

The Communists are aware that even the meanest of men, those, for instance, who distribute handbills or turn the crank on the duplicating machine, have a deep-felt need for intellectual certainty. Like everyone else, they wish to be on the side of Truth; and because this is so the movement must, as it shapes the character of its militants, give them something to believe. The prescription, in short, calls for doctrine as an indispensable ingredient; but the amount of doctrine that goes into the beaker varies from case to case, the correct proportion being determined with an eye to the temperament and the intellectual or cultural level of the prospective militant. At no time in the months and years ahead must the militant be assailed by doubts; and this means that no windows must be left open on that floor of the building (again we vary the metaphor) that corresponds to thought. The militant who is capable of doubting while under fire may find himself incapable of fighting. He cannot

be counted on. You therefore give him, before the battle begins, the defenses he will need in order to resist the germs of
doubt. How? By vaccinating him—by inducing in him just
enough mild thought fever to immunize him against the more
severe forms of the disease. If the vaccination works, he can
be exposed to any amount you like of liberal culture—an
epidemic, if you like—without danger of infection.

The procedures utilized for this purpose are scientific in
the extreme. The men who train the Party's militants make
good—and constant—use of the findings of the sciences of
man, and they are crystal clear about their mission—which is
to produce the "professional revolutionary," who is capable
of forwarding the purposes of the Party and, through those
purposes, the purposes of the Soviet state. The "qualities" the
militant must possess, of course, are to a considerable extent
the qualities that other political and religious movements have
sought to develop in their members, but with this fundamental
difference: The Communists attribute no value to these qualities in and of themselves, or to the man who possesses them
merely in virtue of his possessing them. Intellectual capacity,
courage, probity, all the "virtues," in short, are estimated by
reference to the "interest of the Party," which is itself, of
course, entirely independent of virtue. Their definition accordingly runs in terms not of political ethics but rather political dynamics, and varies with the ups-and-downs of the
political situation.

The ability to think, for instance, is one of a long list of
"resources" which the ideal militant brings together in his
make-up; or, to be more precise, it is at one and the same time
a *resource* that the Party must have at its disposal, a *force* that
the Party must train, and a *danger* that the Party must keep
an eye on. In the closed world of Communist doctrine the
springs from which thought bubbles up are simply ignored,
and attention is fixed upon the "flow," which like the water
supply of an irrigation system must be directed and distributed.
Naturally, therefore, it becomes a world in which the "flow"
tends to peter out as the years pass. What thinking takes place

concerns itself increasingly with tactical problems, and the minds that do that thinking lose their capacity to come to grips with problems of principle. The Truth is one and, on top of that, easy to come by; all else is mere means, mere instrument; and the level on which a man demonstrates his inventiveness is, of necessity, the instrumental level. The problem the Communist sage must continually pose for himself, the problem for which he must always have a ready answer, runs in terms like these: The will of Stalin, as of this moment, is such and such. What must be done in order to subordinate men and situations to that will?

This calls of course for appropriate intellectual pabulum for the militants, for a carefully planned diet. The finished Communist must be, if not the one-book man, at least the these-particular-books man. A complete library for a Communist cell includes only three or four volumes, and can, in a pinch, get along with only one: the *History of the Communist Party of the Soviet Union (Bolsheviks)*, prepared under the personal direction of Stalin, and published—to the tune of several million copies—in many languages. As every non-Communist knows who has examined it, it surpasses all other books in intellectual dishonesty and contempt for facts; and the fact that it has become the *Bible* or, more accurately, the *Summa* of the Communist militant, is a datum of great importance for the man who would understand Communism. Not only must every Communist study it,[1] but study in this case means learn by heart; and having once learned it by heart no Communist is required to study anything else. In the rare case in which someone insists on more books, he is referred either to a couple of other volumes by Stalin (*Foundations of Leninism, Marxism and the National and Colonial Question*) or to certain works of Lenin (*The State and Revolution, On the Road to Insurrection, Left-wing Communism: and Infantile Disorder*); and this completes the list. Master this shelf of books, and you have what the Communists are pleased to call the Marxist-Leninist-Stalinist doctrine—a highly simplified and intellectually sordid catechism which requires no thought or effort on the part of the learner, and satisfies his "cultural" needs just to the point of sealing them off forever.

We must not be misled by the fact that the instructions to the militants constantly reiterate Lenin's phrase: "A revolutionary movement is impossible without revolutionary theory." Lenin would no doubt have understood this to call for the continuous development, within the revolutionary movement, of a corpus of theory; but that is not what the Communists understand by it today. Present-day Communist theory is something that you find all ready for you, cut and dried, in Party "manuals" and "courses of study." The Communist movement itself, if you like, goes forward on a basis of unending improvisation which excludes a priori *no* adaptation to circumstance that may become necessary. Not so Communist theory: it is a given, which all who enter the movement are required simply to assimilate; and the demands in this sense are by no means relaxed when the Party is driven underground and is obliged to leave its militants, for some purposes at least, on their own. "It is precisely during the periods of underground activity," we read in the *Notebooks of Bolshevism*, "that we must take advantage of our opportunity to perfect our mastery of the Party's theoretical and political teachings." [2] The Party's instructions on this point extend even to the methods to be employed: "Study groups of three persons are to be organized on each echelon; and the best-educated member of each group . . . will be required to read aloud and comment on such materials (newspapers, reports, bulletins) as have been forwarded by the Central Committee. . . ." [3] "Each leader, each member, however numerous his responsibilities, must force himself to devote at least one hour daily to study. Work on the first of the courses of study [about to be published] should begin at once; it should be performed pen-in-hand, that is, noting down the central ideas, the words and arguments that are not entirely clear, and the ideas—relating, for example, to our immediate situation—that occur to one as one reads. This scheme of methodical and concentrated study will fix the teachings of the course in one's mind; it cannot fail to develop the theoretical skills of the militant." [4] The course of study in question emphasizes that each Party official, after completing it in the bosom of his group of three, will "take in hand two other militants, and teach the contents to them"—with the result that the Party will have at its disposal "a vast number of tiny schools, whose every pupil will become the teacher of two other Communists." [5] The alternative, the course of study insists, is for the Party to "bog down in the mire of mere practicality." [6]

80. The truths revealed to Marx and Engels and their prophets Lenin and Stalin are not open to discussion: one merely keeps on verifying them by observing the facts of the objective situation. One grasps the truths and one forthwith understands, predicts, and controls the facts. The possessors of these truths, in order to fulfill their mission, learn the idiom of the various social groups that are to be drawn into the stream of the revolution, so that they may speak to them and communicate the message to them. But the flow, from point to point in this series, is all in one direction—from the truths, fixed for all time as of the moment at which they were revealed, down to today's faithful and tomorrow's recruits, never the other way. For your true Communist, revisionism and treason are different ways of saying the same thing, and doubt—even in the land of Descartes—is *one* sin that cannot be expiated. Orthodoxy in the sphere of ideas is the counterpart of discipline in the sphere of action. Neither admits of the slightest departure from the chalk line drawn by wiser and more gifted men; and if the militants are called upon to "think"—as indeed they are—it is nevertheless clearly understood that their thinking shall take place *within* certain clearly defined limits. The leaders watch over the doctrinal posture of their charges with a relentless fanaticism that the Holy Office has never equaled at any time in its long history.

Nor does the Party make any exception here of the intellectuals, who are, as we know, one of the groups that it wishes to draw into the stream. All Communist parties welcome the intellectual, and the French Communist Party more enthusiastically than any other because of his peculiar position in French society; but it is always clearly understood that he comes into the Party to learn, to praise, and to propagate the science of Marxism—not to contribute but to receive. If, because he "has not entirely got rid of his prejudices," he shows any signs of restlessness, he can be sharply reminded that Lenin's *Materialism and Empiro-Criticism* is "the sturdiest and most profound philosophical work of the twentieth century." [7] If he heeds the reminder, he can become an honorary citizen of the Soviet Union,[8] the last refuge of science and his only fatherland.[9] Nor will this be his only reward: he will receive the plaudits of the multitude from a balcony high above the street, and he will be decked out, on these public occasions, with robes tailored to conceal the chains—upon which his keeper, who watches from within the building, will give a sharp tug should his eyes wander off in the direction of any non-Marxist horizon. In a word, the writ of the law of centralization runs to him (and to what he once called his mind) —for all that he is permitted to take the bows that the men further up in the hierarchy modestly forego. If he proves eminently useful, to be sure, they will indulge his whims now and then, as the impresario indulges those of a leading lady who might, otherwise, sign a contract with another theater.

A New Kind of Party

81. The Communist Party is, then, a new kind of party, without precedent in the political and social history of France or of any other country. It differs from all other parties, past and present, in the character of its organization; it is animated by a different spirit; and it uses different methods. The Communists, indeed, say as much themselves: theirs, they insist, is a "party of a new type"—if for no other reason than because of the continuous process of "bolshevization" that goes forward within it. The difference will, in a word, become more pronounced in the future. The Party, conscious of the responsibilities that attach to its historical role, will with each passing day speed the bolshevization process in every way possible until, finally, it is ready to strike down the "enemies of the people." [1]

Such is the balance of political forces in France that if there were no party of the extreme Left it would be necessary to invent one. The French Communist Party is, on this showing, only fulfilling the need once fulfilled by the French Socialist Party (which, in its day, replaced the Radicals in the same way). It has maintained this dominant position on the extreme Left throughout the years since 1920—during the first fourteen of which, however, it was itself undergoing drastic changes. The years 1923–25, for example, were years of bitter struggle over the "bolshevization" issue, i.e., the local version of the battle then in progress within the Soviet Union among the men who surrounded Lenin. One of the stakes in that battle was control of the Communist International, already regarded as an important instrument of power—and thus of each of the "national" Communist parties. In France as well as in the Soviet Union the campaign for "bolshevization" was successful, but with this difference: it took the form of mechanical and unimaginative application of formulae imported from the

Stalinist group in Russia, so that its effect, both on the level of political understanding within the Party and upon the quality of its cadres, was by no means for the better. A genuinely Bolshevist Party is made up, in Lenin's phrase, of "professional revolutionaries" closely tied to the masses; and the French Communist Party, at the end of the period in question, was anything but that: its leaders were professional politicians and/or bureaucrats; its avowed policies tended, at one and the same time, to alienate the masses and to strengthen the Socialist Party and the CGT.

Only after 1934, more precisely, after its shift on the Popular Front issue, does the French Communist Party become capable of leading mass political action—that is, of stirring up social discontent and making it pay political dividends, thus showing that it has fulfilled one of the prerequisites of "bolshevization" by establishing contact with the working classes and the popular masses. The change does not go unnoticed outside France: At the VII Comintern Congress (August, 1935), for instance, George Dimitrov points to the French Communist Party's activities as an example for Communist parties in other countries to follow. And it does not go unrewarded inside France: The Party operates out in the open, uses "legal" methods for seeking power, like any other French political party. Its leaders are comfortably installed in Parliament, in the municipal councils, and in trade-unions. They not only run no serious risks, but occupy positions of profit and honor in French society—besides which they are gaining valuable experience both of the responsibilities of opposition and the responsibilities of power.

The Nazi-Soviet Pact and the outbreak of war in September, 1939, abruptly terminate this privileged position on the part of the Communist Party. In the course of a few days the ax falls on each of the numerous limbs it has put forth; and, for all that the roots are left untouched, the trunk of the tree is itself, as we have seen, badly shaken. It can be stated with complete certainty that, were France in a position to resist the May, 1940, offensive, the damage would be still greater—or, to put the matter more concretely, the Party would steadily be reduced to a small minority of sectarians because of public disapproval of the pact. From the very beginning, that is to say, the Party is the beneficiary of the fall of France, which saves it from complete extinction and sets into motion a train of events that speeds its "bolshevization"—first by making it learn to operate underground, later, particularly after June, 1941, by creating conditions in which, thanks to its neo-patriotism, it can pretend that its heart and that of the French people have a single beat. Nor is that all. The successive sharp changes in the Party line made necessary by that train of events provide valuable training for the Party cadres. Henceforth no other political grouping in France will be able to match them in flexibility and rapidity of movement.

The Party now becomes a "new kind of party" as regards its relation to its individual members, as regards the extent to which it functions as a self-sufficient society within a society, and, finally, as regards the degree to which its propaganda, its organizational structure, and its day-to-day behavior dovetail into one another. It casts off, in large part, its "petty bourgeois" tendencies. Such is the intensity of the repression that no one is likely to remain a Communist for the fun of it, or out of motives of sheer personal vanity or personal interest. The Party, that is to say, ceases to attract the well-born young man who, under the indulgent and world-weary eyes of his friends and relations, begins his political career in the remote reaches of the extreme Left and over the next years moves, in the traditional French manner, discreetly across the board to a point of unimpeachable respectability on the Right. The "parlor pink" still exists, but he no longer calls himself a Communist. The Party's new recruits are men and women whom the established order has not treated kindly, and this becomes increasingly true as the repression proceeds.[2]

Working underground calls for sacrifices none of which can be sidestepped. If one is a Frenchman, one is used to doing things by rote; underground, where one must always be a jump ahead of the authorities, doing things by rote is out of the question. If one is a Frenchman, one loves to chat and gossip; underground the rules demand a close mouth. If one is a Frenchman, one likes to see one's name in public places (this is true of everyone from the literary man who refuses to publish two miserable paragraphs without a by-line to the son of the people who carves his initials on a statue or a cathedral wall); underground the requirement is passionate anonymity, or, worse still, a change of name and identity whenever the heat goes on. If one is a Frenchman, one prides oneself on one's tolerance for weaknesses, vices, crimes even; underground, save as the interest of the party may dictate something different, one must eschew "decadent liberalism" in all its forms,[3] i.e., one must be intransigent, one must be tough, one must take on the habits, accept the constraints, make the choices appropriate to the new kind of man that is needed for the new kind of party.[4]

The Party's publications through this period give us a well-defined picture of this new kind of man which its personnel policy is calculated to produce. "The only things that matter at the present moment," one of them states in August, 1940, "are loyalty and devotion to the cause of Communism, to our glorious International, to our heroic Stalin, and to the USSR . . . The only things that matter are personal courage, political constancy, unshakable confidence in the Party and its leaders, personal initiative, enthusiasm for one's work, and resourcefulness in solving problems."[5]

The qualities listed in the above paragraph are, in point of fact, purely "instrumental," i.e., where a choice must be made between these qualities on the one hand and obedience to the Party and its leaders on the other, it is the former that must give way. We have already called attention to the limits placed, for example, upon individual initiative and individual responsibility, and, for another example, upon theoretical capacity. We must notice, however, that all this constitutes less of an absolute burden upon the militant than one might think. In French politics as a whole, everything goes: principles fade out of sight; programs quickly lose any concrete meaning they may have had at the time they were written. The average Frenchman stands at a political crossroads where all the signposts have been blown down. It is, therefore, easy for him to place himself in the hands of a party, any party, which knows where it is going—even if the knowing is done in faraway Moscow. And it is all the easier if this party is always prepared to tell him what to do next—and to see to it that he does it. The discipline of the Communist Party, the unconditional obedience it exacts, make it, for many Frenchmen, a welcome refuge from a way of life which, because it makes no demands, seems intolerably tame and enervating.

Mystical faith in the Soviet example—the example of the "victorious revolution" and of the "building of socialism in one country"—is what provides automatic before-the-fact justification for every shift in tactics and in the Party line; it is also what keeps these shifts from leaving a bad taste in the mouth. Once the militant, whether out of intellectual conviction or out of sheer party loyalty, has accepted the rules of the game, he soon acquires that faith and, what is more important, derives from it a kind of satisfaction he can find nowhere else. "Ours is a party," declares *Party Life*, "in which each individual carries a marshal's baton in his knapsack. Every comrade can aspire to the highest posts in the Party's organization, and it should, therefore, be every comrade's ambition to become more able, more responsible, so that he can serve our party and our country at his very best. Every member of the Party should realize that advancement and downgrading in the Party's organization depend on the quality of the work performed. He can rest assured that the Party leaders will take cognizance of his efforts and place him where his capacities can be utilized to the utmost." [6] Nor are these promises and assurances wide of the truth. If the militant renounces once and for all certain drives within him, if he allows a certain aspect of his personality to be stunted in the way the Party demands, he can count on making his way up the ladder at a rate that is indeed determined by the qualities he possesses and the results he produces. [7]

Those who underestimate the appeal of this characteristic feature of the Communist Party make a great mistake. The love of power is today endemic even in those social classes which, in other days, were least susceptible to its temptations. It drives men to run risks and to make sacrifices of which they would not otherwise be capable. The structure of the Communist Party recognizes this, and accordingly multiplies posts of command. As one rises in the Party's hierarchy, as one moves closer and closer to the center, one gets more and more power into one's hands. One exercises over one's subordinates a kind of authority that is far beyond that of the employer in the factory or the commanding officer on the battlefield. One can, furthermore, tell oneself that once the Party has won a place for itself in the country's politics, its leaders, perhaps therefore oneself, will exercise a kind of power that far exceeds that of a high official in the government—a power which derives from their status as the true representatives, *in partibus infidelium*, of a great state which is ready to back them up with its prestige and its resources.

The essential fact is that the bolshevization of the Communist Party has led to the creation of *a new kind of Frenchman*, almost without precedent in the previous history of the country. The process by which he has been created involves the simultaneous elevation and degradation of the human beings who are caught up in it—degradation because the principle that underlies the new qualities it gives to those human beings is a principle of death. The point to grasp, in any case, is that this new kind of Frenchman represents a sharp break with the social patterns hitherto dominant in France. The relevant specifications are taken from a blueprint imported from abroad.

Make no mistake about it, however: as far as dealing with the realities of the present world are concerned, this new kind of Frenchman is a marked man as over against the rest of the population, whose eyes are turned toward the past and whose hearts pine for the comforts of other days. He is being turned out by the thousands; and the repression of which we have been speaking in the present chapter merely hastens the pace on the assembly line. And make no mistake about this either: One of the most serious problems France will face tomorrow is that of what to do with its new kind of Frenchmen.

XXVIII

Recruitment

82. The about-face on June 22, 1941, obliges the Communist leaders to set aside their plan for the rapid conquest of power. Henceforth the Party's sole concern is to give every possible aid to the Soviet Union, which is in danger; and the appropriate short-term objective is not revolution but "*national* liberation." Hitherto, of course, the Party has been saying that France can free itself only by carrying out a social revolution. Now, it is to be the other way around.

Does all this mean that the Communists are writing off the conquest of power? Not at all. They will continue to think of themselves as contenders for possession of the government; but they will be obliged, from now on, to use a different set of slogans and to predicate these slogans on a different set of inducements. Yesterday the Communist Party was the only party capable of bringing the French people the peace and well-being they desire, and the argument ran in terms of the intimate relations between the USSR and the triumphant Germans. Today the Communist Party is the only party capable of leading the French people into the war they must fight against the occupying power, and this war is described as part of the struggle forced upon the USSR by German aggression. Revolutionary nationalism takes the place of revolutionary defeatism; and what the Party has been unable to accomplish by working *with* Hitlerite Germany it now proposes to accomplish by fighting *against* it. Its tactics, today and tomorrow as well as yesterday, are dictated by the requirements of Soviet foreign policy; and nothing short of the Soviet Union's losing the war, which with the first battle at Moscow becomes highly improbable, could prevent it from remaining mobilized in the service of that policy. The Kremlin, furthermore, will keep on deciding from moment to moment what form that service is to take. The Party's sudden rededication to French patriotism therefore tells us nothing about its long-term ambition, which is at all times the achievement of power in France at the earliest moment consistent with the intentions of the Soviet Union, from whose point of view France is always mere means.

Does this mean that there will be no Communist revolution in France unless the USSR needs one? Is a Communist revolution possible in France? The answer to both these questions will depend in the long run on the postwar situation in international affairs—or, more particularly, on Russia's power position in Europe and on the condition of France itself. There are, that is to say, various assumptions that we might make about the future international situation on which we might expect a domestic crisis in France to produce a revolutionary "conjuncture" that would result in a Communist victory.

One often hears it said, to be sure, that France's social structure is itself a sufficient guarantee against such a danger. Those who argue in this way are, it seems to me, the victims of the very mixture of chauvinism and unreflecting habit that makes France well-nigh impermeable to the lessons taught by world events—even when it bears their major impact. For, while I am willing to suppose that the composition and spirit of French society tend toward the maintenance of equilibrium and, if you like, toward the restoration of equilibrium once it has been disturbed, I must still insist upon the extent of the injury—both material and spiritual—that France has sustained in the course of the war, the exodus, and the occupation. I must insist particularly on the vast number of people whom these events have uprooted, and on the extent to which they have "proletarianized" the countless men and women who are today living in conditions of insecurity that consume all their energies and exhaust their patience. They live from hand to mouth, and the future promises them nothing.

As this chapter is written (1942) the frustrations of the French people are as the sands of the sea. Their national pride has been deeply wounded by the occupation. Their economic difficulties, the food shortages especially, cramp their lives— leave them, in point of fact, nothing to do but to mark time; and these difficulties are resented all the more because they are regarded as unnecessary, which is to say, arbitrarily imposed on them by the Germans. Their "idealized image" of themselves is being trampled under foot by a regime which repudiates 1789 and proscribes the Republic. For the moment, their frustrations merely paralyze their will. But who is to say what kind of aggressive behavior those frustrations will produce tomorrow?

Two distinct factors are at work here, both of which might well help to produce a Communist revolution. The storm, as we have noticed, has swept away the moorings upon which millions of Frenchmen have been accustomed to depend for their security. That is one factor. The other is the sudden increase of social distance between individuals and between families and the sudden projection of the problem of social distance upon new levels—mainly because money has come to play a decisive role in French life to which Frenchmen simply do not know how to adjust themselves. This last is not, I hasten to add, a matter of subordination to money as such. In France as elsewhere money has been in the past a sure guarantee of prestige and, if you like, of privilege. Today it is that and a great deal more besides: for its power now reaches into the tiniest details of one's daily existence. Those who have little or no money cannot so much as count on keeping themselves alive; and differences in living standards, which yesterday were differences between points *above* the level of mere subsistence, are today differences between points some of which are above, some of which are far below, that level. And because this is true, the new situation is one in which money is a powerful agent of disintegration; for it carves out chasms where a while ago there was good solid earth.

One disquieting possibility that we must consider in estimating the likelihood of a Communist revolution in France is this: All successful revolutions can be traced either to abdication or incompetence on the part of the so-called ruling classes. Revolutions, that is to say, have their opportunities created for them and are, therefore, in an important sense *made from above*. The French Communist Party has eagerly sought, ever since the Armistice, to convince the French people that the "leaders and political parties of the middle class have made a mess of things." [1] The Party knows, in short, that if it can discredit the likeliest present-day candidates for future political preferment—the Gaullists and Socialists in particular —the chances of the French people's rallying behind *it* will be enormously increased. The impotence of the Vichy government is a great asset to the Communists in this regard, because it helps to create a mood of insecurity and thus of anxiety that may ultimately drive all classes of French society to demand a change, however costly, that will relieve the present unbearable tension. It was such a mood—half frustration, half abdication—that made possible the triumph of Bolshevism in Russia and Fascism in Italy. We must remember, too, that where such a mood prevails the balance of political power can shift, with astonishing rapidity, in favor of that political party which is able to convince the bandwagon riders of its strength.

Some writers believe that even if a Communist revolution were to occur in France it would be quite unlike the October Revolution in Russia. I am myself prepared to suppose that the French Communist Party will, if and when its moment comes, make every effort to keep "legality" on its side. Was there ever a revolution that did not? The Revolution of 1789 could not have done without Louis XVI. The "march on Rome" of October, 1922, could not have done without Victor Emmanuel's appeal to Mussolini. [2] Hitler insisted upon—and obtained —Hindenburg's blessing. It would be difficult to think of an exception to the rule suggested by these examples, for the Bolsheviks themselves were glad to point to the Soviets as the "legal" source of their authority, and finally—though they dissolved it very soon—convoked a Constituent Assembly.

But this does not settle, or even illuminate, the point at issue.

Once a Communist government has won power in France, no one, whether from inside or outside, will be able to prevent its following its natural bent, which is that of continuous "radicalization" of a kind that inevitably brings to power whatever group or faction happens to be offering the most extreme proposals. This is the grain of truth in Trotsky's theory of "permanent revolution" (which like everything we have from his pen is abstract and rigid to a fault); it is also one of the insights Marx and Engels gained from their study of the French Revolution and their experiences in Germany in 1848–50. The piecemeal "nationalization" that will be promised in the economic program on which the Party will come to power will lead, rapidly and as a matter of course, to state control of the entire economy, including agriculture—or rather, since the rural regions will automatically provide the operating bases for counterrevolutionary activities, especially agriculture. The French "dictatorship of the proletariat" will, like the Russian, speedily become a dictatorship of the Communist Party and thus the architect of a totalitarian regime. Legal formulae may, for a time, be stretched to cover what is happening; but the final result, regardless of the wishes and intentions of the members of the first Communist Cabinet, is easy to predict.

Nor is there any reason to believe that the methods of the French Communists, once they were in power, would be other than ruthless and violent to an extreme. The Bolsheviks took power in Russia after a revolution that involved almost no fighting and bloodshed. The massacres and physical destruction that accompanied the civil war belong, therefore, to the period *following* their assumption of control; and it is a matter of some interest that their tempo increased in proportion as the Bolsheviks ran up against stiffer resistance on the one hand and economic failure on the other.

83. I have suggested above that without the USSR the French Communists would be helpless. By this I mean that in the absence of direct aid from the Soviet Union, and the strength that accrues to it from the false picture of the Russian

experiment that its adroit propagandists present to the French
people, the Communist Party would have grown far less
rapidly—and would have done notably less harm. It is, to that
extent, an essentially "foreign" or "alien" party—a point
which, stated in this way, cannot be overemphasized. At the
same time, however, it is *not*—and this point cannot be overemphasized, either—a mere importation; and its existence is
not a mere accident of French history. Rather, any complete
explanation of its presence in France and of its remarkable
growth must run, in large part, in terms of certain characteristic features of French society which lend themselves to
exploitation by the possessors of the Soviet myth. These I
shall now proceed to discuss *seriatim*.

a. *The general "drift to the Left" of French politics and
thus of French political parties*. This phenomenon, to which
Charles Seignobos and André Siegfried were already directing
attention many years ago, is not, curiously enough, the result
of any marked "radicalization" of the French masses. Despite
the war, the inflation, and the economic crisis, and despite the
impact of all three on the several groups that make up French
society, the "average Frenchman" is no more "Red" today
than he used to be. He has, however, a greater need to rebel,
to kick over the traces, than he used to have; and the country's
traditional political parties do not minister to this need because they appeal to him with symbols that he no longer finds
meaningful. The typical Frenchman, for all that he may adapt
himself to the realities of life as he goes about his business from
day to day, rejects them to a greater or lesser extent as he casts
his ballot—rejects them, furthermore, in terms of a stubbornly
held basic philosophy which is the constant that underlies (and
in a sense is the cause of) the frequent shifts in the relative
strength of the several parties. There is, as a matter of fact,
considerably greater continuity in French politics than these
shifts would seem to suggest.

From this point of view, the Communist Party has come to
occupy a position which, for most people, used to be filled by
the Socialist Party. Why, for instance, is the electoral strength

of the Communist Party so little affected by its internal crises and its tactical blunders? The number of cardholders fell from 88,187 in 1924 to 52,372 in 1928; but the number of votes the Party polled rose over the same period from 875,812 (9.69 per cent of the total vote) to 1,063,943 (11.37 per cent of the total). These, and more recent data as well, indicate in my opinion that—leaving aside minor fluctuations—there is a solid body of French voters who remain loyal to the Party and its slogans regardless of the policies it is supporting at any given moment. This phenomenon cannot be explained in terms of Party discipline, because it persists even at moments when the Party is losing members. The correct explanation is that—whether because of its own efforts or because of the shortcomings of the other parties—the Communist Party satisfies certain continuing needs that no student of French society and politics dare ignore.

b. *The ever-increasing—and excessive—incidence of discontented and rebellious members of society.* This, I believe, is demonstrably the result of secular trends, and is ultimately independent of, though certainly exaggerated by, the war and the occupation. Its connection with the existence and success of the Communist Party in France is *not*, I hasten to add, direct or simple, and for this reason: In the absence of the Party's methodical and unscrupulous exploitation of the causes of discontent it would not produce Communists (i.e., it provides the occasion for, but does not itself bring about, Communist successes).

c. *The existence—again as the result of trends inherent in French society—of a large "Lumpenproletariat"* whose members support the Communist Party whether they join it or not. Perhaps the crucial point here is the apparent incapacity of the existing order to reabsorb these elements, which may accordingly be accounted a permanent asset of the Communist Party. We must notice, however, that the Party does not rely upon them for its major support, which it is always careful to find among the industrial workers. This brings us to my next point.

d. *The existence within French society of an "advance*

guard" of the proletariat from which the Party can draw its ablest members. The Party of course likes to explain its success on the grounds that it defends the "interests" of the working class; and there is a sense in which it does defend those interests. It *does* midwife (though it subsequently exploits) working-class demands. It *does*, in backing up these demands, vigorously play the champion's role that the other parties, wisely or unwisely, fail to claim for themselves. It *does*, when another party seeks to claim this champion's role, outbid it. It *does*, in this way, maintain close contact with the workers. But this is not the aspect of Party strategy that wins it its hard core of militants, who are notoriously drawn from the least necessitous elements of the working class, i.e., from an advance guard who do not need to have their interests defended in the manner just described. They are men who, in large part because of the relatively *high* standard of living they enjoy, have developed a relatively high degree of awareness vis-à-vis the social and economic situation in which they are caught up. They are men who have come to recognize the "alienation" of the working class from French society—that is, the fact that the workers, under the French capitalist system, are treated as a commodity. They are men who have gained insight into the necessity of escaping from the position of inferiority that alienation implies, have sensed the central importance of the question of property and the question of power, and have caught a glimpse of the values that may one day restore meaning to French life. The influence of the Communist Party, to be sure, tends to dissipate rather than to develop these insights; but that does not alter the fact that the Party has strong attractions for the men who possess them, and is able to recruit considerable numbers of them. Participating in the Party's activities, coming to know the Party's methods, undoubtedly tends to weaken their allegiance to it once they are inside; but even where this occurs the Party continues to benefit from their inability to distinguish between itself and the vision that was awakened (or at least sharpened) within them when they first entered its orbit. The Party, in short, knows how to play upon their hopes and anticipations concerning the future dignity of man, and while it puts those hopes and anticipations to work for ends that are not really theirs, it keeps them convinced that their fidelity to it is fidelity to what is best in themselves.

84, e. *The strategic position of the intellectuals in French society*. In French politics the intellectuals are the pinch of parsley you add to every sauce—which is to say that just as our boards of directors co-opt people with aristocratic names, our political movements seek men with established reputations in the arts and sciences. Why should this be an advantage for the Communists? An adequate answer to that question would run to book length—not because of what we should have to say about the Communists but because of what we should have to say about the intellectuals. But here, at least, are some of the main points such an answer would necessarily include:

(1). The French intellectual of our time is, for one thing, weary of not being able to take sides on the big problems of modern society. He is, for another thing, eager to shake off his feelings of inferiority in the presence of the man of action. The role he has been trained to play is that of doubter, that of constant readiness to reopen any question, that of never permitting oneself any save the most tentative conclusions. The Party offers him, and he gratefully accepts, a dignified way of escaping from this Sisyphean chore. Taking orders from the Party's leaders, knuckling under to Party discipline, gives him a welcome taste of *certainty*. Or, to put the same thing in other words, the Party so to speak enables him to play hooky now and then from the tiresome commitments of the laboratory or the cubicle in the library. How else explain the now familiar spectacle of the man of learning, the tried and tested man of learning, mind you, who would not think of offering an opinion on this or that novel problem in his field without conducting thousands of experiments, but employs the intellectual procedures of the corner grocer when the question put to him is whether Trotsky was an agent of Hitler or whether the Stalin constitution is indeed the world's "most democratic" constitution?

(2). The French intellectual, especially the man of letters, likes to be patted on the back; and as a Party dignitary he sees his name in the papers and, better still, discovers in himself an orator capable of evoking wild applause at great public meetings. As he looks out over the sea of honest faces and hears the clapping of hands he thrills with pleasure, and knows that the tribute to his eloquence and logic is spontaneous— and deserved. Once he has got a little used to this sort of thing, he finds he cannot do without it; he is, therefore, careful not to cut himself off from those who issue the invitations; and soon, oblivious of the responsibilities that attach to his station in society, he is signing pretty much any manifesto or declaration that is put in front of him. The Party, far from asking him to give up his position at the university or the institute, encourages him to have it both ways. If he were to give it up, would he not lose the title that makes his signature valuable?

(3). The French intellectuals have, on the record, proved highly susceptible to the attractions of the Soviet Union and of Marxism, and therefore turn without much urging to the party that speaks in the name of both. This susceptibility can, perhaps, be traced to their predilection for general ideas and their fondness for schematization; so at least one would gather from the kind of thing they end up saying and doing about the Soviet Union and about Marxist philosophy. They concentrate their attention on the "planned society" aspect of the USSR, and, even before they come to the Party, are hardly less eager than the Communists to brush aside, as "mere details" or as "problems that will solve themselves in due time," everything that tends to cast doubt on the success of Soviet planning. What apparently strikes their fancy in Marxism is its emphasis upon offering a simple explanation for everything— the self-same aspect of Marxism, be it noted, that wins it prestige among the workers. The intellectuals, quite independently of urging by the Party, labor mightily to return Engels' compliment: where Engels sought to show that the sciences contain "proofs" that the natural world follows the laws of the dialectic, they seek to show that Marxism contains the "philosophy" of their particular disciplines; and here also they are eager to ignore any inconvenient data.

The central point, however, is the intellectuals' yearning to be in the swing of things along with the man of action, and —let me say it once more—to share with the man of action the luxury of a clearly defined goal about which one has ceased to ask questions. The central point, in other words, is an unwillingness to pursue the search for truth along the steep and rocky road which, as we know, alone leads to it; and this unwillingness is now sufficiently widespread among them to assure a steady flow of France's best-trained minds into the Communist Party.

XXIX

The Psychology of Party Membership

85. The Communist movement, though from some points of view a world all to itself, is like a great river, fed from remote places by dependable tributaries, and swollen by innumerable objects which it tears loose from their moorings and carries along with it. Different people are caught up in it for different reasons, and A's reasons are by no means always compatible with B's. Each recruit, that is to say, has his own motives, reflecting his own loyalties and his own interests, and the Party's task is to provide for him *and* his fellow members a common denominator, a tie, that will somehow hold them together. The man who joins out of devotion to an ideal, the man who joins because he has been overwhelmed by unanswerable arguments in a book or at a dinner party—these and others as well must be kept working together in the common cause, and with at least that minimum of satisfaction that will keep them from "breaking." Sometimes the trick cannot be turned—a fact which is reflected in the continuous turnover in the Party membership. This, however, tends to disappear during emergencies, when, in the Party as in other organizations, the real or potential external enemy or threat acts as a unifying agent.

The permanent solid core of trained militants, however, is little affected by the day-to-day changes in membership and tactics. The Party could not survive without them, and it well knows that in the long run it is no stronger than their loyalty to it. They occupy the strategic positions in its organization, and the Party's constant preoccupation with "sound" personnel policy reflects its determination to choose them wisely. This policy, as we have already intimated, uses devotion to the Party as its major criterion for deciding whom to promote, and is itself, therefore, an effective means of evoking such devotion. The purpose of the present chapter is to set forth the psychological insights upon which the policy rests.

Let us, to begin with, examine the act by which the individual becomes a Party member. This act, as we have emphasized at several points in this book, is analagous not to the act by which one joins other political parties but to the act by which one joins a church, i.e., while it is not necessarily irreversible, it binds the individual, for so long as he remains a member, to a *way of life*—a way of life, furthermore, so different from other ways of life that no man can make the adjustments necessary for it without giving up, in most cases once and for all, a part of his personality. Once the adjustments have been made, therefore, one does not break with the Party save as one is prepared to rebuild one's world and one's "self."

This, incidentally is why the Communist movement tends to thrive in societies whose members are no longer held together by the bond of shared moral principle and purpose, rather than in societies which, like Great Britain, have demonstrated their capacity to effect far-reaching social and economic changes and yet retain or even strengthen that bond. In societies of the former type men tend to divide off into clan-like groupings whose very raison d'être is their repudiation of the ideal of unity over a wider area. The citizen, unable to relate himself meaningfully to the broader constituency, that is, the nation, seeks and finds his "community" in one of these lesser groupings, of which the Communist Party is merely the extreme instance. And having found it, as every Communist who lasts the first stages of the course does, he will not lightly withdraw from it.

This aspect of the Party's role in France cannot be emphasized too strongly. However up-to-date its organization and tactics, the Party ministers to its members' primitive—or, if you like, basic—need to *belong*. The unity of the Party is, in sober truth, the closely knit unity of the primitive clan; and like that unity it has "magical" sanctions, so that breaking with the Party involves committing an act of sacrilege.

86. The Party, then, includes an irreducible minimum of

"regulars," of Lenin's "professional revolutionaries." These are the backbone of the Party; they give it continuity and set its "tone." Above all, they keep control of the center, where the decisions are made that must be carried out at the periphery. They are the Party's bureaucracy, which has more than its fair share of the shortcomings of all bureaucracies. Orders from the center constantly denounce "lack of initiative" and "fear of assuming responsibility," and constantly punish those who, by showing too much independence, have got themselves suspected of heresy.

The Communist bureaucrat, equally with the ordinary Party member, dreads above all things the danger of getting out of step with the Central Committee. His task is to carry out the orders he receives, however foolish he may consider them and however little he may understand the reasons for them. No opportunity is offered for discussion, and thus, in theory at least, the question of divided counsels does not arise. When, despite the elimination of nonconformists by means of successive purges, divided counsels do appear, the dissidents are either brought into line or expelled; and what usually happens is that they are brought into line.

In this respect, the role of personal interest as a factor making for Party loyalty is far greater than one would think, for, admittedly, the facts appear to suggest that the Party, in planning the hard and dangerous life of the militant, makes no allowance for any such interest. We must remember, however, that the Party official, in accepting his post, withdraws from the activity at which he has hitherto earned his living, and breaks off most of his normal associations. In doing so he becomes, to an extent that most of us would find it difficult to imagine, *dependent* upon the Party. This is, I hasten to add, by no means a matter of the modest salary the Party pays him, but rather of the freedom from a routine which he remembers as having offered him little or no opportunity for personally creative work—a matter, in short, of his membership in a social class which, in his eyes at least, is well above that which he has left. Withdrawing from the Party is thus a step downward, a personal defeat whose penalty is renewed subordination to the laws of the work-a-day world. Few militants can bear the thought of the adjustments that subordination would impose.

The Party, for the rest, is like a state within a state. It is not uncommon, in countries that have strong Communist movements, to see a Party leader who is a more powerful man by far than any mere Cabinet minister, and who, when the occasion demands, negotiates with government representatives—directly or indirectly—in an atmosphere not unlike that which surrounds negotiations between two equal powers. Why not? He can bring pressure to bear upon the government if he is not conciliated. He can order demonstrations in the streets, or call the Communist-controlled unions out on strike. He is a force to be reckoned with. This state of affairs is repeated on every echelon of the Communist movement: save when he looks upward, the leader on each level is lord of all he surveys; he disposes of the very lives of the men he commands, whether they be thousands of Party militants scattered throughout a "region" or two comrades in a tiny cell. The Party, in a word, ministers to the militants' lust for power, offers them an opportunity that most of them could not find elsewhere for exercising leadership and developing their personalities. And once a man has acquired a taste for power, he cannot deprive himself of it without suffering a comedown that will prove well-nigh intolerable. One does not withdraw from a race of rulers, a race of men who rule over small things today and will rule over great things tomorrow. Slipping back into the amorphous mass of hewers of wood and drawers of water is unthinkable.

In order to be indifferent to the considerations we have been summarizing the militant would need to be a man of high principles indeed, and this, again if he survives the early stages of Party membership, he is unlikely to be—even if he is the kind of militant who was originally driven into the Party *by* his high principles. Within the Party, he is taught to think less and less of the final goal and more and more of the means by which it is to be realized—until finally the latter wholly monopolize his attention. The time comes when certain symbols, most particularly the "Party" and the "USSR," become absolutes, to which the militant's automatic response is obedience, and about which he ceases even to ask questions. He learns, as Lenin's formula demands, to regard anything that "serves the revolution" as ipso facto morally right. He learns, too, how this formula can be stretched to cover, or even glorify, lying and bad faith and crime. High principles merely get in the way of the man who has learned these heady lessons, and because they get in the way they must be put aside.

XXX

A Foreign Nationalist Party

87. The French Communist Party, founded as recently as December, 1920, must not be regarded as the lineal descendant of nineteenth-century French Communism. It was a creation de novo, the product of forces set in motion by the war and the Russian Revolution; and its ties with the Soviet Union —as students of the subject too often forget—have existed from the very earliest moment of its history.

The Russian Revolution, while it did not produce the chain reaction of "proletarian" revolutions elsewhere that Lenin had expected, did radically transform the character of the working-class movement in certain countries—of which France is one. One way to put it is that the masses in these countries—for all that this did not express itself in positive action—soon came to regard "doing as they have done in Russia" as the only feasible long-term solution of their problems, and largely abandoned their traditional search for new "national" methods of improving their political and social position. They became convinced, that is to say, that in so far as their problems were going to be solved at all they would be solved through an expansion of the Soviet experiment, and that nothing was to be gained, meantime, by canvassing other possibilities. The result? A simultaneous *acceleration* and *impoverishment* of revolutionary trends that can, like it or not, be attributed to the direct influence of the October Revolution. The result in France? The founding of the Communist Party, and the draining off from the French Socialist movement of the energies that might, through the years after the war, have given the country a second Great Revolution along the lines of its first.

Every great movement that looks to the transformation of the existing order must have its "utopia," i.e., its picture of the new world it is striving to create. Sometimes the utopia is situated in the past, and the movement's task becomes that of keeping green the memory of a lost "golden age." Sometimes its locus is the more-or-less remote future. Sometimes, as with the Christians, it lies in both directions, so that yearning for the "lost paradise" of yesterday is combined with hope for the "kingdom of God" of tomorrow. The Communist movement is unique in that its "utopia" is simultaneous with itself, is, so to speak, visible to the naked eye of those whom it inspires. This is its—and thus the French Communist Party's—greatest strength; and because that is true the ties between the Party and the USSR are indispensable to its continuance as a major force in French politics. Without them it would be obliged either to come to grips with the immediate problems of French society, or to make its appeal frankly in terms of a utopia off somewhere in the future. In the first of these two cases, it would find itself competing on more or less even terms with other French parties, and would enjoy only such support as its concrete proposals could command. In the second, it would subside into other-worldliness and futility. In both cases it would lose much of its present inflated following. Because of the USSR, in short, it can have it both ways, and enjoy the immense advantage that having it both ways confers upon any political movement whose opponents do not force it to choose. The USSR is simultaneously the point of departure of the French Communists, their destination, and the road that leads from the one to the other.

There is a second sense in which the French Communist Party is dependent upon the USSR. It, like the Communist parties of many other countries, receives urgently needed material assistance from the Soviet Union, mostly but by no means exclusively in the form of financial grants-in-aid. The absolute size of these payments is often greatly exaggerated. But this does not entitle us to go to the opposite extreme and ignore their relative importance, i.e., the things they enable the Party to do that would, in their absence, be quite out of the question. One sees their effects most clearly during the

Party's "difficult periods," when every man's hand is raised against it: its organization keeps right on functioning, its newspapers keep right on being published, on a scale that would be unthinkable if all the funds were being raised locally. This gap between the Party's "earned income" and its standard of living, the fact that it can budget its activities without exclusive regard to the flow of dues and contributions from its own members and sympathizers, often gives it just the additional striking power it needs in order to confound its enemies. And it follows from all this that the French Communist Party is a party of a very special kind, so that the man who seeks to understand the problems its presence poses for French politics must, at an early moment, face up to that fact.

The Party's critics often accuse it of being "internationalist," but this is to pay it a compliment that the facts do not warrant. The Communist Party is not the spokesman and carrier of internationalism, but rather the spokesman and carrier of *a foreign nationalism*. Far from having transcended patriotic loyalties, it is the prisoner of *patriotic loyalty to the Soviet Union*. Over against this, however, we must set the fact that it cannot arise and grow in any country save as the instabilities, the injustices, and the weaknesses of the existing order in that country create its opportunity for it, and enable it to attribute to itself, however insincerely, *a mission that wants performing*. All Communist parties, that is to say, and thus the French Communist Party as well, have roots that thrust deep into both foreign and domestic soil. The virus is imported from abroad, but it incubates only in a favorable environment. The French Communist Party is at the service of a foreign power, but the forces on which it feeds are nevertheless authentically French.

88. Through the years just following 1917, before the Soviet regime has demonstrated—to the world and to itself—its capacity to survive, the Bolshevik leaders have two aims, the first of which is at a certain point replaced by the second: to widen the October, 1917, breach in the "imperialist front" by bringing about further revolutions, and to establish normal

relations with the Western states. As long as there is any hope of turning the "imperialist" war into "civil" war, the first essential in each country is a Communist Party resolved to make an immediate bid for power. This accounts for the haste with which the Bolsheviks complete their break with the old Social Democratic parties, committed as these are to a "sacred union" with their respective "bourgeoisies"—and paralyzed as they are by their "prejudices" and scruples. Better far to have a homogeneous party which, though small, is well in hand and utterly devoted to the cause of the Russian Revolution, than one of these vast agglomerations whose members are wedded to antiquated methods and, even those of them who are in sympathy with the new Russia, tend to resist orders from Moscow. All bonds with the old International must therefore be severed; and a new International forthwith comes into being, made up of these small, homogeneous parties. The "twenty-one conditions" * are laid down as a principle of selection and a means of imposing the directives and discipline of the Bolshevik Party. Since the world revolution is both imminent and inevitable (wherefore it will await no man's convenience), a time-consuming uphill struggle for majority control of the old Socialist parties and trade-unions is simply out of the question. The result, as far as France is concerned, is the French Communist Party, which promptly proclaims its repudiation of the institutions and practices of bourgeois democracy, and pledges itself to the slogan "Soviets everywhere." The chief obstacle to its conquest of the masses is, as it happens, the Socialist Party (SFIO); and it is therefore upon the Socialists that the new party always turns its heaviest artillery. But the Party never forgets that the Soviets in Russia are being menaced by civil war and intervention by foreign powers, so that the slogan "Defend the USSR" is pressed at least as vigorously as "Soviets everywhere"—and somewhat more successfully. The Party, that is to say, early mobilizes

* The Second World Congress of the Communist International (July, 1920) established a list of "qualifications" that a party must meet in order to be admitted to membership. There were twenty-one items on the list. W.K.

enough support among the popular masses and the intellectuals to hold in check the proponents of anti-Soviet policies.

The world revolution, however, does not arrive on schedule. The Spartacist movement in Germany looks encouraging for a time, then succumbs to its adversaries. The "Soviet" republics of Munich and Budapest capture the front pages for a moment, then disappear. Italy, following its seige of factory occupations, enters upon the political crisis that opens the doors to fascism. The revolutionary tide, in short, mostly does not rise at all, and where it does rise quickly subsides; and the Bolshevik leaders are obliged to remake their plans (few of the old hopes survive the failure—at Warsaw in the summer of 1920—to establish direct contact with the long-overdue German revolution). This is all the more necessary because the old Socialist parties are a much longer time a-dying than Moscow has expected them to be: In France, for instance, where the Communists win over a majority of their followers and make off with their newspaper, *L'Humanité*, they begin finally to recoup some of their losses—besides which the Communists meet increasingly stiff resistance within the trade-union movement. For the rest, things are going none too well in Russia itself, where despite the victory over the Whites the peasants are showing great hostility to the new regime.

The Bolsheviks meet the new situation inside Russia with the New Economic Policy, outside Russia with the Communist International's "united front" stratagem, which, however —the sections have not yet learned to obey without question —runs up against some little opposition within the Communist parties, and more perhaps in France than anywhere else. Everywhere, however, the will of Moscow finally prevails; and one must admit that, in France at least, it represents the wiser counsels. The peasants, for instance, respond much more positively to the idea of a "government of workers and peasants" than to that of a "dictatorship of the proletariat." And the proposal for a "united front" with the Socialists gains the Communists a hearing in quarters which they have not, hitherto, been able to penetrate.

Between 1924 and 1926, as we have seen, the policy and organization of the French Communist Party reflect the struggle being waged by Lenin's successors inside the Bolshevik Party; which is to say that the Party's shifts from Left to Right and Right to Left follow, sometimes with a brief delay, those that Stalin imposes on the Communist International as he presses his bid for personal power. Stalin at first bases his strategy on the "Old Bolsheviks" against Trotsky, then supports himself on the Right (Bukharin, Rykov, Tomsky) against the "Left" (Trotsky, Zinoviev), and finally constitutes a new Left with which to crush his former partners of the Right. We spare the reader an account of the parallel changes back and forth within the French Communist Party, and pause only to notice that the main trend is always in the direction indicated by Stalin.

Stalin's consolidation of his personal power within the Bolshevik Party brings a still further reorientation of Soviet and Comintern policies. Lenin's plan had looked to Russia's remaining, for some while, a primarily agrarian country, which would mark time on the level of *haute politique* until a revolution occurred in some Western nation with a proletarian majority and a modern industrial economy. Stalin, by contrast, resolves to transform Russia itself into a great industrial country that can go about its business independently of the course of events in, say, Germany. The proletariat remains the basis of Soviet policy; but this proletariat is to be created out of nothing within Russia itself, thanks to a process of rapid industrialization for which the countryside is to supply the capital and labor and ultimately the locale. The Communist International's "united front" policy is clearly not appropriate to this new phase. In 1928, the year of the first Five Year Plan, it therefore goes by the board in favor of the new slogan, "class against class."

89. With Hitler's accession to power in January, 1933, a new and extremely disquieting cloud appears on Stalin's horizon; and if he does not at once abandon the Rapallo policy (the 1922 and 1926 treaties remain in force), he does attempt

to shore up his position by bidding for support or, failing support, benevolent neutrality from the "democratic" powers. France promptly becomes a major concern of Soviet foreign policy, and the French Communist Party, always ready to adapt itself to the needs of the Soviet Union, an invaluable ally. Certainly Stalin could not have asked for a more faithful ally. Until August 23, 1939, it subordinates everything to the defense of the USSR against fascism and skillfully puts the Popular Front to work as an instrument of Soviet policy. After August 23, 1939, it does yeoman's service as an apologist for the Nazi-Soviet Pact and the dismemberment of Poland, and as an exponent of "pacifism." When the agreements of September 28, 1939, commit the USSR, as *quid pro quo* for its part of the booty, to support of Hitler's peace offensive, the French Communist Party even goes to the length of demanding that Parliament be called into session to consider the German offer and thus help to end the war. The fall of France and the Armistice are, in its view, windfalls that it can exploit for the purpose of achieving power, making an immediate peace with Germany, and transforming France into a "people's republic" that would owe its very existence to its alliance with the USSR. The Party offers no objection to the Tripartite Pact of September, 1940; it greets with enthusiasm the economic counterpart of that pact (January, 1941), as also the Soviet Union's nonaggression treaty with Japan. The fact that this treaty leaves Japan free to attack England and the United States in the Pacific is of no importance; it means increased security for the USSR. After April, 1941, relations between Hitler's Germany and Stalin's Russia rapidly deteriorate. Both in Central Europe (Hungary) and in the Balkans (Rumania, Bulgaria) Germany embarks on an aggressive policy in an area which the USSR would like to reserve for itself. And the French Communist Party at last turns against the occupying power, though still without in any way jeopardizing the Nazi-Soviet Pact, which remains—pending orders from Moscow—the cornerstone of its policy. The Party launches its first National Front at the end of May, 1941; but it is still concerned, above all, to prevent France from getting into the war, whether on Germany's side or as an ally of England. Once the Wehrmacht divisions have crossed the frontiers of the USSR, however, the Party performs all the indicated somersaults: England, hitherto a country of avid and unscrupulous imperialists, takes its place among the champions of democracy; she is now Russia's ally. The "ruin" and "sorrow" that participation in the war will bring upon "the people of France" are promptly forgotten. The Gaullists, the errand boys of British capitalism, become "brothers" in the struggle for "liberation." Defeatism gives way to patriotism. But make no mistake about it: had Stalin been able to maintain the German alliance, the French Communist Party would have clung to its former position.

The Party, be it noted, at no time makes any secret of its devotion to Soviet interests and Soviet security. How, in addressing itself to Frenchmen, does it avoid the charge of treason? Simply by insisting, in all situations, that the interests of France and the interests of the Soviet Union are identical. After September 1, 1939, and throughout the period of the Nazi-Soviet Pact, France's interest is peace: the people of France must be spared the "ruin" and "sorrow" of further participation in the war. Not until June 22, 1941, does it become the interest of France to free itself from the German occupation. For the Communists, in short, the interest of France is a variable in an equation whose one constant is the interest of the USSR as Stalin defines it.

Does all this mean that the Communists have no love for their country, and are insincere when they pretend otherwise? No simple answer can be given to this question. The slogans the Party puts forward during its ardently patriotic phase reflect a general state of mind which is certainly shared, with greater or lesser reservations, by most Communists; and the common struggle on behalf of those slogans, the common sacrifices it imposes, undoubtedly create new bonds that both Communists and non-Communists will be reluctant to break. The rank and file and the fellow travelers, undoubtedly again, take the slogans at face value, and mean them. The leaders themselves, the best of them at least, would *rather* be acting in accord with national sentiment than against it. The Party, in all these senses, has a right to assert that those who have died in the struggle for its slogans have "died for France." [1] But none of these considerations settles the central question, or disposes of this difficulty: The Party enters upon its ardently patriotic phase because of a shift in the policy of the Soviet Union, and its "patriotism" is a means of forwarding the supreme goal, which is support of the Soviet Union. And the record, e.g., that of 1939–40, shows that when the interests of the USSR and those of France clearly diverge, the interests of the USSR take precedence. When, in short, the Party must choose between French patriotism and Soviet patriotism, it chooses the latter—and must choose it, unless it is to deny its essential character and the purposes that have called it into being. That is why, whatever pose its future tactics may cause it to adopt, it will remain a foreign growth within the body of the nation—a cancer, whose natural function is to destroy healthy tissue and undermine vitality. Those who think it can one day be assimilated are the victims of the most dangerous political illusion of our time.

The Building of Community

90. The Communists, as I have intimated again and again in this book, may one day win power in France. But if they do, it will be because France is a country in which the bonds of community have grown weak, a country in which pretty much everybody is ready, at a moment's notice, to call into question the moral foundations of national unity. For, make no mistake about it, where unity can be had on no other terms men finally seek it in some political movement that is able and willing to *impose* it.

For a quarter of a century now the political pendulum in France has been swinging through a mighty arc, at each extremity of which the nation is, so to speak, split right down the middle. At one extremity, as with the Bloc National, the crisis is somehow negotiated by appeals put forward in the name of the nation. At the other extremity, as with the Popular Front, it is negotiated—again somehow, and with profound dissatisfaction in many quarters—by appeals put forward in the name of social reform. At one extremity we speak of a so-called Rightist "solution," at the other of a so-called Leftist "solution." But no one entertains the illusion that either wins more than grudging acquiescence from the elements clamoring for the other. And the invariable result is a further chipping away at the foundations of unity.

If the moral unity of France (and of other nations similarly situated) is to be restored, it will be through a synthesis of the "national" and "social" drives it harbors in its bosom, not through the triumph of the one at the expense of the other. But, in France at least, no such synthesis is yet in sight, and the question necessarily arises, who is responsible for the failure to achieve one?

I should say that the major responsibility lies necessarily

with the "governing" or "dominant" classes, of whom we may
say that in so far as they fail to achieve the necessary synthesis
they are merely dominant, *not* governing, and that their opposition to social reform is much less a matter of their being
too patriotic, as they like to believe, than of their being not
patriotic enough. When we call upon them to adopt a new
social posture, a new attitude toward the social reforms desired
by the broad masses of the people, we do not ask them to
neglect their obligations as patriots, but rather to begin to
discharge those obligations. The road they would travel toward a meeting of minds and hearts with the masses would
lead them, at the same time, closer to the "fatherland" of which
they are forever reminding us in their political utterances.
They, of course, prefer to state the problem in terms of the
need for "integrating" the proletariat into the life of the nation,
and to take it for granted that they are themselves already
integrated. They can, unfortunately, find *apparent* support
for this view in Marx, who did insist that the proletariat has
no fatherland, and did point to the conditions of misery and
dependence in which the proletariat lives as the explanation of
this fact. But the conclusion they wish to draw cannot ultimately be rested upon Marxism; for even if Marx had been
right on both points (which I do not think he was), it would by
no means follow that those who live comfortably and without
dependency do have a fatherland. Whether or not this or that
group has a fatherland is a matter to be decided by observing
and evaluating its behavior. And what the comfortable classes
in France must be brought to see is that, in situation after
situation over the past years, they have been acting as if they
did not have one—and been blinding themselves to the fact
that the record of the less comfortable classes is, from this
point of view, at least as good as their own.

91. The preceding section must not be understood to mean
that there is no problem of integrating the proletariat into the
life of the nation, or that its record on the point at issue is
notably better than that of the middle class. Let the proletariat
by all means continue to demand a larger share of the national

product. Let it, in view of its numbers, demand the largest share. But let it not forget that its real mission is to eliminate the status of proletarian altogether, and that this calls, in the long run, not only for transforming the country's economic structure, but for bringing about a new kind of relatedness among men within the productive process—*and* for a new outlook on its own part. If what the proletariat wants is merely higher wages, it has no need to be other than proletarian, or to sever the ties that now bind it to the capitalist system. But if what it wants is to create a new kind of society, it must put away the attitudes and habits appropriate to a proletarian status *within* capitalist society, and begin to feel and act as it will be called upon to feel and act in the world it conceives itself to be building.

I say "conceives itself to be building" advisedly, for here, as in other types of creative activity, in the beginning is the Word, that is, the idea of a better, more humane society than that in which we now live. In so far as the workers have truly captured such an idea they must make of it a principle of thought and action. They will, in doing so, find that it carries them far beyond the struggle for higher wages and better working conditions—to a noblesse oblige of the working class. The necessary first step in that direction, in my opinion, is the complete transformation of the trade-unions along lines no less hostile to the traditional doctrine of class warfare than to, shall we say, the doctrine of paternalism.

The above does not mean that the workers must put aside the axiom that the emancipation of the working class is a task that the workers dare not leave to someone else. That axiom, as far as it goes, is correct, though I myself should prefer to state it as follows: the emancipation of the working class must have its beginnings in the activity of the workers themselves, because it is only in the course of activity of a certain kind that the workers can develop the attitude and qualities they will need as participants in the new society. But the workers will find in that new society only such good things as they are able to bring to it, and they will bring good things to it only as they share with others the costs and sacrifices and risks without which it cannot be born. Marxist doctrine on this question, as has often been pointed out, rests upon the false premise that the interests of the workers coincide—out of an inevitability much like that of the "hidden hand" of the economists—with the general interest, a premise from which it follows that the workers have no responsibility for maintaining the coincidence in question: they have only to think and act as a class in order to achieve the classless commonwealth of free and equal men. The workers, in other words, are different from the capitalists. The latter consult their class interests, and in doing so move the world along toward disaster. The former consult their class interests, and move it along toward salvation.

All that, I contend, is root-and-branch wrong. The general interest never results from the enthronement of any or even several sectional interests in a society. The general interest is, rather, the interest of all groups and classes in the building of community, and it must be present in men's minds at the very beginning of the development that is to lead to its realization. What the workers must do is adopt this general interest as their program and accept the building of community as a responsibility that they share with all their fellow countrymen. This is not to ask them to act "unselfishly," because it is only in a genuine community that their essential, long-term interests will be served. Why? Because it is impossible to imagine a community that does not look to eliminating the status of proletarian, which as I have tried to say is the crucial issue.

The Problem of the Trade-unions

92. Until March, 1936, when it "merged" with the "re-formist" CGT, the Communist trade-union movement faithfully followed in the steps of the French Communist Party. Even the 1936 merger was merely a specific application of the new "Popular Front" tactics, and this, in turn, merely a phase of Soviet foreign policy. But as soon as the German-Soviet Pact drives a wedge—however temporary—between the interests of France and those of the USSR, the Communist trade-union leaders copy the example of the leaders of the Party, jettison the "antifascist" cargo that they have accumulated during their long cruise, and, throughout the "phony war," make themselves highly useful to Hitler's fifth column. A new break with the CGT thus becomes unavoidable.

The fall of France forces the CGT leaders to examine their consciences and take under advisement possible changes, not only in the sphere of action but in that of theory as well. Their Toulouse Conference (August, 1940), however, contents itself with a reaffirmation of certain of the principles underlying their 1918 and 1936 positions—as Benoît Frachon was quick to point out. The CGT leaders, he argues, have split up into two rival "teams," one of which, led by Belin, is openly participating in the government of usurpers and traitors at Vichy, and the other, led by Jouhaux (and, within the Socialist Party, by Léon Blum), has joined hands with that section of the bourgeoisie that is supporting British imperialism. "For both teams," he concludes, "the problem is not that of fighting capitalism and imperialism in general, but that of choosing between the rival imperialisms engaged in the war." [1]

This is, to be sure, straight Party-line doctrine for the moment at which it is written. What we must remember, however, is that a few months hence, when Soviet relations with

Germany are growing tense and the French Communist Party is launching its appeal for the first National Front, the Communist trade-unionists will be seeking a new alliance with the CGT. At the same time they will revise their attitude toward the trade-union leaders who are supporting Vichy's labor charter, and ask their cooperation in the struggle over wages and working conditions and in the planning of strikes. On the Communist side, at least, the rupture of September, 1939, when they were expelled, is now regarded as healed, and the Communists can inaugurate a new drive for the conquest of the CGT.

93. The Communists regard the trade-unions as a mere appendage of the Party—as one (undoubtedly the most important) of the many "mass" organizations that the Party needs to control—whether through the indirect method of infiltration or the direct method of open sponsorship. Now it is easy to show that the French trade-unions, if they were to accept any such position of tutelage vis-à-vis a political party, that is, *any* political party, would be repudiating their traditions. But it may be doubted whether their present and future struggle against Communist control can go forward on the basis of rules of thumb borrowed uncritically from the past. The situation to which the available rules of thumb were appropriate no longer exists.

Nor is that all: it is fashionable to exaggerate the nonpolitical character of traditional French trade-unionism. The Amiens Charter,* for instance, was profoundly "political," whatever the slogans to which its authors paid lip service. Did it not aim at the "destruction of the wage-earning and the employing classes," i.e., at the same goal the Socialists have always set themselves? Did it not, by proceeding beyond the day-to-day struggle over wages and working conditions to the idea of a free society for all, pose to itself, willy-nilly, the "social problem" as a whole? And did it not approach that problem with

---

* The Amiens Charter, adopted by the September, 1906, Congress of the CGT at Amiens, emphasized trade-union "independence of political schools." W.K.

its own conception of man and of relations among men? The worker is, to be sure, asked to bring with him neither philosophy nor politics when he joins a trade-union. But let us not overlook the fact that the trade-union, as the "basic grouping" which proposes to bring about a radical transformation of society, cannot itself do without a philosophy and a politics.

The conflict between trade-unionism and the Communist movement is not, I submit, properly speaking a conflict between a so-called economic approach to problems and a political approach. The conflict is of an entirely different kind, and has to do rather with competing conceptions of the state and the character of its relations with sectional associations and with individuals—and ultimately with sharply contrasting notions of freedom and the human personality. Their respective utopias lie at different ends of the world, and neither would find tolerable the type of society the other would build or the kind of human being the other would produce. Of this fact, and of the general character of the trade-unionists' political ideal, we could have no more eloquent reminder than Fernand Pelloutier's profession of faith:

We are the implacable enemies of all kinds of despotism, whether in the sphere of morals or in that of collective organization, that is to say, of all laws and all dictatorships, including those of the proletariat. We are passionately devoted to the ideal of individual development. The revolutionary mission of the enlightened proletariat is to press forward, ever more methodically and with ever greater determination, with the task of man's moral, administrative, and technical education, for this is the indispensable first step toward a society of proud and free men.[2]

94. The problem of the relation between the trade-unions and the political parties has been solved in different ways not only in different countries but also in one and the same country at different times. The First International included the trade-unions among its principal "sections." In Belgium and Great Britain there was a long period during which joining a trade-union meant joining the Labor Party. In Germany and in Italy the Socialist movement and the trade-union movement

worked successfully together on the basis of an agreed division of labor. In France, until the Communists took over the CGT, the trade-unions jealously guarded their independence and avoided all organic ties with the Socialist Party.

It would be difficult, in this background, to venture any conclusions that might be regarded as valid for all countries and all situations. For the rest, we are less concerned here with the general problem of the relation between the trade-unions and the political parties than with the specific problem of the relation between the trade-unions and this "new kind of party," the Communist Party. When the Communist wing of a trade-union gains control over its organization, it does not content itself with changing the faces at union headquarters; it proceeds to transform the actual character of the union, its conception of its function, and its position vis-à-vis other organizations. The union becomes a tool, a repetition in miniature of the Communist Party. Henceforth it will be an element in the Party's mobilization plan, and will be expected to contribute, at whatever cost, to the Party's conquest of power. Communist Party discipline takes the place of policy laid down by the federation or confederation to which the union belongs, and this discipline relates not to the normal business of a trade-union but to a political struggle whose aims and methods are dictated from Moscow. In reality there is no such thing as Communist trade-unionism; there are merely Communists who work for the Party inside the trade-unions. And, once it is taken over by the Communists, a trade-union ceases to be a trade-union, for all that it may retain the charter and outward appearance of a trade-union.

When therefore people in France (or any other country with a strong Communist movement) speak today of trade-union autonomy, what is in question is their first line of defense against "colonization" by the Communists. And it is fortunate, from this point of view, that the French workers have inherited, from the days before 1914, a set of self-denying ordinances calculated to insure the trade-unions against trespassing by the parties, as also against internal bureaucracy and "totalitarianism"—for example, the rule against CGT participation in electoral campaigns. This rule, and others of the same general character, must be maintained at all costs; and other measures, likely to strengthen and extend the democratic process within the trade-unions and prevent their being used for purposes foreign to their nature, must be adopted at the earliest possible moment.

It must be clearly understood, at the same time, that the struggle for trade-union autonomy cannot be won on the trade-union level alone. It is, in the last analysis, a "political" struggle, and must be political because its purpose is to defeat certain political maneuvers and designs. Let the unions, then, continue to regard economic activity as their normal sphere of action. But let them remember that every trade-union activity has consequences for the economy as a whole of which the political process must, at some point, take cognizance, and that, in any case, the working out of the indispensable frontier treaty between the state and the trade-unions is a task of an intensely political character.

Should the trade-unions, then, be absorbed by the state, and become, as in Soviet Russia, mere cogs in the machinery of politics? Certainly not—and least of all when the state becomes sole proprietor and manager of all enterprises and state power even more "totalitarian" than the power of the property owners and great trusts as we know it under the capitalist system. But we must also turn a deaf ear to the anarcho-syndicalists, who think in terms of an unavoidable and continuous clash between the working class and the state pending the "Great Day" when the former will absorb the latter. There is no such clash. Rather, the one constant in this problem is the solidarity—the ultimate identity of interest—between the working class and the nation of which it is a part.

What do we conclude? That the trade-unions and the political parties should remain distinct organizations, neither of which should control the other, but that this should by no means commit the trade-unions to political inactivity or quiescence. The war, the fall of France, the occupation, have "politicalized" French society—with the result that the individual or organization that chooses to be nonpolitical is doomed to ineffectiveness, or, worse still, to continuous self-defeat; and it is only by being political up to an agreed point that the trade-unions can keep themselves from being swamped by politics in its most deleterious form, that is, the Communist Party.

The trade-unions must, above all, write off the myth of "working-class unity." Such unity, in order to be meaningful, must rest upon a basis of shared principles and beliefs, and there are no principles and beliefs that are shared by French trade-unionism, French Socialism, and French Communism. This does not mean that the three cannot act together. It does mean that the long-run use we shall make of our freedom will depend upon the extent to which we have kept ourselves aware of the chasm that divides the first two from the third. When the time comes to make firm decisions as to the kind of France we are going to build, awareness of that chasm will be more important still—lest "working-class unity" be used as camouflage for a Communist monopoly of power.

The Communist Party and Democracy

95. The Communists are, in the last analysis, fighting a war of position; and their rules of action are those of military strategy and tactics. Lenin's classics included, along with Marx, von Clausewitz. And no group of men can—for that very reason—neutralize or overcome the Communist movement unless it is itself highly organized, has a correct, well-studied map of the terrain to be defended or conquered, and has plotted out in detail each move it is going to make.

The Communist movement relies, organizationally, upon the Party, with its network of local and factory cells and its hierarchy of leaders radiating downward from the "Political Bureau" to the lowest echelon. All the remaining elements that go to make up the Communist movement are in one way or another tied into the Party and receive their directives from it.

There is of course nothing to prevent all other political parties from copying the Communists' example in this regard, provided only that they are willing to put forth similar effort and employ similar methods. The political struggle could, conceivably, then continue to be a matter of "free competition" among several parties, each bent upon conquering public opinion and obtaining a majority in the country. These parties might keep on taking turns in power, as the parties do in England, each of them dutifully giving up its portfolios each time the electorate saw fit to repudiate its policies—each of them, if you please, dutifully assuming at such moments the minority's "loyal opposition" role that is indispensable to the smooth functioning of a liberal regime.

For the above to happen, however, another condition would need to be fulfilled: the Communist Party would have to be the same sort of thing as the other parties participating in the competition. Unfortunately for present-day democracy it is not. It cannot play the game of democracy for any purpose other than that of corrupting it and then destroying it. It dons the cloak of legality—or demands the right to do so—where this seems to be good tactics. But power remains its supreme goal, to which all else must be subordinated. What we have said above about the Communists in the trade-unions is equally true of the Communists in other fields of activity. When they manage to get control of a municipality or a trade-union, when they gain preponderant influence in a branch of the army, the police force, or the administrative apparatus of the state, that branch is to all intents and purposes removed from the legal orbit in which it has hitherto moved. Each position the Communists wrest from the enemy becomes a forward base from which to attempt a further advance, a new "facility" to be used in whatever manner the general strategy of the Party may dictate. If it is a local government area, its name will of course continue to appear on the list of local government areas. If it is a branch of the administrative apparatus, it will continue to have its little box on the administrative charts. But this is sheer camouflage; and the reality it conceals is that of an installation that is playing this or that role, offensive or defensive as the case may be, in the war plans of the Communist Party. Other parties stand committed to agreed "rules of the game," which remain in effect whoever has a majority; the Communist Party is inherently incapable of being bound by such rules. It will pay lip service to these rules while it is wearing the cloak of legality, that is, as a means of achieving power; but once it has milked them of every possible advantage it moves promptly to suspend their operation. For reasons that are by no means flattering to the democratic process the Party prefers, in point of fact, to prolong this period of democratic respectability as much as possible, and often does prolong it beyond the moment at which it becomes strong enough to throw the rules into the discard. But that is because—short of taking over the state—it feels most at home in a situation in which it is combining "legal" and clandestine activities and making the former contribute, in a way not always visible from outside, to the latter.

96. Does not this mean, someone will ask, that the Communist Party is incapable of absorption into the national community? If it accepts the rules of the democratic process only while it is too weak to do otherwise, if it demands freedom for itself only in order to carry on its struggle for power, and intends to take away the freedom of everyone else as soon as it can, why should it not be outlawed?

It would be easy, on the level of pure political right, to answer this question with a categorical Yes. When a party does not consider itself bound by any agreed rules, when it is ready to break compacts that do not suit its book, we are entitled to conclude that it has itself chosen the weapon we must use in the duel we are to fight with it, and that that weapon is force. We are entitled to conclude that the positional war it is waging against us justifies us in waging a positional war against it, that, in any case, it must be estopped from using its legal activities as a cover for its clandestine activities, and that, since it is to be a question of force in the long run anyway, the state must not stand with folded hands while freedom, the heritage of all, is being destroyed by the opportunism of the few. All this is unanswerable as far as the logic of political right is concerned. But I, for one, remain convinced that we must not act upon it until it becomes impossible for us to do anything else. Here are my reasons:

a. Freedom involves hazards that free men must learn to live with. A free society demands of its individuals and groups not *less* discipline and self-control than a totalitarian society but *more* discipline and self-control. A free society is *tougher* than a totalitarian society, though with a different kind of toughness that comes into play with respect to a different kind of problem. It must, above all, be tough in resisting the temptation to use force, which is always the easy way out of a predicament.

b. The search for truth cannot go forward in the absence

of heresy and opposition, and not merely because the truth-seekers' muscles go soft when they are not used. When the unity of a democratic society is maintained through arbitrary imposition, even over a very small area, it ceases to be the kind of unity that is appropriate to a truth-seeking society, which is a society that never forgets this: Error is always the result of a defeat suffered by truth on its own territory, so that every attempt to fight error as if it were born beyond the frontiers of truth, every attempt to treat error as a clan treats its external enemy, not only fails as a matter of course but prevents the application of the only effective remedy. Error must, in a word, always be regarded as a crisis in the internal development of truth.

This is not, I hasten to add, to place error and truth and good and evil all on the same level, or to follow the Hegelians in justifying whatever happens as somehow "rational." My point is simply that we can liquidate error only as we absorb and thus transcend it.

c. We are ourselves responsible, in large part, for every error on the part of our adversaries. We are, that is to say, responsible both for the good we have failed to do and for the evil we have failed to prevent.[1] And we must avoid the role of public prosecutor save as we can come into court with clean hands—which, at this juncture, we cannot do.

d. I make no appeal here to Christian ethics, although they are highly relevant to the question of outlawing the Communist movement and tend to support my position. My frame of reference, for the moment, is the national community *qua* national community, and the latter's avowed values and avowed goals. The Communists are bent upon suppressing freedom, and the remedy, we are told, is to pay them off in their own coin. This, I say, is precisely the kind of victory the national community can never afford. The state and the nation, much more easily than the individual, can forego in large part the arbitrament of hand-to-hand combat, and take the long view. If by choosing the longest and hardest road it can avoid contamination by the spirit and methods of its internal enemy, it is always well advised to do so. And it is no answer to this to show that methods borrowed from the enemy will bring quicker results, save as we are sure—which in practice we cannot be—that we are not installing him permanently in our midst and delivering him our souls.

e. The kind of logic that can bear no contradictions is always on the point of becoming "totalitarian," and the danger of its doing so is present even where it is merely calling upon its adversary to be faithful to his own principles. (Mussolini used to say, early in his career, that what he was out to do was force the capitalists to be genuine capitalists and the socialists to be genuine socialists; and his subsequent development was a natural outgrowth of that attitude.) We do not, furthermore, prove that a position is wholly erroneous by proving that those who hold it are confused; and we do not, by any means, dispose of a position by exposing its inconsistencies. This is especially important to remember in connection with the rank and file of the Communist movement as distinguished from its hard core of permanent members. The latter, who subordinate everything to the imperatives of the revolution and equate the revolution with the expansion of the Soviet state, are to all intents and purposes without inconsistencies of the kind I here have in mind. Not so the Communist masses, who are *both* patriotic (in the usual sense of the term) and passionately pro-Soviet—the one because of one set of urges, the other because of another; and they are capable of harboring these demonstrably contradictory sets of urges indefinitely, without ever facing up to their incompatibility. The Party, for the rest, knows how to prevent this incompatibility from coming to their attention in most situations, and, where it fails to do this, it knows how, through skillful manipulation of a certain picture of the Russian Revolution and the Soviet utopia, to make the contradiction bearable. The man who would save the Communist rank and file from their contradictions must, therefore, give them not lessons in logic but a different, i.e., correct, picture of the revolution and the utopia.

f. I have insisted elsewhere in this book on the twofold

character of the French Communist Party, which is at the
service of a foreign power but is, at the same time, fed by forces
that are authentically French. The Party has—partly through
its own tactical brilliance, partly through the tactical stupidity
of its adversaries—reaped incalculable benefits from certain
associations of ideas that it has rarely been called upon to
justify. Immediately after the Armistice of 1918, for instance,
it drew great strength from the two equations: "communism
= peace" and "communism = revolution." From 1934 on it
was the day-to-day beneficiary of the equation "communism
= freedom." These three equations—communism = peace,
communism = revolution, communism = freedom—cannot
of course keep house together. But since the Party was not
called upon to reconcile them, their very incompatibility was
an advantage (each enabled the Party to appeal to some group
that would not have been attracted by the other two). For
the rest, both individual and group psychology are much more
a matter of watertight compartments than most people imagine, i.e., both the individual and the group achieve and maintain unity by tapping the compartments one at a time rather
than by breaking down the walls, mixing the contents, and
eliminating unassimilable elements. Certainly a considerable
number of Frenchmen today react positively to each of the
symbols, Communist Party, Peace, Freedom, Fatherland, and
Social Justice, and permit any one of the five to evoke the other
four, without becoming aware of any clash among them. The
problem of French unity is, on one level, precisely that of driving wedges between these Communist symbols and the deeply
rooted values that cause men to be attracted—and deceived—
by them.

It follows from the above analysis that the struggle against
the Communists must take a certain definite form, namely,
that of day-to-day effort to guard the essential processes of
collective living against infiltration and subsequent control by
Communist militants and sympathizers—and we must not de-
ceive ourselves as to the extent to which responsibility for
this effort can be entrusted to the state. The latter must, to be

sure, see to it that the army, the police, and the courts remain free of Communist control. The French Communist officer will not hesitate to betray his country in any future war in which the USSR, or one of its allies, is on the other side; that is as certain and predictable as tomorrow's sunrise.[2] The Communist policeman is not going to defend the "order" his Party is out to destroy. The Communist magistrate will consult no code save that which defines the interests of his party. All these, just to the extent that they are Communists, are incapable of performing the functions for which they are retained. And this poses problems of which the state can and should take cognizance.

Save within the restricted area just mentioned, however, the struggle against the Communist movement should have its center of gravity not in the state but in the nation itself, that is, in its private citizens. Most of the latter would of course prefer not to assume the responsibilities for which this calls: they ask nothing better than to be left alone so that they may go about their business. They must, however, be made to understand that the conditions under which the political struggle now takes place do not admit of a right to be left alone. Any state in which there is a strong Communist movement, as there is in France, urgently needs the active help of its citizens— not only in what it does to maintain order but also in what it does to correct the social malaise that leads to disorder. The citizens must confront the Communists in the factories, in the streets, in the villages; they must show the Communists that they not only disagree with them but are prepared to resist them for every inch of the territory they propose to conquer. The state should step in only when Communist action takes a form that private citizens simply cannot cope with.

Someone may object that if the danger is indeed so great as this book suggests we should not continue to cherish principles that render the struggle more difficult, and certainly should not concern ourselves with the conversion and reassimilation of those who threaten us. I can only repeat, by way of reply, that the fight for freedom cannot, in the very nature of the case, be won by adopting the methods of the enemy—or, if you like, that it ceases to be worth winning unless freedom's champions maintain their moral and spiritual superiority over freedom's foes. If we advance upon those foes with hatred in our eyes, those of them whose faith in Communism is sorely taxed (as the Communists' faith often will be if the opposition takes the form envisaged here) will, as they did in France after August, 1939, shake off their doubts and carry on as before.

By Way of a Conclusion

97. The struggle against the Communist movement must be conceived as an attempt to persuade the masses of men to accept an ideal other than that which the Communists have offered them, and to create for the society of the future a structural basis different from that which a Communist victory would entail. Such a struggle is both necessary and right; but it can go forward only in the name of an ideal, and as a means to a social structure, that can make a stronger appeal to man's spontaneity and sense of justice than that made by Communism itself.

For this, three things are needed: an appropriate socio-political program; an organizational effort calculated to assure popular participation in the achievement of that program; and a political theory that will define the ends the program is to serve and determine the methods by which they are to be accomplished. We must, above all, avoid the temptation to deny the claims of the last point. There is no such thing as a fact that is "accomplished" so long as the idea that fact expresses has not been successfully defended on the level of theory; nor is there such a thing as a fact that has been wiped out of existence so long as the idea that it expresses survives every theoretical attempt to demonstrate its harmfulness or sterility.

The political theory of Bolshevism rests, as is well known, on premises drawn from Marxism. An initial task, therefore, is to restudy Marxism and arrive at a decision as to which of the theoretical conclusions to which it leads are worth salvaging. This process of revaluation cannot, I suggest, take the now familiar form of showing (a) that Bolshevism has pushed this or that emphasis of Marx and Engels "too far" and in doing so has crossed the line that divides truth from error, and (b) that it has neglected to take this or that emphasis of Marx and Engels into account, e.g., the extent to which they themselves repudiated certain opinions they had held in, say, the years 1847–50. (Both of them lived to confess, for example, that certain passages in the *Manifesto* needed restating; and they went so far as to plan an introduction to a new edition which, as they hoped, would "bridge the gap between 1847 and the present time." Engels, both in his preface to the second German edition of *The Condition of the Working Classes in England* and in his article, "Socialism in Germany," [1] insists upon the fact that universal suffrage has made it necessary to reconsider the whole question of the tactics and prospects of the working-class movement.) I give it as my opinion that some at least of the "totalitarian" aspects of the Soviet regime, particularly the hypertrophy of the state and the withholding of a whole series of individual liberties, are the unavoidable consequences of positions that are demonstrably present in the writings of Marx and Engels. Marx, humanitarian that he was, undoubtedly would if he were alive today profoundly disapprove of the Stalinist version of "socialism"; but he would be disavowing his own handiwork, and the disavowal would by no means acquit him of responsibility for it. My quarrel with Bolshevism—I speak as a French Socialist—is that it remains faithful to a certain internal logic of Marxism and at the same time goes far beyond it.

French Socialism, we must notice in connection with the third of our three "musts," is by no means open to the charge of having neglected its responsibility to create a reasoned political theory. During the nineteenth century it produced a literature which I do not hesitate to describe as one of the most brilliant manifestations of man's spirit, and which, in the field of political theory, quite overshadows that of any other country over a period of similar length. Fourier and Saint-Simon and the Saint-Simonians; Babeuf and Blanqui; Pécqueur and Considérant; Proudhon and Jaurès—what other country can point to a group of writers who, within the space of a few decades, have thought so deeply and creatively about the problems of society? They worked by preference in uncharted regions on the map of political theory, and each of them made it his business to open up new roads into those regions. Some of those roads, to be sure, lead only to an impasse; others lose themselves in the jungle—though even these are likely to surprise you by reappearing at some point further on. But this, at least, seems to me undeniable: any forward steps man is to take in the years ahead with regard to the problems of collective living he will take by resuming the labors of the French Socialists, by adopting the values they sought to win acceptance for, and by projecting his thought on the level of penetration they achieved. (I am not forgetting here that Marx seized upon many hints from the writers I mention, and incorporated them in his system; but without exception they turned sterile in Marx's hands.)

I am not saying that French Socialism has nothing to learn from the Marxists. It would, for example, be well advised to take over certain Marxist methods of analysis and certain Marxist notions regarding the evolution of contemporary society—though in taking them over it would also be well advised to rethink and sharpen them. What it would *not* be well advised to do is *become* Marxist, whether orthodox or revisionist; for its real task is to press forward with its own conception of the life of man, as it was worked out by its own thinkers through more than a century of brilliant investigation and speculation.

98. Let me point out here that it is no accident that the school of writers to which I allude appeared in France rather than somewhere else, and, particularly, that the ideas set forth in their books are in no sense pollen deposited in France by winds from other countries. France, as the record plainly shows, had at one time the kind of soil that is most congenial to the seeds of socialist thought. No one, pending further historical and sociological investigation, could hope to say either why France once had it or why it ceased to have it; but I feel quite sure that when the investigation is completed it will show that the decline of the country's socialist thought was merely

one aspect of a process of disintegration and waning vitality on the part of French society as a whole.

My thesis is, then, that the Socialists of France have at their disposal, whether they know it or not, the elements that would need to be combined in order for them to pose the question of a "national" revolution in fruitful terms. This does not mean at all, however, that the answer to the question, once it was posed, would be "nationalist" in character. If it were, it would be faithless to one of the central long-term emphases of French socialist thought. As early as 1814 Saint-Simon was calling upon France and England to turn their backs upon nationalist rivalry and to concern themselves with the "reorganization of European society" along lines that would "bring the peoples of Europe together in a single political unit and at the same time preserve the national independence" of each. And as recently as the early years of the present century Jaurès was insisting upon the "twofold duty" of creating a new social order and organizing peace.

To reduce socialism to the national level, I insist, is to make it over into something other than itself—even when the nation in which the reduction is attempted covers one sixth of the globe. And this is not merely because of that meshing of the interests of any one country with those of all other countries which has become so much more pronounced with the emergence of a world-wide economy. (Some countries, whether because of their natural resources or because of their political regimes, are of course less vulnerable in this sense than others. Even Charles Maurras took cognizance of this meshing of interests, as may be seen from the fact that he never went so far as to propose a policy of complete isolation for France.) Rather I should say that the basic objection to all professedly socialist schemes of "integral nationalism" flows from some such premises as the following: Socialism is the affirmation of a particular set of human values. This set of values constitutes a standard by which one judges the nation-state, rather than the other way around. This is not to deny, of course, that nationhood involves a certain degree of autonomy and, along with it, a consensus, itself autonomous to some extent, among the nation's citizens. It is not to deny, either, that the nation must, in order to exist and develop, impose upon its members its own forms of discipline and correction and, at the same time, keep an eye on the possibilities and dangers inherent in the current international situation. And it is not to deny, finally, that the nation (within certain limits, of course) confers upon the individual who grows up within its frontiers a "human nature" tailored, so to speak, to its own specifications (it determines, for example, the extent to which the individual can live his life behind private and familial and occupational barriers). But we can concede all this and still assign a higher priority to the imperatives of a true science of politics, whose task it is to lay down the rules of individual and collective living which a nation must observe upon pain of ceasing to exist, rather than to the imperatives of nationalism. Not, I hasten to add, the highest priority: for that science of politics will itself be subordinate to *principles*, and in the course of the adjustments, the precaution taking, and the expedients which will be its central business it must keep these principles in sight. But it will not, by subordinating itself to principles, in any sense lessen its own dignity: the principles will provide the ultimate justification of which it will stand in constant need. Politics, on this showing, is the science by which we infuse principles into a given national reality-situation.

99. The term "national revolution" has been associated with so many ventures of a stupidly reactionary or even traitorous character that, in France at least, one hesitates to make use of it. But this does not dispose of the fact that a national revolution *is* what France needs to effectuate before she can get back on her feet and resume her place in world society.

This—since it means creating a *people* where, strictly speaking, today there is no people, and thus hammering out both the economic and social structure and the spiritual bonds which alone can give that people unity—is no easy task. Every group that goes to make up the population of France today carries a part of the burden of responsibility for the June, 1940, defeat, in the sense that it is impossible to point to any group which did not, in the course of the events leading up to the defeat, fail to measure up to even minimum standards of civic virtue. This does not mean, of course, that they are all equally culpable, or that there are no clearly definable responsibilities to be laid at the door of particular individuals. It does mean that the sickness that reduced France to impotent helplessness at that time is so deeply rooted and so generalized that nothing short of a revolution can make the country whole again.

Will not a "social" revolution suffice? If we could carry through a genuine social revolution, would it not (as the Communists were saying it would back in June, 1941) automatically confer upon us the advantages of the other revolutions that might otherwise need to be made?

My answer to this question is an unhesitating No. It is indeed possible to imagine a historical and social context in which a change in the ownership of property and a transfer of power from one class to another would be a step in the direction of progress. These conditions are, however, no guarantee that the march will continue in that direction. They offer no assurance, for one thing, that the resultant regime, new foundations and all, will not be overthrown, or, for another, that a tyranny will not be built upon those foundations. In the last analysis, moreover, the way to judge the results of a revolution is to ask whether it has brought about a genuine and permanent change in the relations among men and in the meaning of their freedom and their solidarity. If there is no such genuine and permanent change, the revolution is pointless. And no revolution can go far, in the sense I have just indicated, if it is the handiwork of a class or party which relies upon the automatism of institutional structures to bring about the regeneration of the people to whom it belongs; and this becomes doubly true if we posit a people that is sick in mind and heart. Froth, which is all such a revolution can produce, does not cease to be froth because it is red with blood. There is no such thing as a revolutionary technique capable of producing a new national consciousness. The latter, if it is there at all, is there prior to the revolutionary technique, seeks to express itself through it and the new institutions it builds, and remains effective just to the extent that those new institutions faithfully embody it.

The Communist approach to the problem of society rests unabashedly on the assumption that by installing a new set of political and economic machinery you can carry your fellow citizens with you and, in the long run, "transform" them—whether they wish to be transformed or not. The Communists count on dictatorship to confer the gift of freedom, on universal proletarianization to eliminate the proletariat, on totalitarian economic controls to usher in personal liberty, on a monopoly of the means of expression to defend the claims of the mind and the spirit. Where Communism takes power, however, what it in fact does is create new social inequalities —and then consolidate them in a context whose major characteristics are that the liberties of the person are wholly absent and that the struggle for existence and for power, though it indeed goes forward under new rules, is if anything more cruel and implacable than before.

That is the kind of revolution France—and other countries also—must avoid. But this it can do only by carrying its own revolution through to its logical conclusion, which is to say, by attacking the sickness of France in the very soil in which it has its old roots and is each day putting down new ones. That means, first of all, attacking that sickness in the minds and hearts of its sons, who must relearn the human values that are France's most precious possession—and the gage of its greatness.

NOTES

INTRODUCTION

1. Paris, Editions Self, October, 1948.

2. I refer to the letter, signed by 22 members of the faculty of the Yale Law School, to the President, Secretary of State, and Speaker of the House of Representatives, as reported in the *New York Times* and the *New York Herald Tribune* of November 27, 1947. The letter condemned the House Committee on Un-American Activities and the President's loyalty program as "suppression" and "persecution" endangering the nation's liberty. It is high time, the letter said, for the government "to forswear its belief in witches, begin practicing democracy, and set examples to those parts of the world which we hope to have embrace its principles."

3. Mr. Truman developed this theme further still in the weekly press conference reported in the June 27, 1949, issue of *Time*. Some of the arguments he used suggest that he might have been reading Thomas I. Emerson and David M. Helfeld, "Loyalty among Government Employees," *Yale Law Journal*, December, 1948.

4. Thus Paul G. Hoffman, Economic Cooperation Administrator, reports that "Participating countries increased production to virtually the prewar level," and goes on to list specific achievements in steel, fuel, textiles, crops, exports, and financial stability (*New York Times*, April 3, 1949). In a speech at Occidental College, Los Angeles, he asserts that Russia's drive for world domination has been "stopped cold" in Western Europe and that economic recovery by 1952 will "more than probably" force the Kremlin into a "live-and-let-live" policy (*New York Times*, March 30, 1949).

5. Between the Constituent Assembly elections of June 2, 1946, and the elections to the Chamber of Deputies of April 18, 1948, in Italy, for instance, the Christian Democratic Party increased its percentage of seats from 37.2 to 53.1 (Republica Italiana, Istituto Centrale di Statistica, *Compendio Statistico Italiano*, 1947–48, Serie 2, II, 182, 187). For French statistics, see n. 13, *infra*.

6. See his *An American Dilemma* (New York, Harper & Brothers, 1944), pp. 8–9.

7. The full text of the speech appears in the *New York Times*, June 20, 1949.

8. See his article, "Stop Russia's Subversive War," *Atlantic*, May, 1948, p. 27.

9. *New York Times*, June 9, 1949. The Commission's report, finally adopted by the National Education Association's plenary session (*New York Times*, July 7, 1949) goes on to say: "Such membership . . . involves adherence to doctrines and discipline completely inconsistent with the principle of freedom on which American education depends. Such membership, and the accompanying surrender of intellectual integrity, render an individual unfit to discharge the duties of a teacher in this country."

10. See his article, "How We Won the War and Lost the Peace," *Life*, August 30, 1948, and September 6, 1948.

11. At p. 1096 (emphasis added).

12. Thus the political correspondent of the *Daily Telegraph* writes on June 27, 1949: "There is little possibility that Sir Stafford [Cripps] will be able to offer

any concession despite the strong pressure of Mr. Harriman and the E.C.A. [Economic Cooperation Administration] in America, who think that the dead-lock threatens the continuance of Marshall aid."

13. In France the anti-Communist parties polled 71% of the popular vote in the 1946 elections to the National Assembly and Communists and sympathizers 29%; in the 1949 local elections the government parties and Gaullists polled 76% of the vote and Communists 24% (Foundation for Foreign Affairs, *A Constitution for the Fourth Republic*, Washington, 1947, Appendix VII; *New York Times*, March 20, 1949). For Italy, see n. 5.

14. Cf. *New York Times*, October 11, 1947: "Are the Chilean miners well paid, well fed, well housed, with sufficient medical care and a reasonable hope of security in their old age? The answer is obviously in the negative. . . . That is the soil in which it is easy for communism to take root and flourish."

15. Thus Mr. Truman, who surely knew better as a judge in Missouri (i.e., before his accession to the presidency delivered him into the hands of his present, more expensively educated advisers): "A slash in the funds available for European recovery at this time would be the worst kind of false economy . . . a great gain for Communism" (*Time*, June 20, 1949).

16. The *locus classicus* is General Marshall's speech at Harvard: "Our policy is directed not against any country or doctrine but against hunger, poverty, desperation, and chaos. The purpose should be the revival of a working economy in the world so as to permit the emergence of political and social conditions in which free institutions can exist. . . . Any assistance that this government may render in the future should provide a cure rather than a mere palliative" (*New York Times*, June 6, 1947).

17. Cf. Mr. Paul Porter's pronouncement in the *New York Times*, June 8, 1947: "Europe cannot be on its feet politically because it is not yet on its feet economically. . . . Food and fuel are our best weapons against totalitarianism. We will soon be throwing them into Greece. I hope that before long we will be throwing them in tremendous volume into other parts of Europe. We will use them in favor of economic security and political liberty . . ." Cf. an edi-torial in the *New York Herald Tribune*, September 12, 1947: "The lamentable consequences in both inflation and threatened starvation are apparent to all. . . . Communism will fall heir to Western Europe unless our democratic economy [sic] can prove its strength in meeting human needs."

18. And made incalculable levies upon the time of a colleague, Mr. Henry Wells, to whom I am indebted for a first draft translation of Chaps. XVI and XVIII; a research assistant, Mr. John Ponturo, who has prepared the index and performed countless chores for me at the library; and the following students in my political theory seminar at Yale, who have prepared first-draft translations of the chapters listed following their names: Miss Anne E. Brunsdale (Chaps. I–XII), Mr. Frederick C. Engelmann and Mr. Charles M. Lichenstein (Chaps. XIII, XXIII, and XXIV), Mr. Duane Lockard (Chaps. XVII, XIX, and XX), Mr. Dankwart A. Rustow (Chaps. XXI and XXII), Mr. Alfred Diamant (Chaps. XXV and XXVI), Mr. Karl H. Cerny (Chaps. XXVII and XXIX), Mr. Mauro B. Lopes (Chaps. XXX–XXXIII). I dare not, however, attribute to them any responsibility for the translation in its present form.

19. Note that he is thus equating Europe and the West, and therefore, *mutatis mutandis*, the European and Western man. Let us not tell ourselves, then, that he is not talking about us.

20. José Ortega y Gasset, *The Revolt of the Masses* (New York, W. W. Nor-ton & Co., 1932), pp. 198–200 (emphasis added).

21. As also, by implication at least, has Sebastian de Grazia. See every last

disturbing word of his *The Political Community* (Chicago, University of Chicago Press, 1948).

22. Richard M. Weaver, *Ideas Have Consequences* (Chicago, University of Chicago Press, 1948), *passim*.

23. *Ibid.*, p. 122.

24. *Ibid.* (emphasis added).

25. *Ibid.*, p. 60.

26. *Ibid.*, p. 124.

27. *Ibid.*, p. 9.

28. *Ibid.*, p. 23.

29. *Ibid.*, p. 2.

30. *Ibid.*, p. 30.

31. *Ibid.*, pp. 32–33 (emphasis added).

32. G. E. G. Catlin, *The Science and Method of Politics* (New York, Alfred A. Knopf, 1927), pp. 84–85.

33. "The Record of French Communism," *Economist*, June 4, 1949.

34. Paris, Somogy, 1948.

35. London *Times Literary Supplement*, April 9, 1949.

36. W. Lloyd Warner (ed.), Yankee City Series (New Haven, Yale University Press, 1941–47), 4 vols.

37. Robert S. and Helen M. Lynd, *Middletown* (New York, Harcourt Brace and Co., 1929). I am not forgetting *Middletown in Transition* (*ibid.*, 1937), which did in a sense bring *Middletown* up to date. But let the reader say which of the two volumes he oftener takes off his bookshelf and to which of the two he finds the more frequent references in his reading.

38. R. G. Collingwood, *The New Leviathan* (London, Oxford University Press, 1942), p. 4.

39. See the bibliography in Edward Shils, *The Present State of American Sociology* (Glencoe, Ill., The Free Press, 1948), p. 36.

40. Rossi, *op. cit.*, p. xxxi.

41. Thomas I. Emerson and David M. Helfeld, "Loyalty among Government Employees," *op. cit.*, pp. 142–143.

42. *Ibid.*, pp. 67–79 and 134–135.

CHAPTER I

On the Eve of the Defeat

1. *Pour sauver notre pays*, published as a pamphlet in June, 1940.

CHAPTER II

After the Armistice: Communist Collaboration with the Occupation

1. This and the preceding quotations are from *Appel au peuple de France*, published as a pamphlet at Bordeaux, June 18, 1940.

2. This handbill bears no title.

3. June 26, 1940.

4. *L'Humanité*, July 1, 1940.

5. *La Doctrine communiste de Marx-Engels-Lénine-Staline en six cours*, Part I, p. 21.

6. *Ibid.*

7. *Ibid.*

8. *Les Premières Instructions du P.C.F. après l'armistice*, June or July, 1940. These instructions are reproduced in their entirety in the French edition of this book, pp. 395–399.

9. "Lettre aux militants communistes," November, 1940, reprinted in *Cahiers du Bolchevisme*, 1st quarter, 1941, pp. 6–10.

10. *Vie du Parti*, September, 1940.

11. Both quotations are taken from *La Gazette des démobilisés*, October, 1940.

12. See n. 4, *supra*.

13. See n. 8, *supra*. The phrase "aid from the Soviet Union" is from a handbill, published in October, 1940, without a title.

14. See n. 8, *supra*.

15. *Ibid.*

16. *Ibid.*

17. The French edition of this book carries a full account of these negotiations in an appendix, p. 402 ff., under the title, "Démarches communistes à l'ambassade d'Allemagne en juin 1940." For corroborative evidence see Edouard Daladier, *Réponse aux chefs communistes* (Paris, 1946), and the parliamentary debates for December 5–11 in *Journal officiel*, pp. 5520–5624.

18. *Les Tâches du Parti pour septembre–octobre*, published as a pamphlet in August, 1940. It is reproduced in the French edition of this book, pp. 399–402.

19. *Nous accusons*, published as a pamphlet in October or November, 1940.

20. See n. 18, *supra*.

21. *Il faut en finir avec l'incurie et le désordre*, published as a pamphlet in July, 1940.

22. See n. 4, *supra*.

23. *Appel au peuple de France*, mid-August, 1940.

24. *Ibid.*

25. *Attention*, published as a pamphlet around July, 1940.

26. *Vie du Parti*, October, 1940.

27. *La Politique communiste*, February, 1941.

28. Both quotations are from *ibid.*, December, 1940.

29. *Jeunesse de France*, published as a pamphlet in autumn, 1940.

30. See Section 12, *supra*.

CHAPTER III

The Conquest of the Unorganized Masses

1. This and the preceding quotation are taken from *Appel au peuple de France*, August, 1940.

2. This and the preceding quotation are taken from *Vie du Parti*, August, 1940.

3. *L'Humanité*, October 12, 1940.

4. *Ibid.*, December 30, 1940.

5. *Ibid.*, May 10, 1941.

6. *Ibid.*, May 25, 1941.

7. *Les Tâches du Parti pour septembre–octobre 1940*, published as a pamphlet in August, 1940, p. 1.

8. *Le Guide*, March, 1941.

9. *L'Enchaîné*, July, 1940.

10. *Vie du Parti*, August, 1940.

11. The Communists at first make only the most cautious references to the requisitions by the Germans. It is only later, when their plans for intimate col-

laboration have clearly failed, above all, of course, after June 22, 1941, that they exploit them in their propaganda.

12. *Vie du Parti*, August, 1940.

13. *Le Problème du chômage reste entier*, published as a pamphlet in January, 1941.

14. *Nos droits sur eux*, published as a leaflet in September or October, 1940.

15. *Vie du Parti*, August, 1940.

16. *Ibid.*

17. "Rendus a leurs foyers," *La Caserne*, October, 1940 (special edition).

18. *Aux soldats de l'armée d'armistice*, published as a pamphlet in May, 1941.

19. "Rien de ce qui interesse les jeunes . . . ," *L'Humanité*, August 5, 1940.

20. *Pour le salut du peuple de France*, published as a pamphlet in January, 1941.

21. *Vie du Parti*, August, 1940.

22. *Ibid.*

23. *La Liaison* and *Le Trait d'union*.

24. *Le Trait d'union*, March, 1941.

25. This circular was distributed in September and October, 1940.

CHAPTER IV

The Call to the Workers, the Peasants, and the Middle Class

1. The notebooks are made available to the leaders of factory cells in a circular, without title, bearing the date of March 21, 1941. In general, the notebooks are based on careful research. The most important and, at the same time, the most impressive, is the *Cahiers des revendications des métallurgistes*, also distributed in March, 1941.

2. *Vie du Parti*, August, 1940.

3. *La Vie ouvrière*, August 10, 1940.

4. *L'Humanité*, April 12, 1941.

5. *Ibid.*, February, 1941 (special edition).

6. Some examples are: *Aux paysans de France*, September, 1940; *Camarade paysan*, February, 1941; *Paysan, mon frère, écoute l'un des tiens*, March, 1941; *Ni Londres ni Berlin, la terre aux paysans*, June, 1941; *Paysans, unissons-nous pour le respect de nos droits*, June, 1941.

7. For example, *Jeunes paysans, jeunes paysannes*, January, 1941.

8. For example, *Vignerons, unissez-vous*, spring, 1941.

9. For example, *Aux militants des syndicats*, January, 1941.

10. Some examples are: *Paysans creusois*, September, 1940; *Paysans du Nord, luttez avec le Parti Communiste*, February, 1941.

11. This and the preceding quotations are taken from *Paysans, unissons-nous contre la loi du baillon*, published as a pamphlet in January or February, 1941.

12. *L'Humanité*, February, 1941 (special edition for the rural districts).

13. Both quotations are taken from *Camarade paysan*, published as a pamphlet in February, 1941.

14. *Paysans de France*, published as a pamphlet in January, 1941.

15. *Ibid.*

16. *Paysan de France, redresse-toi*, published as a pamphlet in February, 1941.

17. *Ibid.*

18. See n. 12, *supra*.

19. See n. 14, *supra*.

20. Cf. the following pamphlets: *Le Parti Communiste avec les classes moyen-*

nes, January, 1941; *Aux petits commerçants et artisans*, January, 1941; *Comité de défense des petits commerçants et artisans français*, March, 1941.

CHAPTER V

The Communists, the Intellectuals, and the Principles of 1789

1. See the following pamphlets: *Appel aux instituteurs, aux professeurs de l'enseignement*, January, 1941; *Aux instituteurs français, pour la défense de l'école laïque*, February, 1941; *La Défense de l'école française*, February, 1941; *Contre le sabre et le goupillon, pour l'école laïque*, March, 1941; *Aux éducateurs du peuple*, June, 1941.

2. See the following pamphlets: *Pour la défense de la science française*, December, 1940; *La Défense de la culture: le Cas Langevin*, April, 1941.

3. *Appel aux étudiants*, January, 1941.

4. *Aux étudiants de France*, published as a pamphlet in May, 1941.

5. *Appel aux intellectuels français*, March, 1941.

6. *La Pensée libre*, January, 1941.

7. *Ibid.*

8. *Ibid.*

9. *Ibid.*

10. *Ibid.*

11. *Ibid.*

12. *Révolution et contre-révolution au XXe siècle*, published as a booklet in January or February, 1941. (We may notice, in this connection, that the French Communist Party has reissued this booklet since the war. The reprints bear the date 1947.)

13. *Ibid.*

14. *Ibid.*

15. *L'Esprit européen*, published as a booklet. This publication bears no date, but we may be sure, on the basis of internal evidence, that it is posterior to June 22, 1941. I have reason to believe that it was published early in July and distributed in the course of that same month.

CHAPTER VI

Social Revolution and National Liberation

1. *Appel au peuple de France*, June, 1940.

2. *L'Humanité*, September 10, 1940.

3. *Ibid.*, October, 1940 (special edition).

4. "Lettre aux militants communistes," November, 1940, reproduced in *Cahiers du Bolchevisme*, 1st quarter, 1941, pp. 6–10.

5. Cited in *Vie du Parti*, October, 1940, p. 7.

6. See n. 4, *supra*.

7. *Une Lettre du Comité Central du Parti aux militants emprisonnés, internés, deportés*, May 1, 1941.

8. *Cahiers du Bolchevisme*, 1st quarter, 1941.

9. "Déclaration du Parti Communiste Français à propos de l'annexion de L'Alsace-Lorraine," *L'Humanité*, November, 1940 (special edition).

10. See the article, "Pour le droit des peuples coloniaux à disposer d'eux-mêmes.—6,000 Annamites assassinés en Indochine sur l'ordre des traîtres de Vichy," *L'Humanité*, November, 1940 (special edition); *Cahiers du Bolchevisme*, 1st quarter, 1941, p. 50.

11. *Lutte sociale,* November, 1940; cf. *Pour l'indépendance nationale de l'Algérie,* published as a pamphlet in January, 1941.

12. *L'Humanité,* November 10, 1940.

13. *Etudiants,* published as a pamphlet in January, 1941.

14. This leaflet bears no title. It begins with the words: "When in 1937–1938 . . . etc."

15. *Révolution et contre-révolution au XXᵉ siècle.* See Chap. V, n. 12, *supra.*

16. *Comment se défendre,* published as a pamphlet in January, 1941, p. 26.

17. This and the preceding quotation are taken from *Révolution et contre-révolution au XXᵉ siècle.* See Chap. V, n. 12, *supra.*

18. *Cahiers du Bolchevisme,* 2d and 3d quarters, 1941, p. 83.

19. *Pagaïe à Vichy,* published as a pamphlet in February, 1941.

20. See n. 13, *supra.*

21. *Ibid.*

22. The source is a July, 1941, leaflet of which these words constitute the entire text. The author has in his possession evidence proving that the slogan originated with Ilya Ehrenburg.

CHAPTER VII

The March to Power: the Committees of the People to Become Soviets

1. This and the preceding quotations are taken from *Les Premières Instructions du P.C.F. après l'armistice,* June or July, 1940.

2. *Vie du Parti,* September, 1940.

3. *Ibid.,* September, 1940 (supplement).

4. *Ibid.,* September, 1940.

5. Cf. *L'Humanité,* July 1, 1940.

6. *Vie du Parti,* August, 1940.

7. *L'Humanité,* September 14, 1940.

8. *Pour le salut du peuple de France,* published as a pamphlet in January, 1941.

9. *Ibid.*

10. *Vie du Parti,* 1st quarter, 1941.

11. Lenin develops these theses in the two books, *The Threatening Catastrophe and How to Fight It,* and *Will the Bolsheviks Retain State Power?* (New York, International Publishers, 1932). The Party chooses this moment to publish French translations of both books under the title, *Sur la route de l'insurrection* (Paris, Librarie de l'Humanité, 1924).

12. See n. 8, *supra.*

13. *History of the Communist Party of the Soviet Union (Bolsheviks)* (New York, International Publishers, 1939), pp. 189–191.

14. *L'Humanité,* August, 1940 (special edition).

15. See n. 8, *supra.*

16. *L'Humanité,* July 27, 1940; see also *Vie du Parti,* September, 1940 (supplement).

17. This and the preceding quotation are taken from *Il faut en finir avec l'incurie et le désordre,* published as a pamphlet in July, 1940.

18. *Pour sauver notre pays,* published as a pamphlet in June, 1940.

19. *Appel au peuple de France,* June, 1940.

20. *A bas le gouvernement de la trahison et de l'asservissement de la France,* published as a pamphlet in February, 1941.

21. *Ni Berlin, ni Londres*, published as a pamphlet in April, 1941.
22. *Les Capitalistes français sont* . . . , published as a pamphlet in January, 1941.
23. *Appel aux étudiants de France*, May, 1941.
24. *Notre propagande*, October, 1940.
25. See n. 8, *supra*.
26. See, for example, *L'Humanité*, January 2, 1941.
27. *Les Deux Frances*, published as a pamphlet in October, 1940.
28. These words are taken from a leaflet distributed in October, 1941. It bears no title.
29. *L'Humanité*, December, 1940 (special edition).

CHAPTER VIII

Eliminating the Competition

1. *Vie du Parti*, August, 1940.
2. "Lettre aux militants communistes," November, 1940, reproduced in *Cahiers du Bolchevisme*, 1st quarter, 1941, pp. 6–10.
3. *Appel au peuple de France*, mid-August, 1940; *L'Humanité*, August, 1940 (special edition).
4. *L'Humanité*, July 1, 1940.
5. See n. 2, *supra*.
6. *L'Humanité*, June 20, 1941.
7. See "Tous dans le bain," *L'Humanité*, July 1, 1940.
8. *Pour sauver notre pays*, published as a pamphlet in June, 1940.
9. *La Grande Trahison*, published as a pamphlet in March, 1941.
10. *L'Humanité*, October 4, 1940.
11. *Appel au peuple de France*. See n. 3, *supra*.
12. *L'Humanité*, August, 1940 (special edition).
13. *La Gazette des démobilisés*, October, 1940.
14. *Vie du Parti*, August, 1940.
15. As it does in *Pour le salut du peuple de France*, published as a pamphlet in January, 1941. For intermediate versions, see *Notre propagande*, October, 1940; *L'Humanité*, January 2, 1941.
16. *L'Humanité*, September 19, 1940.
17. *Ibid.*, July 27, 1940.
18. *Travailleur socialiste*, published as a pamphlet in July, 1940.
19. *Notre propagande*, October, 1940.
20. *Lettre à un travailleur socialiste*, October 8, 1940.
21. *L'Humanité*, October 1, 1940 (Allier edition).
22. This quotation is from a leaflet published early in 1941. It bears no title. The reference to Blum and his lawyer is from the pamphlet, *La Vie de château pour les uns*, published in March, 1941.
23. *L'Humanité*, April 6, 1941.
24. *Frère, ouvrier socialiste, à l'action*, published as a pamphlet in January, 1941.
25. See n. 20, *supra*.
26. *La Doctrine communiste de Marx-Engels-Lénine-Staline en six cours*, Part IV, March, 1941.
27. See n. 19, *supra*.
28. *Lettre à un travailleur radical*, published as a pamphlet in October or November, 1940.

29. See n. 15, *supra*.
30. See n. 19, *supra*.
31. See n. 4, *supra*.
32. *Ibid.*, January 21, 1941 (Normandy edition).
33. "Pour la formation d'un front national de lutte pour l'indépendance de la France," May 15, 1941. Reproduced in *Cahiers du Bolchevisme*, 2d and 3d quarters, 1941, p. 27.
34. For this and the two preceding quotations see *ibid.*
35. *Ibid.*
36. *L'Humanité*, January 9, 1941.
37. See Section 30, *supra*.
38. See Section 36, *infra*.
39. *Cahiers du Bolchevisme*, 3d quarter, 1940, pp. 18–19.
40. See Section 37, *infra*.
41. See Section 38, *infra*.
42. See Section 37, *infra*.
43. See Section 38, *infra*.
44. *Ibid.*
45. *Ibid.*
46. *Ni Berlin, ni Londres,* published as a pamphlet in June, 1941.
47. See Section 39, *infra*.
48. *La Doctrine communiste de Marx-Engels-Lénine-Staline en six cours,* Part 5, p. 47.
49. *L'Humanité*, October, 1940 (unoccupied zone edition).
50. *Vie du Parti*, September, 1940.
51. See n. 2, *supra*.
52. See n. 3, *supra*.
53. *L'Humanité*, October, 1940, special edition for Haute-Garonne.
54. See n. 33, *supra*.

CHAPTER IX

The Communists, the Nazi-Soviet Pact, and the Foreign Policy of the USSR

1. The most important of these are: "La Politique de paix des communistes," *Cahiers du Bolchevisme*, 3d quarter, 1940, pp. 14–25; *Nous accusons*, published as a pamphlet in October or November, 1940, pp. 3–20; *Jeunesse de France*, published as a pamphlet in autumn, 1940, pp. 20–34; and *La Doctrine communiste de Marx-Engels-Lénine-Staline en six cours*, Part 5, pp. 60–74.
2. "Un an après le déchaînement de la guerre impérialiste," *L'Humanité*, September, 1940 (special edition).
3. *L'U.R.S.S. et la guerre*, published as a pamphlet in August, 1940.
4. *La Vérité sur l'U.R.S.S.*, published as a pamphlet in May, 1941.
5. *Nous accusons*, p. 5. See n. 1, *supra*.
6. This and the preceding quotation are taken from *L'Humanité*, October, 1940 (special edition).
7. *Lettre du groupe ouvrier et paysan*, republished as a pamphlet (it had appeared in numerous Party newspapers in October, 1939) immediately following the Armistice in 1940.
8. The two quotations are taken from *La Doctrine communiste de Marx-Engels-Lénine-Staline en six cours*, Part 5, p. 68.

9. This and the preceding quotation are from "La Politique internationale au seuil de 1941," in *Cahiers du Bolchevisme*, 1st quarter, 1941, p. 47; cf. *La Doctrine communiste de Marx-Engels-Lénine-Staline en six cours*, Part 4, p. 29.

10. *Cahiers du Bolchevisme*, 3d quarter, 1940, p. 16.

11. *Russie d'aujourd'hui*, January, 1941.

12. *Pour sauver notre pays*, published as a pamphlet in June, 1940.

13. *Appel au peuple de France*, June, 1940.

14. See the following pamphlets: *Pour sauver notre pays*, see n. 12, *supra; Pour un gouvernement populaire luttant contre le fascisme hitlérien*, published as a pamphlet in June, 1940; *Appel au peuple de France*, June, 1940; *Trahison et responsabilités*, published as a pamphlet in June 20, 1940.

15. *Cahiers du Bolchevisme*, 3d quarter, 1940, p. 18.

16. For these quotations see *ibid.*, p. 23.

17. *Ibid.*, p. 37.

18. See n. 3, *supra*.

19. For this and the preceding quotation see *ibid.*

20. *Cahiers du Bolchevisme*, 3d quarter, 1940, p. 37.

21. Molotov's speech on August 1, 1940, is reproduced in *ibid.*, 3d quarter, 1940, pp. 38–43.

22. The leaflet was distributed in August, 1940.

23. The point is dealt with in Article 5 of this treaty.

24. *L'Humanité*, November, 1940. This issue of *L'Humanité* omits the day of the month from its masthead. It may have been published by one of the Party's regional headquarters.

25. This and the two preceding quotations are taken from *L'Humanité*, November 21, 1940.

26. *Russie d'aujourd'hui*, January, 1941 (special edition).

27. *L'Humanité*, January 18, 1941.

28. *Ibid.*

29. "L'Extrême-Orient et la guerre imperialiste," *La Politique communiste*, March, 1941.

30. *Vie du Parti*, 2d quarter, 1941, p. 4.

31. This and the two preceding quotations are taken from "La Politique internationale au seuil de 1941." See n. 9, *supra*.

32. *Ibid.*

33. This and the preceding quotation are taken from *Les Evénements de Bulgarie et l'attitude de l'U.R.S.S.*, published as a pamphlet in March, 1941.

34. The foregoing quotation and the line of argument summarized in this sentence are both taken from *L'Humanité*, April 12, 1941.

35. *Du pain, de la viande* . . . , published as a leaflet in April, 1941.

36. *Vie du Parti*, 2d quarter, 1941, p. 3.

37. "Pour la formation d'un front national de lutte pour l'indépendance de la France," May, 1941.

38. *Appel au peuple de France*, mid-August, 1940.

39. See the following pamphlets: *Accord avec l'U.R.S.S. pour que le peuple de France mange à sa faim*, April, 1941; *Alerte à toutes les femmes de France*, February, 1941; *Le Pain va manquer*, February, 1941.

40. These posters bear such titles as "La France meurtrie par la guerre impérialiste"; "Pour sauver la France de la famine"; "La France affamée veut un pacte économique avec l'U.R.S.S."

41. *L'Humanité*, October 27, 1940.

42. *Ibid.*

43. *Ibid.*, October 12, 1940.

44. *Ibid.*, January 18, 1941.
45. "Le Communisme, seul espoir de la France," *L'Humanité*, February, 1941. This issue of *L'Humanité* does not bear the day of the month on the masthead.
46. This and the preceding quotation are from *La Pensée libre*, January, 1941, p. 9.
47. *Cahiers du Bolchevisme*, 3d quarter, 1941, p. 24.
48. This and the preceding quotation are from *Révolution et contre-révolution au XXᵉ siècle*, p. 45.

CHAPTER X

The Turning Point: June 22, 1941

1. *L'Humanité*, July, 1941 (special edition).
2. *Ibid.*, June, 1941 (Loire edition).
3. *Ibid.*, June 27, 1941 (Seine-Inférieure edition).
4. *Cahiers du Bolchevisme*, 2d and 3d quarters, 1941, p. 131.
5. *Vie du Parti*, 4th quarter, 1941, p. 14.
6. *L'Humanité*, July 2, 1941.
7. *Ibid.*, July 12, 1941 (Seine-Inférieure edition).
8. *Cahiers du Bolchevisme*, 2d and 3d quarters, 1941, p. 32.
9. These quotations are taken from *L'Humanité*, July, 1941 (special edition).
10. See Section 35, *supra*.
11. *Révolution et contre-révolution au XXᵉ siècle*, p. 44.
12. *La Pensée libre*, late January, 1941, p. 8.

CHAPTER XI

New Forms of Struggle

1. *L'Humanité*, July, 1941 (special edition for unoccupied zone). See Chap. IX, n. 45.
2. *Ibid.*, August 12, 1941 (unoccupied zone edition).
3. *Ibid.*, July 2, 1941 (unoccupied zone edition).
4. *Qui est Hitler?* published as a pamphlet in October, 1941.
5. *L'Humanité*, June 22, 1941.
6. *Appel à tous les travailleurs*, July or August, 1941.
7. *L'Humanité*, August 7, 1941 (special edition).
8. See n. 2, *supra*.
9. See n. 3, *supra*.
10. *Ibid.*, July 7, 1941.
11. *Français, organisez le sabotage*, July, 1941.
12. *Tribune des cheminots*, August–September, 1941.
13. See, for example, the pamphlet *Sabotage*, September, 1941.
14. See Section 55, *infra*.
15. See n. 13, *supra*.
16. *L'Humanité*, August 7, 1941.
17. *Cahiers du Bolchevisme*, 2d and 3d quarters, 1941, p. 51.
18. *Enchaîné du Nord*, December, 1941.
19. See the pamphlets *Métallurgistes parisiens* and *Aux métallurgistes de la région parisienne*. Both these pamphlets belong to late 1941, but I have been unable to fix the exact date.

20. *La Vie ouvrière*, December 6, 1941.
21. *Vie du Parti*, 4th quarter, 1941, p. 20.

CHAPTER XII

Action on the Trade-union Front: the Labor Charter

1. *La Vie ouvrière*, September 8, 1941.
2. *Vie du Parti*, October, 1940.
3. *La Vie ouvrière*, December 21, 1940.
4. *Ibid.*, November 15, 1941.
5. *Tribune des mineurs*, November, 1941.
6. *La Vie ouvrière*, November, 1941 (special edition).
7. See n. 2, *supra*.
8. This and the preceding quotation are taken from *La Vie ouvrière*, November 15, 1941 (unoccupied zone edition).
9. On Communist policy regarding the committees of the people, see *La Vie ouvrière*, November, 1941 (special edition). Cf. *Vie du Parti*, 4th quarter, 1941, pp. 23–24.

CHAPTER XIII

The Rural Areas and the Food Problem

1. *L'Humanité*, June 22, 1941.
2. *Ibid.*, July 12, 1941.
3. *Ibid.*, July 2, 1941.
4. *Paysans de France, contre l'oppresseur, unissez-vous!*, published as a pamphlet in July, 1941.
5. *Aucune livraison à l'Allemagne nazie*, published as a pamphlet in autumn, 1941. The date cannot be fixed more precisely.
6. *Hitler ordonne, Pétain-Charbin obéissent*, published as a pamphlet in December, 1941.
7. *Appel aux paysans de France!*, September–October, 1941.
8. *Ibid.*
9. *Ibid.*
10. *Ibid.*
11. *Où conduit l'inflation?* published as a pamphlet in December, 1941.
12. This and the preceding quotation are taken from *Vie du Parti*, 4th quarter, 1941, pp. 45–46.
13. *Selon la volonté d'Hitler*, published as a pamphlet in November, 1941.

CHAPTER XIV

The Mobilization of Youth

1. *Vie du Parti*, 4th quarter, 1941, p. 27.
2. *Ibid.*, pp. 27–29.
3. *Ibid.*, p. 29.
4. *Notre jeunesse*, September–October, 1941, p. 5.
5. *Ibid.*, p. 5.
6. *L'Avant-garde*, October–November, 1941.

7. This and the preceding quotations are taken from *Notre jeunesse,* September–October, 1941, pp. 9–14.

8. *L'Humanité,* June 22, 1941.

9. *Vive la France,* November, 1941.

10. *Aux Français de l'armée d'armistice,* published as a pamphlet in November or December, 1941.

11. *Aux soldats de l'armée d'armistice,* published as a pamphlet in May, 1941.

12. *Vie du Parti,* 4th quarter, 1941, pp. 32–33.

13. *Ibid.;* cf. *Notre jeunesse,* September–October, 1941, p. 7.

CHAPTER XV

The Mobilization of the Intellectuals

1. *L'Esprit européen,* July, 1941.

2. *Ibid.*

3. *Déclaration des intellectuels français,* published as a pamphlet in September, 1941. Cf. "Appel aux intellectuels français," *L'Université libre,* September 23, 1941.

4. *A tous les professeurs français,* published as a pamphlet in October, 1941; cf. *L'Université libre,* October 5, 1941.

5. "Appel aux intellectuels français," see n. 3, *supra.*

6. *Hommage du Parti Communiste à l'Université de Paris,* published as a pamphlet in December, 1941.

CHAPTER XVI

Mass Demonstrations and "Terrorist" Activity

1. See, for example, *14 Juillet: 1941–1789,* published as a pamphlet in July, 1941.

2. See *A nos frères de gaullistes,* published as a pamphlet in July–August, 1941, where the "Marseillaise" and the "Internationale" are mentioned in the same sentence.

3. *L'Humanité,* August 21, 1941 (italics mine).

4. *Ibid.,* August 20, 1941 (Loire-Inférieure edition). Italics mine.

5. *11 Novembre 1941: Honorons nos morts,* published as a pamphlet in October, 1941.

6. *Ibid.*

7. *Ibid.*

8. *Aux combattants des guerres 1914–1918, 1939–1940,* published as a pamphlet on November 5, 1941.

9. *La Bretagne ouvrière, paysanne, maritime,* September, 1941.

10. *Juges français,* September, 1941.

11. The leaflet in which this threat is made, distributed in October, 1941, bears no title.

12. *Front national,* November 11, 1941.

13. *Notre jeunesse,* September–October, 1941, p. 4.

14. *Vie du Parti,* 4th quarter, 1941, p. 12.

15. *Après les incidents de Versailles: Une Déclaration du Parti Communiste,* published as a pamphlet August 27, 1941.

16. Cf.: *L'Humanité*, September 4, 1941; *La Vie ouvrière*, September 8, 1941; *Déclaration des intellectuels français*, published as a pamphlet in September, 1941.

CHAPTER XVII

The Defense against the Repression

1. The relevant decree, signed by General von Stülpnagel, bears the date September 14, 1941.

2. The question of hostages was first posed in an announcement from General von Shaumburg's headquarters on August 22, 1941: "1. Beginning August 23, all Frenchmen taken into custody, either by the German authorities in France or on orders originating with them, will be regarded as hostages; 2. Should any further criminal action occur, hostages will be shot in a number corresponding to the seriousness of that action."

3. *L'Ouvrier français André Masseron a été assassiné par la Gestapo*, published as a pamphlet in August, 1941.

4. *Français, unissons-nous contre l'assassinat des patriotes*, published as a pamphlet in September, 1941.

5. See, e.g., *Libération*, December, 1941.

6. *L'Humanité*, September 4, 1941.

7. *Nous les vengerons*, August, 1940.

8. See, e.g., *L'Humanité*, August 31, 1941.

9. *Patriotes français*, published as a pamphlet in September, 1941.

10. See, e.g., the following pamphlets: *Arrêtons la main criminelle des bourreaux du peuple*, August, 1941; *On assassine les patriotes*, September, 1941; *La Terreur blanche*, October, 1941; *Alerte, population du XIVe*, October, 1941.

11. See, e.g., the following pamphlets: *Autour de Jean Catelas et de Gabriel Péri, rassemblement des Français*, early June, 1941; *Arrachez la libération de Gabriel Péri*, June, 1941; *Appel aux jeunes français*, June, 1941. Cf. *L'Avantgarde*, December 25, 1941.

12. *Les Derniers Moments des fusillés*, published as a pamphlet in early December, 1941.

13. *Contre l'assassinat des patriotes, action des ouvriers*, published as a pamphlet in November, 1941.

14. *Métallos, Jean Timbaut a été assassiné*, published as a pamphlet in October, 1941.

15. *Ibid.*

16. *L'Humanité*, August 16, 1941.

17. *Juges français*, published as a pamphlet in September, 1941.

18. *Aux agents et inspecteurs de police*, published as a pamphlet in January, 1941.

19. *Aux fonctionnaires de la police française*, published as a pamphlet in June, 1941.

CHAPTER XVIII

The New "National Front"

1. The text of Stalin's speech appears in *Cahiers du Bolchevisme*, 2d and 3d quarters, 1941.

2. Thus *L'Humanité* publishes its July 17 edition under the title "Anglo-Soviet Accord against Hitler." *La Tribune des cheminots* speaks, in its August–September edition, of "the struggle of the most powerful army in the world, the Red Army, allied with the most powerful navy in the world, the British Navy, and supported by the American people."

3. "L'Union des R.S.S. et l'Angleterre," published as a poster in August, 1941.

4. The text of Stalin's speech appears in *L'Humanité*, December, 1941 (special edition).

5. *Hitler sera battu*, published as a pamphlet in July, 1941.

6. *Nous, les travailleurs*, published as a pamphlet in September, 1941.

7. *L'Humanité*, September 11, 1941.

8. Walter Citrine, *I Search for Truth in Russia* (London, G. Routledge & Sons, Ltd., 1936).

9. *Le Front national de lutte pour l'indépendance de la France est constitué*, published as a leaflet in July, 1941.

10. *Ne pas mourir pour la machine nazie*, published as a pamphlet in July, 1941.

11. See, e.g., *Assez de morts. Au sujet du bombardment du Havre*, published as a pamphlet in October, 1941.

12. *L'Humanité*, May 12, 1941 (Caen edition).

13. *Ibid.*, August 28, 1941.

14. *Soldats, marins, aviateurs*, published as a pamphlet in June, 1941.

15. *Vie du Parti*, 4th quarter, 1941, p. 5.

16. See particularly *Hitler est l'ennemi de la France. Ce qu'il a écrit dans Mein Kampf*, published as a pamphlet in September, 1941.

17. *Paysan de France, redresse-toi*, published as a pamphlet in February, 1941.

18. *Paysans de France, contre l'oppresseur, unissez-vous!* published as a pamphlet in July, 1941, p. 26.

19. *Cahiers du Bolchevisme*, 2d and 3d quarters, 1941, p. 104.

20. *L'Humanité*, June 20, 1941 (occupied zone edition).

21. See n. 15, *supra*.

22. *France libre*, August, 1941.

23. *L'Etudiant patriote*, early November, 1941.

24. *Le Front national de lutte pour l'indépendance de la France est constitué* (*zone non occupée*), published as a leaflet in November, 1941.

25. *L'Enchaîné*, December, 1941.

26. This and the preceding quotation are taken from *Le Front national de lutte pour l'indépendance de la France est constitué*, published as a leaflet in July, 1941.

27. See n. 24, *supra*.

28. *Jeune travailleur chrétien*, published as a pamphlet in August, 1941.

29. *M. le curé*, published as a pamphlet in August, 1941.

30. *Catholiques: Pour la manifestation du 11 novembre*, published as a leaflet in November, 1941.

31. The usual formulation speaks of a National Front extending from the Gaullists to the Communists.

32. *Notre Jeunesse*, September–October, 1941, p. 5.

33. *Français, patrons, ouvriers, paysans, intellectuels, anciens combattants, retraités, ménagères, unissons-nous pour chasser l'envahisseur*, published as a pamphlet in October, 1941.

34. *L'Humanité*, June 27, 1941 (Seine-Inférieure edition).

35. *Cahiers du Bolchevisme*, 2d and 3d quarters, 1941, p. 131.

CHAPTER XIX

"Organization Is What Counts"

1. *Comment se défendre?* published as a pamphlet in December, 1941.
2. *Les Premières Instructions du P.C.F. après l'armistice*, June or July, 1940. See Chap. II, n. 8.
3. This and the preceding quotations are taken from *ibid.*
4. *Vie du Parti*, September, 1940.
5. See n. 2, *supra.*
6. See n. 4, *supra.*
7. *Ibid.* (supplement).
8. See n. 2, *supra.*
9. *Vie du Parti*, August, 1941.
10. *Bulletin d'Information du Secrétariat Européen de l'I.S.R.*, December, 1940.
11. See n. 1, *supra.*
12. My source here is the circular, a copy of which I hold in my files, in which the Center embodied the plan.
13. *Vie du Parti*, October, 1940, p. 25.
14. See n. 10, *supra.*
15. See n. 1, *supra.* Cf. *Vie du Parti*, 1st quarter, 1941, p. 13.
16. My source is the circular distributed by the various headquarters. I hold a copy in my files.
17. *Vie du Parti*, 2d quarter, 1941, pp. 9-12.
18. *Ibid.*, pp. 13-17.
19. See Chap. XX, *infra.*
20. See Section 75, *infra.*

CHAPTER XX

The Rules for Underground Activity

1. *Vie du Parti*, 2d quarter, 1941, pp. 6 ff.
2. *Ibid.*, p. 8.
3. I hold an original copy of this questionnaire in my files.
4. The following instructions are included: "Recently a sector report fell into the hands of the police. The ensuing repression impels us to remind everyone of the numerous precautions we must take to cut our risks to a minimum, while at the same time seeing to it that we keep up our communications, as keep them up we must. Your weekly reports must be brief and concrete. . . . Include in your reports only the [indispensable] facts and events of the current week, along with a statement of the accomplishments to which you can point. For purposes of clarity arrange your report under distinct headings. Write all family names and give names either in code or in abbreviated form. Reread your report, raising with yourself the following questions: What would happen if the police got hold of this? . . . Keep your report as short as possible. Never include the names and given names either in code or in abbreviated form. Reread your report, should be signed with a number, which in your case is ——. . . . Remember that in a pinch the courier must above all save your report . . . by destroying it, usually by chewing it up and swallowing it."

My source here is the Party circular, a copy of which I hold in my files.

5. See the same Party circular.

6. *Vie du Parti*, 1st quarter, 1941, p. 22.

7. *Ibid.*, pp. 22–23.

8. *Vie du Parti*, 2d quarter, 1941, p. 9.

9. *Ibid.*

10. *Comment se défendre?*, published as a pamphlet in December, 1941. The pamphlet adds: "The dilemma posed to us by the bourgeoisie at the present time is this: the concentration camp, or the prison, where one will see one's wife and children through bars, or freedom, which one will enjoy far from one's family but which will enable one to keep on fighting for the emancipation of the people, which can alone create the opportunity for genuine family life."

11. *Vie du Parti*, 2d quarter, 1941, p. 10.

12. *Comment se défendre?*, p. 10, see n. 10, *supra*.

13. *Soyons hardis, soyons prudents*, published as a pamphlet in September, 1940, p. 3.

14. *Ibid.*

15. *Ibid.*

16. Cf. *Comment se défendre?*, p. 22, see n. 10, *supra.; Vie du Parti*, 2d quarter, 1941, p. 11.

17. *Soyons hardis, soyons prudents*, p. 3, see n. 13, *supra*.

18. *Ibid.*

19. *Comment se défendre?*, p. 10, see n. 10, *supra*. Cf. *Vie du Parti*, 4th quarter, 1941, p. 59.

20. *Soyons hardis, soyons prudents*, pp. 5–6, see n. 13, *supra*. Cf. *Comment se défendre?*, p. 10, see n. 10, *supra*.

21. *Vie du Parti*, 4th quarter, 1941, pp. 59–60; Cf. *Soyons hardis, soyons prudents*, p. 4, see n. 13, *supra*.

22. *Comment se défendre?*, p. 5, see n. 10, *supra*. Cf. *Vie du Parti*, 2d quarter, 1941, p. 10.

23. *Ibid.*

24. *Renforçons la surveillance*, published as a pamphlet in November, 1940.

25. *Soyons hardis, soyons prudents*, p. 5, see n. 13, *supra*.

26. *Vie du Parti*, 2d quarter, 1941, p. 10.

27. See n. 4, *supra*.

28. *Soyons hardis, soyons prudents*, p. 5, see n. 13, *supra*.

29. *Ibid.*

30. *Vie du Parti*, 4th quarter, 1941, pp. 59–60.

31. *Soyons hardis, soyons prudents*, p. 4, see n. 13, *supra*.

32. *Ibid.*

33. Louis Andrieux, *Souvenirs d'un préfet de police* (Paris, 1924). 2 vols.

34. *Vie du Parti*, October, 1940.

35. *Ibid.*

36. *Comment se défendre?*, pp. 1–9, see n. 10, *supra*.

37. *Ibid.*, p. 9, see n. 10, *supra*.

38. *Vie du Parti*, 4th quarter, 1941, p. 60.

39. *Soyons hardis, soyons prudents*, p. 6, see n. 13, *supra*.

40. *Ibid.*, pp. 6–7.

41. *Comment se défendre?*, pp. 7–8, see n. 10, *supra*.

42. *Soyons hardis, soyons prudents*, p. 7, see n. 13, *supra*.

43. *Comment se défendre?*, p. 15. see n. 10, *supra*.

44. This and the preceding quotation are taken from *Vie du Parti*, 1st quarter, 1941, p. 34.

45. *Comment se défendre?*, pp. 15–17, see n. 10, *supra.*
46. *Ibid.*
47. *Ibid.*, p. 18, see n. 10, *supra.*
48. *Soyons hardis, soyons prudents*, pp. 11–12, see n. 13, *supra.*
49. *Comment se défendre?*, p. 18, see n. 10, *supra.*
50. *Soyons hardis, soyons prudents*, p. 11, see n. 13, *supra.*
51. *Comment se défendre?*, p. 16, see n. 10, *supra.*
52. This and the preceding quotation are taken from *Vie du Parti*, 2d quarter, 1941, pp. 20–21.
53. Reprinted in *ibid.*, p. 28.

CHAPTER XXI
Political and Military Organization

1. *Circulaire n⁰ 11*, January 6, 1942, from National Police Headquarters (Direction Générale de la Police Nationale) to police prefects and intendants throughout France.

CHAPTER XXII
The Press

1. *Vie du Parti*, September, 1940, p. 6.
2. *Ibid.*, 1st quarter, 1941, p. 39.
3. Circular to sector and section leaders in the Nord region, January, 1941.
4. *Les Tâches du Parti pour septembre-octobre*, published as a pamphlet in August, 1940. See Chap. II, n. 18.
5. *Vie du Parti*, September, 1940.
6. *Ibid.*, August, 1940.
7. *Ibid.*
8. *Vie du Parti*, August, September, October, 1940; *ibid.*, May, 1941, pp. 50–53; *Notre propagande*, May, 1941. Cf. *Quelque mots aux militants pour la diffusion du matériel*, published as a pamphlet June, 1941; *Vie du Parti*, 1st quarter, 1941, p. 52.

CHAPTER XXIII
Party Finances

1. My source here is the circular sent out from the Center. I hold a copy in my files.

CHAPTER XXIV
Personnel

1. *Cahiers du Bolchevisme*, 1st quarter, 1941, p. 60.
2. *Etude au sujet de la propagande communiste, au cours des mois de juin, juillet et août 1940*, prepared by the Ministry of the Interior, Paris, September 1, 1940.
3. *Ibid.*

4. *Vie du Parti*, October, 1940, p. 26; cf. *ibid.*, 4th quarter, 1941, p. 64.

5. *Ibid.*, August, 1940, p. 15.

6. *Ibid.*, 4th quarter, 1941, pp. 68–69.

7. *Cahiers du Bolchevisme*, 2d and 3d quarters, 1941, p. 128.

8. *Vie du Parti*, 2d quarter, 1941, p. 12; cf. *Cahiers du Bolchevisme*, 2d and 3d quarters, 1941, p. 131.

9. This and the preceding quotation are taken from *Cahiers du Bolchevisme*, 1st quarter, 1941, p. 62; 2d and 3d quarters, p. 129.

10. *Vie du Parti*, August, 1940, pp. 15–16; cf. *ibid.*, 2d quarter, 1941, p. 18.

11. *Ibid.*, 4th quarter, 1941, pp. 65–66.

CHAPTER XXV

Party Training and Party Mystique

1. See "Il faut trouver des cadres pleins d'initiative . . . ," *Cahiers du Bolchevisme*, 2d and 3d quarters, 1941, pp. 127–131.

2. *Ibid.*, p. 12.

3. My source here is the circular, *Plan d'organisation et de travail d'une cellule*, sent out from the Center. I hold a copy in my files.

4. See *Vie du Parti*, October, 1940, p. 28.

5. See "Développons notre esprit de parti," *Vie du Parti*, 4th quarter, 1941, p. 51.

6. *Ibid.* p. 49.

7. Cf. the present writer's *The Rise of Italian Fascism* (London, Methuen & Co. Ltd., 1938), pp. 328–329: "The socialists of the extreme left . . . invoked at every step their final aim of 'proletarian revolution.' On principle everything was sacrificed to this. For them there was no question as to whether their aim was consonant with the general interest; it was an accepted dogma, an historical fact, that it was so. Henceforward human emancipation was the work of the proletariat, and of the industrial proletariat in particular, acting through its leaders and its political party. And in their turn the party leaders became the trustees of the general interest and identified themselves with its progress and its demands. To look back and see if the sanctity of the apostolic succession had survived so many stages was pointless. There resulted a sectarian frame of mind dominated by a theological hatred of all who refused to recognize the divine quality of their mandate."

8. *Vie du Parti*, 4th quarter, 1941, p. 49; cf. *Cahiers du Bolchevisme*, 2d and 3d quarters, 1941, p. 128.

9. *Vie du Parti*, September, 1940.

CHAPTER XXVI

The Role of Doctrine

1. See the Biographical Questionnaire in Section 64, A.

2. *Cahiers du Bolchevisme*, 2d and 3d quarters, 1941, p. 131.

3. *Ibid.*

4. *Vie du Parti*, 1st quarter, 1941, pp. 32–33.

5. *La Doctrine communiste de Marx-Engels-Lénine-Staline en six cours*, Part I, p. 33.

6. *Ibid.*

7. *La Pensée libre*, p. 24. This issue bears no date, but it appears to belong to January, 1941.

8. *Ibid.*, p. 10.

9. *L'Humanité*, March, 1941 (special edition).

CHAPTER XXVII

A New Kind of Party

1. *Vie du Parti*, 4th quarter, 1941, p. 49.

2. For example, the Jews. A Jewish professor, when asked by a trial judge why he has been distributing Communist pamphlets, replies: "You people have read me out of society." It is worthy of note, in passing, that the French Communist Party, although its central organization is made up almost entirely of non-Jewish Frenchmen, takes a firm stand against antisemitism in its newspapers, and devotes several pamphlets to the problem of antisemitism: *L'Antisémitisme, arme de la réaction*, November, 1940; *A bas l'antisémitisme*, June, 1941; *Brisons l'arme de l'antisémitisme, unissons-nous!*, June, 1941; *L'Antisémitisme, le fascisme, le problème juif*, November, 1941.

3. *Vie du Parti*, 2d quarter, 1941, p. 11.

4. *Ibid.*, 2d quarter, 1940, p. 18.

5. *Ibid.*, August, 1940, pp. 15–16.

6. *Ibid.*, 4th quarter, 1941, pp. 65–66.

7. This is also true within the Soviet Union. Indeed, the man who has not grasped this fact about Soviet politics and administration will never understand the course of events within that country.

CHAPTER XXVIII

Recruitment

1. *L'Humanité*, September, 1941 (special edition).

2. A. Rossi, *The Rise of Italian Fascism*, pp. 292 ff.

CHAPTER XXX

A Foreign Nationalist Party

1. For a statement to this effect see *L'Humanité*, September 4, 1941.

CHAPTER XXXII

The Problem of the Trade-unions

1. *Cahiers du Bolchevisme*, 1st quarter, 1940, pp. 25–26.

2. For a full discussion of Pelloutier's views see Edouard Dolléans, *Histoire du mouvement ouvrier* (Paris, 1939).

CHAPTER XXXIII

The Communist Party and Democracy

1. Cf. A. Rossi, *The Rise of Italian Facsism,* p. 325: 'Responsibility for evil committed is always shared by those who have failed to prevent it; and we have no right to connive at others' actions unless we are prepared to step in at the right moment and succeed where they have failed."

2. Cf. "Resolutions of the VI World Congress of the Communist International, July–August, 1928," published under the title, *The Struggle against Imperialist War and the Tasks of the Communists* (New York, Workers Library Publishers, 1932), p. 29: The Soviet Union is the "fatherland of the international proletariat"; in the event of war against the Soviet Union, "the proletariat in the imperialist countries must not only fight for the defeat of their own governments in this war, but must actively strive to secure victory for the Soviet Union. . . . The Red Army is not an 'enemy' army, but the army of the international proletariat . . . the workers in capitalist countries must not allow themselves to be scared from supporting the Red Army and from expressing this support by fighting against their own bourgeoisie, by the charges of treason that the bourgeoisie may hurl against them."

CHAPTER XXXIV

By Way of a Conclusion

1. See the 1872 Preface, written by Marx and Engels, to a German edition of *The Communist Manifesto;* the Preface can be found in D. Ryazanoff, *The Communist Manifesto* (London, Martin Lawrence, Ltd., 1930), Appendix C. See also Engels' 1892 Preface to his *The Condition of the Working Class in England in 1844* (London, G. Allen and Unwin, Ltd., 1936); his 1895 Preface to Marx's *The Class Struggles in France* (New York, International Publishers); and his article, "Le Socialisme en Allemagne" in *Almanach du Parti ouvrier,* 1891.

2. Jean Jaurès, Introduction to *Histoire socialiste, 1789–1900* (Paris), I, 6.

Index